Business and Finance for

CW00409212

Springer
London
Berlin
Heidelberg
New York
Barcelona
Hong Kong
Milan
Paris
Singapore
Tokyo

Michael Blackstaff

Business and Finance for IT People

Springer

Michael Blackstaff, FCA, MBCS

Michael Blackstaff is a chartered accountant with over thirty years' practical experience in the IT industry

ISBN 1-85233-264-6 Springer-Verlag London Berlin Heidelberg

British Library Cataloguing in Publication Data
Blackstaff, Michael, 1939–
Business and finance for IT people.
1. Business 2. Business enterprises – Finance
I. Title
650
ISBN 1852332646

Library of Congress Cataloging-in-Publication Data
Blackstaff, Michael, 1939–
   Business and finance:/Michael Blackstaff.
     P. cm --
   Includes bibliographical references and index.
   ISBN 1-85233-264-6 (alk. paper)
   1. Corporations–Finance–Data processing. 2. Business enterprises–Finance–Data processing.
   3. Managerial accounting–Data processing. 4. Management information systems. I. Title.
   HG4012.5 .B57 2000
   658.15–dc21   00–058309

Typesetting: Florence Production Ltd, Stoodleigh, Devon
Printed and bound at the Athenæum Press Ltd., Gateshead, Tyne & Wear
34/3830-543210 Printed on acid-free paper SPIN 10755291

Contents

Acknowledgements

I should like to thank the four companies that have kindly agreed to let extracts from their published annual reports and accounts be reproduced and used for illustrative purposes in this book. I believe that their willingness to do so will have increased substantially its value to readers by helping them to relate principles to real-life practice. In alphabetical order they are the following: Glynwed International plc, Logica plc, J Sainsbury plc and Severn Trent plc.

The extract from *Travesties* by Tom Stoppard on page 1 is reproduced, slightly modified, by kind permission of the author and of the publishers, Faber and Faber Limited, London.

Finally, I should like to thank the following people:

- Professor Ray J. Paul, BSc MSc PhD, Dean of the Faculty of Science, Brunel University for suggesting that I write this book;
- Rebecca Mowat and Catherine Drury of Springer-Verlag for their help and guidance in producing the book;
- My wife Jenny for reading and commenting on the draft.

Introduction

The purpose of this book is to give people, especially but not exclusively those who are studying computing and information systems, or who work in those fields, an insight into the world of business and finance. *Finance* simply means money resources.

I know from long experience that there are three keys to imparting an understanding of business and the financial principles upon which it is based. The first is to demonstrate the many similarities between business transactions and personal transactions, business finance and personal finance. The second is to take things step by step, one transaction at a time, and the third is to recognise that understanding of the principles comes from learning how transactions are recorded. These three keys are the basis of the approach that I have adopted in this book.

The book includes two topics that are often regarded as "advanced" – cost/benefit analysis and investment evaluation methods. I do not regard them as advanced but as fundamental. Chapter 1 explains the purpose of business. What is the point in being told the purpose of anything if one is not also shown as many as possible of the methods by which, in practice, people try to achieve that purpose?

If anything is worth saying, then it is worth saying in plain English. However, jargon is as inevitable in business and finance as it is in any other profession. Where it is either useful or unavoidable I use it, but when I do I define it, both in the text when it is first introduced and in the glossary in Appendix 2. A word defined in the glossary is italicised when, or soon after, it first occurs in the text, as with the word "finance" above. Two jargon words that, in my view, are neither helpful nor unavoidable are "debit" and "credit". They are quite unnecessary and, unless used by consenting adults in private, can be thoroughly confusing. I neither use them nor define them. However, at the end of the book I do offer an explanation of how they came about.

There are five other conventions that I have adopted throughout the book except where the sense demands otherwise. They are these: I use the word "company" to mean any kind of business organisation; as abbreviations for "thousand" I use "k" in the text, as in "£25k", and £000 as headings in tables; as an abbreviation for "million" I use "m" both in the text and in table headings, as in £m; where I wish to refer to "computing" or "information systems" or "information technology" I use the common shorthand "IT"; finally, I use the phrase "IT people" to refer to anyone, whether buyer, seller, technician or manager, whose occupation or interest is in the world of IT.

The book is full of practical examples. Where appropriate, examples specific to IT are used. Indeed, some whole chapters are devoted to aspects of finance that I know from experience to be of particular, although not exclusive, interest to IT people. However, I have not tried slavishly to put things into an IT context where other examples would be more appropriate or easier to understand.

While this book was written especially for IT people, the principles that it sets out to explain are universal. It is therefore my belief that the book will be of use to anyone who wishes to understand business and the financial principles on which it is based.

1 What Is Business?

Purpose – Sole Traders – Partnerships – Limited Companies

> *"For every thousand people there's nine hundred doing the work, ninety doing well, nine doing good, and one lucky blighter who's the artist."*
>
> Tom Stoppard, *Travesties*

It's a nice line, and most of us are indeed just doing the work, in order to make a living. From a financial viewpoint, there are only two legal ways to make a living – that is, if you have neither sufficient wealth nor a patron, and you do not wish to beg. You can work for yourself or you can be employed. In other words, you can run your own business or you can work in someone else's. For this purpose the word "business" can be taken as meaning any enterprise that requires a person or people to achieve its objectives. It therefore includes, for example, government departments, academic institutions and charities, also artists – of whatever kind, however much this may offend against what they might regard as the purity of their art. It should also include our own personal lives. For any enterprise to succeed, it should be run in a businesslike way.

The Purpose of Business

Whether you decide to run your own business or work in someone else's, your main immediate purpose will be to earn an income sufficient for your essentials – food, a roof over your head and warmth. However, unless you are a particularly saintly person, you would like more than that. In fact, you would probably like as much as you can get. This is for two reasons. First, so that you can enjoy luxuries, by which I mean anything that is not a necessity. Second, so that you can save or invest for the future when, eventually, you may no longer be able to earn a living.

1

Investment is simply the process of forgoing consumption of goods and services now in order to be able to enjoy them in the future; a way of accumulating wealth which, in turn, is capable of generating income.

We could say that the financial aim of almost all individuals is to maximize their personal wealth. If that is true of individuals, it had better also be true of the business in which they work or which they operate. People who work as employees try to obtain the highest wage or salary they can in return for their labour, but high wages can only be paid if the business in which they work is doing sufficiently well to be able to afford them. People who run their own businesses try to maximize their profits. A simple definition of *profit* is: the amount by which the earnings of a business exceed its expenses. We shall elaborate on this definition later but it will do for now. We shall also look later at more precise meanings of "earnings" and "expense", however the everyday meanings of these words will also suffice for the time being.

The primary purpose of a business – what it is for – is to maximize the wealth of its proprietor or proprietors. That is not to say that other things to do with a business are not also important. Of course they are. It is important that a business should not pollute the environment; it is important that it should pay its taxes; it is important that the person or people running it treat their employees, customers and suppliers fairly. However, these are obligations of businesses, not the reasons why they exist. The cynic might even say that these, too, are actually ways of helping to achieve the main objective, because they help to show the business in a good light. All this may seem obvious. However, if true, it has some implications that are often lost sight of by both employees and proprietors of businesses.

First, employees: unless employees contribute more to a business than they are paid, a rational employer will sack them. While writing this I have been expecting an employee of an office furniture company to ring me back with the answer to an enquiry. He said he would, but three days later he has not done so. Because he has not done what he said he would do, I have gone elsewhere, and he has lost for his company not only my small piece of business but the possibly larger orders from people whom I might otherwise have recommended. This person is not *adding* to the wealth of his employer, he is *reducing* it.

Second, proprietors: just as money spent on employing people should contribute to maximizing the wealth of the proprietor or proprietors, so should anything else that a business spends money on – information systems, for example. The investment of a business's limited supply of money, in information systems or anything else, should be subjected to the test of whether, of all the possible investments the business might make, this is the one that is most likely to contribute to maximizing the wealth of the proprietors. Precisely how this test is applied we shall see in later chapters.

In this book I shall have little more to say about being an employee, except insofar as it is one aspect of the way in which we may choose to run that most important of "businesses" – our own lives. Much of what follows, however, will look at business from the other side, from the viewpoint of the proprietor or proprietors. First, we should consider what we mean by "proprietors".

Sole Traders

Most businesses are run by individual people as "sole traders". A sole trader is obviously the sole proprietor, the owner, of the business. One could think of many examples: craftsmen of various kinds, market stallholders, couriers, taxi drivers, small shopkeepers, builders and decorators, professional people of many kinds from doctors to musicians – and a growing number of people who provide a variety of IT services on a freelance basis. Notice the main categories of business represented in that sample list and the generic names by which they are usually known, i.e. making and selling things (manufacturing); buying and selling things (retail or wholesale); and various occupations that are not about things (goods) at all, but services. Later we shall look in more detail at the financial characteristics and requirements of these different types of businesses.

There are many advantages of running a small business as a sole trader. They include being in charge, for better or worse, of one's own destiny, relative freedom – compared with some other ways of running a business – from regulation and bureaucracy and, perhaps above all, not having anyone else tell you what to do or when to do it. Any profit you make as a sole trader is yours, or at least what profit is left after the tax authorities have taken their slice. By the same token, any loss is also down to you.

The price that an employee pays for receiving a wage or salary is tax. The price that a business pays for making a profit is also tax. Most sole traders have to make periodic withdrawals of money, representing part or all of the profit, from the business in order to meet their living expenses. However, whether this is done or not, the profits of sole traders are regarded as part of their personal income for tax purposes. Sole traders can and do employ people to work for them.

Partnerships

If the business starts to get too big for you to handle as an individual, you can bring in one or more others as partners, who will usually put some of their own money into the business. The business is then known as a *partnership*, and the partners are now the proprietors or owners. Partnerships have almost the same relative freedom from regulation and bureaucracy as do sole traders. However, you are now reliant on at least one other person, usually both financially and for getting the work done, and so at least some of your freedom has been sacrificed. Also, your partners will expect a share of the profit if they have put in money. Their shares will usually be proportionate to the money that they have put in, but may be in some other proportion by mutual agreement.

In most respects, including taxation, partnerships are treated just like sole traders. Partners' shares of the profit are regarded as part of their personal income for tax purposes, whether drawn out of the business or not. For partners, like sole traders, the business is often their only source of income, so they too usually make periodic withdrawals of money from the business in order to live.

Depending on the kind of business, there is one particular aspect of being a sole trader or partnership that may involve considerable risk – a risk that may outweigh all the benefits. That is the risk of *bankruptcy*, or at least of losing all one's personal assets to avoid it. The reason is this. Just as, for tax purposes, there is no separation of business profit from personal income, so in law there is no separation of business assets from personal assets. An *asset* is simply something of value that is owned. A possible effect of this is illustrated in the following paragraph.

Suppose that, through negligence or accident, a sole trader causes injury to a person or loss to a business and is sued successfully for compensation. If the trader cannot afford to pay the compensation out of the business, then their non-business assets – house, car, investments – must be used. If even these are not enough, then the trader may be made bankrupt. Bankruptcy is a legal procedure for making public the fact that a person has become unable to pay their debts, and for ensuring a fair distribution of what assets they have among their creditors. A *creditor* is a person or a business to whom a debt is due.

A second disadvantage of trading as a sole trader or partnership is that there are practical limits to the amount of money that you can raise. Bringing in additional partners is certainly a way of introducing more money into the business. However, the choice of willing and able potential partners with money to spare is probably not great. Furthermore, the bigger the business becomes, the greater the potential risks should it be sued, and each partner is usually liable for all the debts of the business.

A third disadvantage lies in the question of succession. Many small businesses are family owned businesses. For example, imagine a family business that runs a shop as a partnership, all the partners being family members. They have each left their interest in the business to their children, and they hope that the business will continue through future generations. However, this wish is dependent on the willingness of the children to leave what may be a substantial part of their inheritance money in the business. One or more of them may wish to take the cash and run. If so, and no acceptable and willing successor can be found, the business may not have enough money to continue.

The point here is that a willing successor, perhaps outside the family and therefore without any emotional attachment to the business, is more likely to be found if they can somehow avoid the unlimited liability of being a partner, and if the process of buying into the business can be made as simple as possible. This is especially so if they are willing to put in money as an investment, but have no wish to be active in running the business. The answer to this, and to the other disadvantages of partner-ships and sole traders is the *limited liability company*, or more commonly just *limited company* or *company*.

Limited Companies

Business as we know it would simply not be possible without the concept of limited liability. The idea was developed in the middle of the nineteenth century to facilitate the growth of business consequent upon the Industrial Revolution. The principle is described in the following paragraphs.

Suppose that I have a good idea for making money by starting a busi-ness, and that I invite you and other people to invest in it – put money into it – in addition to my own investment. As an incentive for you to do so, I produce a detailed brochure, called a prospectus, describing the business, my plans for it and the total amount of money that I shall need to get started. The prospectus includes a detailed forecast of how much profit I believe the business will make over the next few years. If it is an existing business, for which I am seeking more money for expansion, then the prospectus will also include a summary of the past few years' results.

Suppose that to get started I need £1 million, and that you are prepared to invest £1,000. In return for your £1,000, your *share* of the total, you receive a piece of paper certifying that you are indeed the owner of a £1,000 share in my company. Predictably, this piece of paper certifying a share is called a *share certificate*. In practice, the *nominal* or *par value* of each share will often be a much smaller amount, for example £1, in which case your share certificate will state that you are the owner of one thousand £1 shares; or two thousand 50 pence shares, and so on.

Most shares in companies are just like the ones described here – just ordinary shares, with nothing special about them. For this reason, and to distinguish them from other possible kinds of share, they are often called *ordinary shares*. As the owner, in this example, of one-thousandth of the ordinary shares in the company, you will also be the owner of one-thousandth of all the profits that the company makes, but you also run the risk of suffering a one-thousandth part of any losses. This is why another name sometimes given to money invested in ordinary shares is *risk capital*. Capital, used in this sense, is simply another word for money; we shall define other meanings later. Yet another name for ordinary shares is *equity shares*. Notice how you stand a better chance of confusing people with several different jargon phrases all meaning the same thing than if you merely use one.

I may not ask you for all the money at once, because I may not need the whole £1 million at once. It will, after all, take time to acquire my premises and equipment, and to employ people. So I may, for example, ask you for only 20 pence per share initially (£200), to be followed by 40 pence per share (£400) 3 months from now, and finally 40 pence, 6 months from now. However, by making your initial payment, £200 in this example, you have committed to make the other payments on the due dates. In the jargon, you have a liability to make the remaining payments. A *liability* is something owed – an obligation to do something that you have undertaken to do.

However – and this is most important – your liability to the company, of which you are now a *shareholder* or member, is limited to the amount as yet unpaid for your shares. This is what is meant by limited liability, and it is the main plank upon which much of modern business stands. If the company goes bankrupt, or for any other reason is wound up (ceases to exist) you will have to pay that amount, but nothing else. Your private assets are untouchable, provided of course that you have not been party to some fraud that caused the company to go bankrupt in the first place. So, the concept of limited liability limits the liability of the individual shareholders of a company to the amounts, if any, unpaid on their shares. It does *not* limit the liability of the company to others – its external creditors. That remains unlimited, to the full amount of their debts. However, the limit on the liability of individual shareholders obviously puts a practical limit on the money available for paying those debts.

Companies may thus have thousands, or even millions of individual shareholders. Even if they were all capable of contributing actively to the running of the business, it would be quite impracticable for them to do so. A committee of six is often a pretty inefficient way of getting things done, but imagine a committee of a 1,000. It is, of course, unthinkable. What happens in practice is this. A company is a democracy in which each share usually carries one vote, so that the power of each shareholder is directly proportional to the number of shares held. At least once a year, a company is required to hold a general meeting – the annual general meeting – which all the members are entitled to attend and at which they are entitled to vote, in person or by proxy. A vote is passed on a simple majority, so if one shareholder holds one share more than 50% of the total, then that person's view prevails.

One of the most important things decided at the annual general meeting is the appointment or reappointment of people called *directors* to run the business on the shareholders' behalf. Not only do the directors run the business, delegating some of the day-to-day authority to managers; they also have to keep records of the business activities and produce *annual accounts* at the end of each year which are summaries of those records. Another important thing decided at the annual general meeting is the appointment of *auditors*, who are professional accountants. Their job is to report back to the shareholders at the next annual general meeting whether, in their opinion, the accounts produced by the directors represent accurately the business activities of the company during the intervening year. Yet another decision usually made at the annual general meeting is whether to accept the directors' recommendation of the amount of dividend to be paid. A *dividend* is that part of the profit paid to the shareholders as a cash *return* on their investment.

Shares in companies can be bought and sold, which makes it easy to pass ownership from person to person or, because companies can hold shares in other companies, from company to company. It is this aspect of companies, as well as limited liability, that can make the problem of succession in, for example, a family business, easier to solve. Shares in any company can be bought and sold privately. For this reason, most companies are called *private limited companies*. However, in order to be allowed to offer its shares to the public generally, and for its shares to be buyable and sellable on a *stock exchange*, which is simply a market for trading in shares, a company must be a *public limited company*, often abbreviated to *plc*. "Stock" is another term meaning shares. Plc's are subject to more stringent regulations than are private companies.

If the liability of shareholders in companies is to be limited, through the mechanism of limited liability, it follows that companies must be subject to strict regulation. If this were not the case, then unethical business people would find ways of setting up companies that had no hope of ever being financially viable, using them to make a fast buck, not caring if they failed, and then repeat the process, leaving a trail of unpaid debts behind them at every step. This does of course happen, but it is becoming more and more difficult, because the regulation of companies and company directors is becoming ever more stringent. In the UK, the main Acts of Parliament governing companies are the Companies Act 1985 and the Companies Act 1989. Between them they occupy about a thousand pages, and there are equivalents in every country.

In summary, then, the main purpose of a business is to maximize the wealth of its proprietor or proprietors. Although there are other possibilities, the great majority of businesses are run by individuals (sole traders), groups of two or more individuals (partnerships) or by limited liability companies. Limited liability means that shareholders of a limited company cannot be held personally liable for the company's debts beyond the amount of money, if any, not yet paid for their shares. Without this concept, no rational person would invest in other than a very small business, because the investor would be personally liable for all its debts.

While the word "business" tends to be used mainly in the sense of a commercial enterprise, it can be taken as meaning any enterprise that involves a person or people in achieving its objectives. Any enterprise, if it is to be successful, should be run in a businesslike way. This is obviously true of commercial enterprises. It is equally true of a government department, a university, a charity, a local football club, a professional musician and . . . individuals concerned to make a success of their own lives. In a very real sense, we are all in business – the business of living. Fortunately, the same set of business principles is applicable to all these enterprises, as we are about to discover.

2 The Business of Living – Part 1

Assets – Liabilities – Net Worth – Balance Sheet – Capital

This and the three chapters that follow are really a single chapter divided into four, simply in order to have chapters of a reasonable length. The same practical example is used to illustrate the principles discussed in all four. In all of them, we shall explore the fundamental principles of business and finance by looking, step by step, at different kinds of transactions, their financial implications, their effect on wealth, and how they are recorded or accounted for. Above all, we shall be using examples that are familiar to all of us because they concern our own lives.

Assets

We are all in business, whether we like it or not – the business of living. With the possible exception of some latter-day St Francis, whatever our goals in life might be, we need some material resources with which to achieve them. Whether rich or less rich in such things, we all have *some* material resources, and the objective for most of us is to maximize the return we receive from them. As mentioned already, the word often used for such things is assets, and you will no doubt recall our working definition of an asset as something of value that is owned. Examples might be a house, a car, a stock of food in the freezer, or fuel for the car. It may be that all our assets have been paid for out of our own resources. If so, when for example we bought the car, we conducted a transaction that converted one kind of asset called "cash" into another kind of asset called "car"; likewise when we bought the house, and so on. A *transaction* is simply a piece of business done, especially commercial business.

Most of us however, from time to time at least, have to raise money temporarily by borrowing in order to be able to afford assets that we either need or want – "temporarily" because money borrowed has the annoying characteristic of needing to be paid back. Money borrowed from others is one example of what are collectively called liabilities. Recall that a liability is something owed, an obligation. Examples might be a bank overdraft, a credit card balance, or a loan from a friend; or a liability could be non-monetary, such as the obligation to do something for which we have been paid in advance. I am aware that some people have a moral objection to borrowing; I have a friend who left the world of business mainly for that reason. However, the fact is that the majority of individuals, and almost all businesses, do borrow from time to time. Notice what we are doing when we borrow money. We are conducting a different kind of transaction from the one described above. The difference is that this transaction has the effect, not of converting one kind of asset into another, but of creating an asset – cash – by also creating a corresponding liability, a loan, the liability being the obligation eventually to pay it back.

Although the two transactions considered so far – buying the car for cash and taking out the loan – were different, they nevertheless have one particular characteristic in common. What is it? The answer is that these, and indeed all, transactions have two sides. In the first case, the asset cash was converted into another asset – the car. No liabilities were involved at all. In the second case, however, a new asset, cash, was created by also creating a corresponding liability, a loan. This two-sidedness of transactions is of fundamental importance when we come to record transactions that we have entered into. It is the cornerstone of all accounting systems in use today.

If our financial affairs are not to be totally out of control, we all need to keep some kind of record, however rudimentary, of our transactions. For example, we should note the fact that we owe the bank £500 or we shall soon be in trouble; and if we haven't been keeping records as we go along of how much cash we've got, then we might not even know whether we need the loan in the first place. We could say that we all need to account for our transactions, and our accounting system, if not too grand a description, should ideally be such that it records both sides of every transaction. For example, if we record the fact that we have paid £100, but fail to record the fact that it was a loan to a friend, and as a result forget it, we may eventually learn the hard way the truth of Shakespeare's admonition that "loan oft loses both itself and friend".

In practice, in our own personal accounts, we may be able to get away with not always recording both sides of every transaction, although our accounts will be better if we do not take such short-cuts. A business, however, cannot get away with short-cuts because too many other people besides the owners are interested in it – for example: the tax authorities, banks and other lenders, suppliers and customers. All these people will expect to see full and accurate accounts. So, from this point we shall regard it is as a fundamental rule that *an accounting system should always record both sides of every transaction*. That raises the question: does every transaction have two sides? The answer is yes, and while you are welcome to challenge me, I believe that I would be able to answer any challenge to that assertion. You give, I receive; I lend, you borrow; you provide a service, another person receives that service, and so on.

Assets can be categorized in various ways. For example, in the sample list of assets described above, what essential differences could you discern between the assets "cash" and "stock of food" on the one hand, and the assets "house" and "car" on the other? I would suggest that there are three essential differences, and they are encapsulated in answers to the following three questions: how long are the assets likely to last?; how much do they cost?; and would people typically be able to buy these particular assets using their own cash, or would they usually have to borrow in order to be able to acquire them?

First, consider the house and the car. I suggest that the answers would usually be as follows. These are assets that are likely to last quite a long time – almost certainly more than one year. They cost what most people, in the context of their personal finances, would regard as quite a lot of money, and most people would not have that kind of money lying around; it would usually have to be raised by borrowing. The everyday phrase to describe such things would be long-term assets. However, business people, often with a distaste for ordinary words where a good jargon word might do instead, would usually call them *fixed assets* or, sometimes, *capital assets*.

By contrast, with regard to the stock of food, and fuel for the car the answers to the questions would usually be as follows. These are short-term assets, most unlikely to last as long as a year; they are used up and need to be replenished quite frequently. In the context of their owner's financial resources, their cost is probably quite modest. Finally, most people would expect to be able to afford such assets out of their regular income. If, temporarily, they cease to have regular income, then they have a problem, and short-term borrowing might be necessary, even for these assets.

We might well call these things short-term assets. Business people would refer to them as *current assets* or, sometimes, *circulating assets*, the latter precisely because they are continually being circulated – used and replenished. There is one further distinguishing characteristic of these short-term assets. That is that they are often, as in this case, a consequence of an earlier decision to acquire long-term assets. If you do not have a freezer, then while you certainly need food of some kind, you would not buy freezer food; if you do not have a car, there are not many non-criminal uses for petrol.

So far we have looked at two quite common ways of classifying assets – long-term and short-term. Although we discerned some substantial differences between them, there is one characteristic that all our examples so far have in common, and that is that they are things, or tangible assets.

Now, however, suppose that you have lent £100 to a friend. First of all, what are the two sides of that transaction? You have certainly paid out cash, but what is the other side of it? Have you created a corresponding liability? I think not, because our definition of liability is that it is something that we owe to somebody else. In this case, on the contrary, it is the friend who has an obligation to us – the obligation to repay us the loan. The answer is that this is another example of a transaction that has converted one asset, cash, into another asset – the right, in this case, to receive cash in eventual repayment of the loan. A right to receive cash is just as much an asset as is cash itself or a stock of freezer food. However, it is an example of an intangible asset. Let us suppose that the loan is interest-free. What happens when the friend repays the loan? What are the two sides of that transaction? The answer is, of course, the reversal of the original one – the asset called "right to receive cash" is converted back into cash. However, instead of that rather long-winded phrase, "right to receive cash", the term *debtor* is usually used, or *receivable* in US terminology.

Now let us consider an example of a non-monetary right. Whether you own a house or live in rented accommodation you have, directly or indirectly, to pay the local authority for the provision of services such as street lighting and rubbish collection. In the United Kingdom this is called council tax. It is payable on 1 April for the following 12 months. You can pay in monthly instalments, but we shall ignore that for the purpose of this illustration. Suppose that on 1 April you pay £400 for council tax. You have obviously reduced the amount of your cash by £400, but what is the other side of this transaction? Having learnt from the previous example, it is perhaps a fair bet that you have converted the cash paid into another kind of asset. But what is the nature of that asset? The answer is that you have made a payment in advance, or *prepayment*, for the right to have the streets lit and rubbish collected for the next twelve months. This is a non-monetary asset, but an asset nevertheless. The right eventually to receive a service, or goods, in return for cash paid in advance is just as much an asset as is the right eventually to receive payment for goods or services delivered.

Having paid the council tax, during the year that right will gradually be used up, as services are provided day-by-day, until at the end of the year there is none of it left. It has all been used up. The process of using up assets, whether stocks of food, rights to services, or cars, is what is meant by the term expense. An *expense* is the extent to which an asset has been used up during a period. A special term – *depreciation* – is used to describe the expense represented by the gradual using up of long-term assets, such as cars or computers. Both of these terms – expense and depreciation – have the unusual merit of being ones that we use in everyday speech to describe just such things as the paying of council tax or the phone bill, or the gradual using up of a car. We shall cover depreciation in a little more detail in Chapter 4.

Do all expenses represent the using up of assets? The answer is yes, although it may sometimes be necessary to think a little in order to connect the expense with its corresponding asset, as we shall see in the next chapter. Meanwhile, we shall extend our consideration of liabilities.

Liabilities

Liabilities, like assets, may be long-term or short-term. Where liabilities such as loans are incurred in order to finance a particular asset, their term should ideally correspond with the expected life of that asset. For example, it makes reasonable sense to finance the purchase of a house with a long-term loan over 25 or 30 years because that is the kind of period over which the house is likely to be useful to us, and over which we are likely to be able to afford repayments out of income. It does not make sense to take out a 5-year loan to finance a 3-week holiday, because we shall still be repaying the loan long after the asset – the right to holiday travel and accommodation – has been used up.

All liabilities are intangible, and they are mostly monetary. They represent where the money has come from with which to finance our lives – or our business. Most European languages use a particularly expressive word to mean liabilities. Translated, it is the word "passives", used as a noun. It means simply "where the money comes from", quite regardless of what we do with it once we've got it. Their corresponding word for assets is "actives", also used as a noun, and it refers to what, for the time being, we are doing with our money, what it is currently "invested in".

Not all liabilities are monetary, however, just as not all assets are monetary. Suppose that you are pretty useful at servicing cars, and that you have agreed to service a friend's car for £50, which the friend pays in advance. What are the two sides of this transaction? Obviously, you have received £50 in cash, but what is the other side of the transaction? The answer is that you have incurred a corresponding liability – the obligation to do the work for which you have been paid. So, just as some assets represent the right to receive services, or goods, for which we have paid in advance, so some liabilities represent the obligation to provide services, or goods, for which we have *been* paid in advance.

Net Worth

It is sometimes instructive to make a list of all our assets and liabilities in order to see how much we are worth, in purely financial terms of course. With luck, our assets will exceed our liabilities, at least by a small margin, so that our *net worth* or simply wealth is positive. If we sold all our noncash assets, that is to say, converted them all into cash, and paid off all our debts, that is the amount that we would be left with; provided, of course, that our estimates of asset values were accurate in the first place – a big proviso. If you have a car, you do not know exactly what it is "worth" until you come to sell it. In that sense, any asset can be said to be worth what a willing buyer is prepared to pay for it. But that is only one meaning of worth or value. Your car may be an old wreck, but if it goes, and especially if it is a lovingly maintained old wreck, then it has a worth, or value, to you that is much greater than its market value. Your PC may be so old that you would have to pay someone to take it away, so that its market value is negative. But if it still works, and still does the things you need it to do, then its value to you is positive.

At this point, I suggest that you pause, and write down all the assets that you have that are capable of being expressed in monetary terms, and, in a separate list, all your liabilities. Add up the amounts in each list, then subtract the total of the liabilities from the total of the assets. The difference will be your net worth in monetary terms. While I said that you can't know exactly what your car, for example, is worth until you come to sell it, I do suggest that in valuing your assets you make a reasonable guess at their market value, because that is the only objective value that they have. You may love your old car so much that nothing less than £10,000 would persuade you to part with it. However, in working out your net worth, it might be unwise to include it at a valuation of £10,000 if you know that you could only get £500 for it. £500 might not give you such a warm feeling, but it might contribute more realistically to the calculation of your net worth.

In case you feel that your current financial situation is such as to make that particular exercise both futile and depressing – a temporary situation almost certainly – then how about doing the exercise with made-up numbers? It will achieve much the same, albeit in a less personal way. Suppose that you are indeed interested in finding out your net worth. In order to do so, you have jotted down your assets and liabilities in the order in which they occur to you, and your jottings are as shown in Table 2.1.

To find out your net worth, first decide whether each item in Table 2.1 is an asset – something you own, or a liability – something you owe. Then add up all the assets, and all the liabilities. Finally, subtract the total of the liabilities from the total of the assets, and the result will be your net worth. With luck, this will be a positive number. The likely result of this work, your statement of assets and liabilities, appears in Table 2.2, and it shows that your net worth is indeed positive, an amount of £4,689. The references, in this and some subsequent tables, are there only as navigational aids, should you need them.

A negative net worth would usually only be caused by a fall in value of a major asset. For example, if a loan of £50,000 had been taken out to buy a house for £60,000, and the value of the house subsequently dropped to £45,000, then the house-owner would be said to have *negative equity* of £5,000 in the house, because its value had fallen below the amount borrowed. Unless the total of the house-owner's other assets less other

Table 2. 1 List of personal assets and liabilities

	£
Car, at estimated value	6,000
Hire purchase debt on car (will be paid off within 1 year)	2,880
Freezer (cost from memory)	409
Investment (long-term savings account)	41
Stock of food in freezer, at cost*	843
Loan to Sam (repayable this year)	249
Loan from Granny (long-term)	812
Investment (short-term – instant access deposit)	114
Cash – current account and in hand	725

* You have expensive tastes and you are very precise

Table 2. 2 Personal statement of assets and liabilities

	Ref.	£
Assets		
Car		6,000
Freezer		409
Investment (long-term)		41
Stock (of food)		843
Debtor (loan to Sam)		249
Investment (short-term)		114
Cash at bank and in hand		725
Total assets	(a)	8,381
Liabilities		
Hire purchase loan		2,880
Loan from Granny		812
Total liabilities	(b)	3,692
Net worth	(a–b)	4,689

liabilities was £5,000 or more, then that person would, for the time being, have negative net worth.

The Balance Sheet

What you have just done is to subtract total liabilities from total assets, and described the difference as your net worth: it amounts to £4,689. In

Table 2.2 we have simply listed the assets and liabilities in the order given. However, the reason why we had the earlier discussion about various categories of assets and liabilities was because it is often quite useful to distinguish between them according to these categories. So let's now modify Table 2.2 by categorizing our assets and liabilities into those that are long-term and those that are short-term and, in the case of the long-term assets, those that are tangible and those that are not. You might wish to try it for yourself. Whether you do or not, one way of setting out the result would be as in Table 2.3. As an alternative to the rather long-winded "statement of assets and liabilities", I have used the shorter, and more common, term *balance sheet*, which means the same thing. As we have seen already, business people have the infuriating habit of letting you get familiar with one jargon word or phrase, only to then coin another one which means the same thing. I have also, in Table 2.3, appended supplementary labels to the terms current liabilities and long-term liabilities. You will see why in just a moment. Meanwhile, the supplementary labels do actually describe a little more precisely the meanings of the two terms.

Table 2.3 Categorized personal statement of assets and liabilities or balance sheet

	Ref.	£
Fixed assets		
Tangible assets (car and freezer)		6,409
Investment (long-term)		41
		6,450
Current assets		
Stock (of food)		843
Debtor (loan to Sam)		249
Investment (short-term)		114
Cash at bank and in hand		725
		1,931
Total assets	(a)	8,381
Current liabilities (creditors due within one year)		
Hire purchase loan		2,880
Long-term liabilities (creditors due after one year)		
Loan from Granny		812
Total liabilities	(b)	3,692
Net worth	(a–b)	4,689

At this point, you may be wondering when in this chapter, in a book that you thought was about business and finance, we are going to get round to mentioning business, by which I, and probably you, really mean commercial business. If so, I have good news for you. Some of the *essential* concepts of commercial business, finance and accounting have already been covered. Not convinced? Please look at Figure A1.1 in Appendix 1, ignoring for now the last three columns. Do you recognise it? Except for a few obvious differences, the text and the numbers look much the same as those in Table 2.3, although if you look carefully at the numbers you will see that they represent millions of pounds rather than pounds.

What you have just looked at in Appendix 1 is the balance sheet of J Sainsbury plc, the well-known UK based retailer, as it appears in that company's Annual Report for 1999. Of course such differences as there are in text and numbers need to be explained, and they will be. However, the point is that the balance sheet of a commercial business is no different in concept from the balance sheet of an individual. The numbers are usually bigger, but these days even that is by no means always the case.

There is another thing that you should, perhaps, be wondering about. As I made such a big thing about the need for accounting systems to record both sides of every transaction, you might complain that the exercise I just invited you to do of drawing up lists of assets and liabilities was *one*-sided. If so, you would be quite right. A photograph of a building shows how the building looked at the time the picture was taken, but tells us nothing about how it was built. In the same way, your personal balance sheet, indeed any balance sheet, is just a snapshot of assets and liabilities at a particular moment in time. It tells the reader nothing about how the situation it describes came about. In order to understand that, it would be necessary to look, step by step, at the various transactions that had given rise to the situation. That is what we shall now do.

To return to our personal example – so you are currently "worth" £4,689. A reasonable question to ask is: where did that wealth come from? The answer is that for individuals wealth comes legally from only four possible sources: we inherit it, we are given it, we win it or we earn it. Let us suppose that, for some time, Granny had been saving up small change and from time to time paying it into a deposit account, her purpose being to help you make a start when you left home. She is a prudent old lady and, recognizing that one day, once you are established, she may need the money back again, she lets you have it as an interest-free loan for 5 years, repayable on demand at any time thereafter.

We shall suppose that the money in Granny's deposit account at the time she lets you have it amounts to £812. Let us also suppose, no doubt unrealistically but for the purpose of example, that up to that point you had no resources of your own. So, receipt of Granny's £812 loan could be regarded as the financial beginning of your life as an independent person. We could say that it represents the financial start of your life

Table 2.4   Personal balance sheet

	£
Transaction: receive Granny's long-term loan £812	
Assets	
Cash	812
Total assets	812
Liabilities	
Loan from Granny	812
Total liabilities	812

"business". From the viewpoint of that "business", what are the two sides of that transaction? Certainly your "business" has acquired an asset of £812 cash. However, you will by now know that it has also acquired a liability, a long-term liability – the obligation eventually to repay the loan to Granny. Table 2.4 shows the initial balance sheet of your life "business". For simplicity, in this and in later balance sheets in which we shall record subsequent transactions, we shall revert to the original unclassified format of the balance sheet, although we shall continue to show the various assets and liabilities in the same sequence as that in which they would usually be shown.

Capital

Now let us suppose that Granny 2 is also kindly disposed towards you. She too has been saving up over the years, a grand total of £1,839. She too has to be careful with her money, but unlike Granny 1 she feels confident enough to make you an outright gift of that amount. It is for the same reason – to help you make a start in life. What is the nature of this transaction? Obviously your life "business" has acquired a further asset of £1,839 in cash. Equally obviously it must have acquired a further liability, but what is the nature of this liability? Is it a loan? If it is, it is not a loan from Granny 2, because her £1,839 was an outright gift to you. And there is the clue. Once Granny 2 has given you the money, it is yours, so from the viewpoint of your "business" this further £1,839 was received from you, its proprietor. You, the individual, have paid £1,839 of your personal money into your "business".

However, that money still belongs to you, the individual, and at some time you may want it back. You might, for example, choose to give it all away and indeed become a latter-day St Francis, living on charity and ministering to the poor. That is about the only circumstance in which, so long as you live, you might reasonably be described as *not* being in the "business" of living. So, *is* your £1,839 a loan to the "business"? In a sense it is, because we have just agreed that it is money that you the individual might want back at some time. However, because it is obviously different in nature from the loan from Granny 1, or a loan from the bank or from any other external source, it had better be given a different name. The liability of a business to its owner for the money paid into it is usually called its *capital*. Capital has several meanings, but in this sense it just means money contributed by the proprietor or proprietors of a business to enable it to function – the business of life or any other business. So, the capital of a sole trader might be called *proprietor's capital*, while that part of a company's money belonging to its shareholders might be called *shareholders' capital, share capital* or, sometimes, just capital. Finally, because "capital" has such a broad meaning, long-term loans such as Granny 1's would sometimes be referred to as *loan capital*.

This discussion has led us to another fundamental rule of finance – that *any business should be thought of as separate from its owner or proprietor*. Take the case of the one-person taxi business. To the customers, the taxi driver and the business are much the same thing, and you may recall that this is also the case legally if the business is not a company. However, for purposes of finance and accounting, the business should always be thought of as a separate entity from the individual. This is really just another aspect of the principle of two-sidedness already discussed.

A reasonable question now is: how can we reconcile the two-sided way of looking at things with the, apparently simpler, one-sided approach that we adopted in working out your net worth in the first place? After all, in the two-sided view, total assets must always equal total liabilities; so, isn't net worth, which is total assets less total liabilities, always nil? The answer to this impeccable logic is to slightly modify our definition of net worth to the following: net worth is total assets less total *external* liabilities, where this means all liabilities except proprietor's capital.

The balance sheet of your life "business" at this point is as shown in Table 2.5. From that balance sheet we can see that the total of your assets is £2,651, while the total of your external liabilities is £812 – Granny 1's long-term loan. Subtracting this external liability from the total assets leaves £1,839, which, at this point, is your net worth. At the level of this simple example, net worth and capital mean the same thing, and they often do in practice. Net worth is the term usually used when looking at things in the one-sided way; capital is the term usually used when looking at things from an accounting point of view, that is in the two-sided way. In working through the various transactions of your "business", all subsequent balance sheets will, like the one in Table 2.5, contain a note in italics of the transaction being recorded and will also, as an aid to clarity, show the "before" and "after" situations.

Let us now suppose that your first priority is to acquire a car. Incidentally, I am sorry if you are one of the significant number of people who choose not to drive a car, and are irritated by the frequent mention

Table 2.5 Personal balance sheet

	Before £	Transaction £	After £
Transaction: proprietor's capital paid in £1,839			
Assets			
Cash	812	1,839	2,651
Total assets	812		2,651
Liabilities			
Loan from Granny	812		812
Capital		1,839	1,839
Total liabilities	812		2,651

of cars, but the car is a useful example of a long-term asset used by individuals, so I trust you are prepared to accept it for the purposes of this example. Suppose that you find a car that costs £7,500 and that you spend £1,000 on the deposit, the balance being borrowed under a hire purchase (HP) agreement. How many transactions are involved here? I suggest that there are two. The first one is the acquiring of an additional £6,500 in cash by the raising of a loan from the HP company (Table 2.6); the second is the converting of £7,500 of one asset called cash into another asset – the car.

Table 2.7 shows your balance sheet after both of these transactions. Note that neither your capital nor Granny 1's loan which, together, represent the original long-term money used to get the "business" started, has changed. This should not be a surprise. Remember that liabilities are

Table 2.6 Personal balance sheet

	Before £	Transaction £	After £
Transaction: hire purchase loan arranged £6,500			
Assets			
Cash	2,651	6,500	9,151
Total assets	2,651		9,151
Liabilities			
Hire purchase loan		6,500	6,500
Loan from Granny	812		812
Capital	1,839		1,839
Total liabilities	2,651		9,151

Table 2.7   Personal balance sheet

	Before £	Transaction £	After £
Transaction: car bought for £7,500			
Assets			
Car		7,500	7,500
Cash	9,151	−7,500	1,651
Total assets	9,151		9,151
Liabilities			
Hire purchase loan	6,500		6,500
Loan from Granny	812		812
Capital	1,839		1,839
Total liabilities	9,151		9,151

passive – collectively they represent where the money being used in a business came *from*, but they say nothing about what it is being used *for*. For that, we look at the "active" side of the balance sheet – the assets. Granny 1's loan, for example, will not show any change unless you were to make a full or partial repayment, in which case you would have extinguished all or part of that liability by correspondingly reducing the value of the asset called cash. As for your capital, we shall see shortly some of the things that might cause that to change.

We shall suppose that your next purchase is the freezer, which you buy with cash for £509. Unfortunately your memory was at fault in the initial list of assets and liabilities that you drew up (Table 2.1), in which you believed that it cost £409. Let us assume that you have rented a furnished flat, and that a freezer is the only thing that it lacks. This transaction converts more of the asset cash into – the freezer. This only affects the "active" side of things; the passives remain – well, passive (*see* Table 2.8). Next you go on a spending spree, buying your initial stock of freezer food for £843. We shall assume that it is a large freezer and that, as already suggested, you have expensive tastes. Your intention is to fill the freezer initially, and then each month replace the food that you have used. Table 2.9 shows the situation after this transaction.

This is all very well, but a slight problem is brewing. In your enthusiasm for your new-found independence, you hardly notice that your cash has fallen to quite a low level; you need some income quite soon. Earnings are the subject of the next chapter, together with expenses – those manifestations of the unfortunate fact that earnings rarely, if ever, come free.

Table 2.8 Personal balance sheet

	Before £	Transaction £	After £
Transaction: freezer bought for £509			
Assets			
Car	7,500		7,500
Freezer		509	509
Cash	1,651	−509	1,142
Total assets	9,151		9,151
Liabilities			
Hire purchase loan	6,500		6,500
Loan from Granny	812		812
Capital	1,839		1,839
Total liabilities	9,151		9,151

Table 2.9 Personal balance sheet

	Before £	Transaction £	After £
Transaction: Initial stock of freezer food bought for £843			
Assets			
Car	7,500		7,500
Freezer	509		509
Stock of food		843	843
Cash	1,142	−843	299
Total assets	9,151		9,151
Liabilities			
Hire purchase loan	6,500		6,500
Loan from Granny	812		812
Capital	1,839		1,839
Total liabilities	9,151		9,151

3 The Business of Living – Part 2

Earnings – Expenses

This chapter is a continuation of Chapter 2. It continues our consideration of various kinds of transaction and our treatment of your personal balance sheet or statement of assets and liabilities as the primary accounting document. You now have all the assets that you need, and at this point you could say that your life "business" is set up, and that you are ready to face the world. However, your cash has fallen to quite a low level, and we noted that you do need some income quite soon. Fortunately, you have been offered a job, which will pay you £1,250 per month after tax and other deductions. Given your impending cash crisis, you are fortunate that it is the kind of job – and there are some – that pays your salary monthly, in advance. However, in coming to record the receipt of your first month's pay we appear to have a slight problem. A balance sheet only records assets and liabilities. Earnings do not seem to fit into either category – or do they?

Earnings

Being paid for work done is certainly a transaction, to which therefore there must be two sides. As before, one side is obvious – you have received cash of £1,250, so your cash has increased by £1,250. What, however, is the other side of the transaction? Is this the kind of transaction that has converted some other asset into the asset called "cash"? I think not. You still have the car, the freezer and the stock of food. Is it, on the other hand, the kind of transaction that creates an asset, cash in this case, by creating a corresponding liability? Indeed it is, but not a monetary liability this time. The liability is the obligation that you have to do the work for which you have been paid. Remember that obligation is an alternative word for liability. Table 3.1 shows how that liability – the obligation

Table 3.1 Personal balance sheet

	Before £	Transaction £	After £
Transaction: salary paid in advance £1,250			
Assets			
Car	7,500		7,500
Freezer	509		509
Stock of food	843		843
Cash	299	1,250	1,549
Total assets	9,151		10,401
Liabilities			
Obligation to work		1,250	1,250
Hire purchase loan	6,500		6,500
Loan from Granny	812		812
Capital	1,839		1,839
Total liabilities	9,151		10,401

to work – might be recorded. I say "might be", because the reality is usually slightly different, as we shall see. In a commercial business, the terms *deferred income* or *deferred revenue* would usually be used instead of the more descriptive but rather clumsy "obligation to work".

What happens as, day by day, you do the work? The obligation is obviously reduced, because there is less work still to do. For example, halfway through the month, you have done half the work for which you have been paid, so the obligation is now only £625 and the amount should be reduced accordingly. One half of the obligation to work has been fulfilled. While you have indeed been *paid* in advance for all of a month's work, you have only *earned* that reward to the extent that the work has been done. As work is done, you are converting the obligation to work into earnings. Business people too use the word earnings, but they also often use the word *revenue*, which for practical purposes means the same, but has the comforting ring of jargon about it.

So what is the other side of this transaction of reducing by a half the obligation to work? The perhaps surprising answer is that in reducing your obligation to work, you have correspondingly increased your capital. A clue as to the reason why this should be so lies in the £1,839 of your own money – Granny 2's gift – that you paid into your life "business" at the start. That was a liability – called capital – representing what the "business" owes to you, its proprietor. So, anything else belonging to the proprietor that is generated by the "business" should be handled in the same way. Halfway through the month, only half (£625) of the salary you received at the beginning truly belongs to you, the half representing the work done, and that is the amount that is added to your capital. After all, if you chose to leave your employer after two weeks you would almost certainly be required to repay the half of the salary not earned. So, here we have an example of yet another kind of transaction – one that converts one kind of liability into another, the obligation to work into capital.

Now, the earning of your salary could indeed be recorded by being added to your capital. However, perhaps it would be a better idea to keep on showing your original capital as a separate amount. Certainly in a commercial business you would need to do so. Why? One reason would be that you would want to keep track of how well the business is doing. As you can probably imagine, one method of doing this would be from time to time to compare the profit that you have made so far with the amount of capital you provided. In order to be able to do so, you had better keep note of what that original capital was, and the way of doing so is indeed to continue showing it as a separate item in the balance sheet. Profit, you may recall, is simply earnings (or revenue) less expenses over a given period. It happens that we do not normally use the term profit to describe the difference between earnings and expenses of an individual during the "business" of living, but we could if we wished, quite accurately.

If we are going to show earnings and, later, expenses separately from the original capital, then we had better give a name to that separate item. Anything that is really part of proprietor's capital, but needs to be shown separately from it, is usually called a *reserve*. Because this particular reserve is one in which only income and expenses will be accumulated, things which together contribute towards profit or loss, it is usually called the *profit and loss reserve* or, more commonly, the *profit and loss account*. Table 3.2 shows how the above transaction might be recorded – as a decrease in the obligation to work and an increase in capital, but shown separately under the heading "profit and loss account". At the end of the month, the obligation to work will have been wholly fulfilled. To reflect this, the remaining £625 would also be added to the capital, as shown in Table 3.3

You might think that all that was rather a long-winded way of recording the simple fact that you had received a salary payment – cash – in exchange for your labour, and you would be right. You will understand, I think, that we have done it that way in order to illustrate some particular points of principle. However, I also said above that in reality a slightly different method is usually adopted. If you remain employed for the whole year, then by the end of that year, how much salary will you have been paid? The answer is $£1,250 \times 12 = £15,000$. Assuming that you have indeed earned your money, how much will you have *earned* during the year? Once again, the answer is £15,000. Over an extended period, what you are paid will equal what you have earned.

Table 3.2   Personal balance sheet

	Before £	Transaction £	After £
Transaction: half of salary paid has now been earned £625			
Assets			
Car	7,500		7,500
Freezer	509		509
Stock of food	843		843
Cash	1,549		1,549
Total assets	10,401		10,401
Liabilities			
Obligation to work	1,250	−625	625
Hire purchase loan	6,500		6,500
Loan from Granny	812		812
Capital	1,839		1,839
Profit and loss account		625	625
Total liabilities	10,401		10,401

Table 3.3   Personal balance sheet

	Before £	Transaction £	After £
Transaction: remainder of salary paid has now been earned £625			
Assets			
Car	7,500		7,500
Freezer	509		509
Stock of food	843		843
Cash	1,549		1,549
Total assets	10,401		10,401
Liabilities			
Obligation to work	625	−625	0
Hire purchase loan	6,500		6,500
Loan from Granny	812		812
Capital	1,839		1,839
Profit and loss account	625	625	1,250
Total liabilities	10,401		10,401

This should suggest a short-cut to use when recording your salary. It is to miss out the intermediate step of recording each month the "obligation to work" and, for accounting purposes, to assume that the salary is *earned* instantaneously at the same time that it is *received*. We could say that we are assuming that the obligation is fulfilled as soon as it is created. The effect of this short-cut is to combine what are really two transactions – earning the salary and being paid it – into a single transaction. The way that the two sides of this artificial transaction are recorded is to increase cash on the one hand, and to increase capital, via the profit and loss reserve, by a similar amount on the other. Such willingness on the part of the business community to accept that accounting need only approximately represent reality, rather than attempting to represent it precisely, is a considerable convenience to all concerned. It allows us to cut out a lot of unnecessary detail. It is also one of the things that gives rise to the often-used description of accounting as being an art rather than a science.

What would the differences be if, instead of being paid in advance, you were paid in arrears – at the end of each month? Do you agree that halfway through the month, the amount that you had *earned* (£625) would be exactly the same as it would if you had been paid in advance? If so, then at that midway point your capital would have increased by that same amount of £625; but what would then be the other side of that transaction? You would have acquired a corresponding asset – the right to be paid, eventually, for the work that you had done. You could simply call this a debtor, which is the general term meaning "right to be paid". However, in a commercial business this particular kind of debtor, if significant – "material" – enough to be treated separately from other debtors, would usually be called *accrued income* or *accrued revenue*.

I used the words "significant enough" above because of another, rather convenient, general rule in accounting – the rule of *materiality*. This means that items that are insignificant in the context of the business as a whole can be lumped together with other items rather than being shown separately. By the end of the month, just before payday, your right to be paid would amount to exactly £1,250. On receipt of your salary, this right would, of course, be converted into the asset cash. Notice how, by applying the rule of two-sidedness, all possible kinds of transaction can be recorded. With practice, only a little thought will be needed to work out the logic for any particular transaction, either in your personal "business" or a commercial one.

Let us now go back to the beginning of the month. Flush with your first salary, paid in advance before you have even done a day's work, you are feeling generous. Assume that a friend, Sam, has a sorry tale to tell of temporary financial embarrassment and persuades you to help out with a short-term interest-free loan of £500. By so doing, you have converted part of the asset called cash into another asset called "right to receive cash" – repayment of the loan – in the future. Once again, the general term used for "right to receive cash" is debtor, but if the amount is significant then it might be shown separately from other debtors and be described as "loan", or perhaps more specifically "short-term loan".

Also, later that day, realising that you should be setting some money aside, in order to avoid in the future just the kind of financial embarrassment that Sam is experiencing now, you are prompted, by an advertisement in the window of a local bank, to open a long-term savings account. You open the account with all the spare cash that you have with you, which happens to be £41. By doing so, you have converted more cash, this time into an asset called *investment*, a long-term asset, or at least it is your intention that it should be long-term. You intend to make out a bank standing order to transfer money regularly into the investment account, but somehow you never quite get round to it. These two transactions are very similar, so Table 3.4 shows both of them together. Because the "obligation to work" now has a value of zero and will no longer be required, this line that appeared in the last three balance sheets has been deleted.

Expenses

The question now is: did your earnings come without incurring any expense? Remembering that you are now an independent person, the

Table 3.4 Personal balance sheet

	Before £	Transaction £	After £
Transaction: loan to Sam £500 and long-term investment £41			
Assets			
Car	7,500		7,500
Freezer	509		509
Investment (long-term)		41	41
Stock of food	843		843
Debtor (loan to Sam)		500	500
Cash	1,549	−541	1,008
Total assets	10,401		10,401
Liabilities			
Hire purchase loan	6,500		6,500
Loan from Granny	812		812
Capital	1,839		1,839
Profit and loss account	1,250		1,250
Total liabilities	10,401		10,401

answer is – of course not. We have already noted that you have to eat, so that your stock of food will have to be replenished, that you live in a flat, for which you must pay rent, and that you have to get around, for which purpose we have assumed that you have chosen to run a car. Taking these in order, suppose that by the end of Month 1 you have used £300 worth of the food in your freezer. What is the nature of that transaction? First, the value of your stock of food has been depleted by £300, so this reduction in value must be recorded. What is the other side of the transaction? It is our first example, in your personal "business", of an expense. Do you recall the earlier definition of an expense as being a used up or consumed asset? Well, in this case part of the asset has indeed been consumed – literally; this is a good way of remembering what an expense is.

If, as just discussed, the effect of earnings is to increase capital, then what do expenses do? They reduce it. We could indeed show the expense as a reduction of capital, but it would be rather silly to have set up our profit and loss reserve for just such a purpose and then not to use it. So, on the one hand, the value of the food stock is reduced by £300 and, on the other, the value of the profit and loss reserve is also reduced, by the same amount. Table 3.5 shows the position after this transaction. You then replenish your food stock by buying, for cash, another £300-worth (Table 3.6).

Notice that the *cost* is incurred at the time you buy the stock of food. The cost only becomes an *expense* when you consume it. Expenses, the

Table 3.5 Personal balance sheet

	Before £	Transaction £	After £
Transaction: food consumed £300			
Assets			
Car	7,500		7,500
Freezer	509		509
Investment (long-term)	41		41
Stock of food	843	−300	543
Debtor (loan to Sam)	500		500
Cash	1,008		1,008
Total assets	10,401		10,101
Liabilities			
Hire purchase loan	6,500		6,500
Loan from Granny	812		812
Capital	1,839		1,839
Profit and loss account	1,250	−300	950
Total liabilities	10,401		10,101

Table 3.6 Personal balance sheet

	Before £	Transaction £	After £
Transaction: food stock replenished £300			
Assets			
Car	7,500		7,500
Freezer	509		509
Investment (long-term)	41		41
Stock of food	543	300	843
Debtor (loan to Sam)	500		500
Cash	1,008	−300	708
Total assets	10,101		10,101
Liabilities			
Hire purchase loan	6,500		6,500
Loan from Granny	812		812
Capital	1,839		1,839
Profit and loss account	950		950
Total liabilities	10,101		10,101

using up of assets, always have the effect of reducing the proprietor's capital – what we earlier described as what the "business" owes to its proprietor. Most commercial businesses also have to maintain items of stock – for example raw materials, spare parts, goods for resale. These stocks too have to be regularly replenished as they are used. Their acquisition, use and replenishment are accounted for in exactly the same way as we have just accounted for your food stock.

Now let us look at the rent, your share of which we shall suppose is £200 per month. Let us also suppose that the tenancy is on a monthly basis. If so, when you signed the agreement and paid the first month's rent in advance you acquired an asset. What was it? By now you should have little difficulty in deciding that it was the right to live in someone else's property for one month. You have paid in advance, or prepaid, for that right and, as already discussed, such rights are indeed usually called prepayments. You have converted part of the asset "cash" into the asset "right to accommodation". Table 3.7 shows the effect of this transaction.

Using the same logic that we applied to your salary, but in reverse, how does your "business" stand mid-month with regard to the rent? How much of the "right to accommodation" has been used up? Half of it, of course, so that the asset is now only worth £100 – half of what you paid for it. We now know that a used-up asset is what is called an expense, and that expenses always have the effect of reducing capital, usually being shown as a reduction from that "reserved" part of the capital called the

Table 3.7   Personal balance sheet

	Before £	Transaction £	After £
Transaction: rent paid in advance £200			
Assets			
Car	7,500		7,500
Freezer	509		509
Investment (long-term)	41		41
Stock of food	843		843
Debtor (loan to Sam)	500		500
Prepayment (of rent)		200	200
Cash	708	−200	508
Total assets	10,101		10,101
Liabilities			
Hire purchase loan	6,500		6,500
Loan from Granny	812		812
Capital	1,839		1,839
Profit and loss account	950		950
Total liabilities	10,101		10,101

profit and loss account. Table 3.8 shows how this might be recorded but, as with your salary, we would in practice use a short-cut. By the end of the month, your right to accommodation has been entirely used up, so we had better reflect that fact by showing it at a value of zero, and further diminishing your profit and loss reserve (*see* Table 3.9).

As with your salary, so with the rent, but in reverse. By the end of the twelfth month, how much rent will you have paid? £2,400. How much right to accommodation will you have used up? Once again, the answer is £2,400. Over an extended period, what you pay in rent will equal the value of the right to accommodation that you have used. The short-cut this time is to miss out the intermediate step of recording each month the prepaid "right to accommodation" and, for accounting purposes, to assume that that right is *used* instantaneously at the same time as the rent is *paid*. Also, as with your salary, the effect of this short-cut is to combine what are really two transactions – paying for the right to accommodation, and using it – into a single transaction. The way that the two sides of this artificial transaction are recorded is to decrease cash on the one hand, and to decrease capital, via the profit and loss reserve, by a similar amount, on the other.

What would the difference be if, instead of paying the rent in advance, you were able to pay it at the end of each month – in arrears? Halfway through the month, the amount of the right to accommodation that you

Table 3.8 Personal balance sheet

	Before £	Transaction £	After £
Transaction: half of the prepaid right to accommodation is used up £100			
Assets			
Car	7,500		7,500
Freezer	509		509
Investment (long-term)	41		41
Stock of food	843		843
Debtor (loan to Sam)	500		500
Prepayment (of rent)	200	−100	100
Cash	508		508
Total assets	10,101		10,001
Liabilities			
Hire purchase loan	6,500		6,500
Loan from Granny	812		812
Capital	1,839		1,839
Profit and loss account	950	−100	850
Total liabilities	10,101		10,001

Table 3.9 Personal balance sheet

	Before £	Transaction £	After £
Transaction: the remainder of the prepaid right to accommodation is used up £100			
Assets			
Car	7,500		7,500
Freezer	509		509
Investment (long-term)	41		41
Stock of food	843		843
Debtor (loan to Sam)	500		500
Prepayment (of rent)	100	−100	0
Cash	508		508
Total assets	10,001		9,901
Liabilities			
Hire purchase loan	6,500		6,500
Loan from Granny	812		812
Capital	1,839		1,839
Profit and loss account	850	−100	750
Total liabilities	10,001		9,901

had used up (£100) would be exactly the same as if you had paid the rent in advance. Therefore, at that midway point your capital would have decreased by that same amount of £100. What would be the other side of that transaction? You would have acquired a corresponding liability – the obligation to pay, eventually, for the accommodation that you have used. This could be called a creditor, which is the general term meaning a person to whom a debt is due. However, in a commercial business, this particular kind of creditor would, if significant enough to be treated separately from other creditors, usually be called an *accrued expense* or simply an *accrual*.

At this point I should perhaps challenge you to try and think if there are any expenses which cannot be expressed as "used up assets". Here are a few examples to think about – a train ticket, your electricity bill, interest on your bank overdraft, income tax. These are all things that we usually think of as expenses. In each case, what is the asset, the using up of which represents the expense? My suggested answers are in Table 3.10.

The principle illustrated above is to show as an expense an amount representing how much of the value of a particular asset has been used up during a given period. In practice, what I have called the short-cut methods are nearly always used for the day-to-day recording of income and expenses. Also in practice, adjustments are made at the end of the year, or other accounting period, to account for any significant accrued expenses, prepayments, accrued revenue or deferred revenue. However, if you can remember the principles illustrated by the long-winded methods, you should never have a problem either accounting for transactions yourself or understanding accounts produced by others. Having used the long-winded approach to illustrate the simple logic of accounting for transactions, from now on we shall use the short-cuts, just as commercial businesses do.

Mention of commercial businesses leads us to the fact that all commercial businesses are required by law to produce accounts annually, and public limited companies publish them as part of an *Annual Report*. In Chapter 4 we shall complete your personal balance sheet. Having done so, we shall then compare it with the published balance sheet of J Sainsbury plc and, in doing so, discover just how similar the two documents are.

Table 3.10 Examples of expenses as used-up assets

Expense	Asset
Train ticket	The right to be conveyed from one place to another
Interest	The right to use someone else's money
Electricity bill	The right to use the output from the power company's generating equipment
Income tax	The right to the benefits provided by the state

4 The Business of Living – Part 3

Other Transactions – Depreciation – Published Balance Sheets

In the two previous chapters we have followed step-by-step the logic of a series of perfectly ordinary personal transactions and how they can all be recorded on a single accounting document – the balance sheet or, if you prefer, the statement of assets and liabilities. In doing so, we have covered many of the main principles of finance and – as a means to an end – accounting. Having covered the main principles, we can now speed things up by summarizing all your transactions for the remaining months of the year. Our purpose now is simply to complete our record of how, typically, you might have arrived at the personal balance sheet that we drew up in Table 2.2 at the beginning of Chapter 2. You will appreciate that by summarizing transactions, for example by treating your monthly salary payments for the remaining 11 months as though they were one single payment, we shall be distorting the true dynamics of your bank account, your stock of food and other elements of your balance sheet. However, the means are justified by the saving of time and the avoiding of unnecessary further detail.

Other Transactions

Let us suppose that, at various times during the year, you have paid into, and withdrawn amounts from, a bank instant-access deposit account, the net deposits amounting to £114. We would think of such an account as a short-term investment, so let's call it that. Summarizing the various deposits and withdrawals into a single transaction, what is the nature of that transaction? Simple, I hear you say. One asset, cash, has been converted into another asset called short-term investment (*see* Table 4.1). Next, Sam, still in trouble but wanting to pay off at least slightly more

Table 4.1 Personal balance sheet

	Before £	Transaction £	After £
Transaction: net payment into instant-access deposit account £114			
Assets			
Car	7,500		7,500
Freezer	509		509
Investment (long-term)	41		41
Stock of food	843		843
Debtor (loan to Sam)	500		500
Investment (short-term)		114	114
Prepayment (of rent)	0		0
Cash	508	−114	394
Total assets	9,901		9,901
Liabilities			
Hire purchase loan	6,500		6,500
Loan from Granny	812		812
Capital	1,839		1,839
Profit and loss account	750		750
Total liabilities	9,901		9,901

than half the loan, pays you £251, so that £251 of the asset called "debtor" has been converted into cash (*see* Table 4.2). Because the prepayment now has a value of zero, and will no longer be required, the relevant line that appeared in the last few tables has now been deleted.

The next few transactions are simply repeats in summary form of transactions that we have already discussed in detail. I suggest that you use the opportunity to recall how each kind of transaction was dealt with last time and, in advance of looking at the answer, to work out for yourself how it should be dealt with.

Assuming that you remain employed for the rest of the year but with, sadly, no salary increase during that time, your salary for the remaining 11 months will be £1,250 × 11 = £13,750. If we treat this as though it were a single transaction, and if we use the short-cut method of recording it, ignoring the timing difference between earning your salary and being paid, what changes should we make to the balance sheet to reflect this transaction? The answer is that cash will have increased by £13,750 and that, because your earnings will also have increased, your capital will have gone up by a corresponding amount, the increase being recorded in the profit and loss reserve (*see* Table 4.3).

For the sake of simplicity we shall now assume that each month for the remaining 11 months of the year, you consume £300-worth of food

Table 4.2   Personal balance sheet

	Before £	Transaction £	After £
Transaction: partial repayment of loan by Sam £251			
Assets			
Car	7,500		7,500
Freezer	509		509
Investment (long-term)	41		41
Stock of food	843		843
Debtor (loan to Sam)	500	−251	249
Investment (short-term)	114		114
Cash	394	251	645
Total assets	9,901		9,901
Liabilities			
Hire purchase loan	6,500		6,500
Loan from Granny	812		812
Capital	1,839		1,839
Profit and loss account	750		750
Total liabilities	9,901		9,901

Table 4.3   Personal balance sheet

	Before £	Transaction £	After £
Transaction: receive 11 months salary £13,750			
Assets			
Car	7,500		7,500
Freezer	509		509
Investment (long-term)	41		41
Stock of food	843		843
Debtor (loan to Sam)	249		249
Investment (short-term)	114		114
Cash	645	13,750	14,395
Total assets	9,901		23,651
Liabilities			
Hire purchase loan	6,500		6,500
Loan from Granny	812		812
Capital	1,839		1,839
Profit and loss account	750	13,750	14,500
Total liabilities	9,901		23,651

and that, also each month, you replenish the freezer fully, in line with the policy that you decided upon at the outset. So, total consumption and total replenishment during the 11 months come to £3,300, ignoring inflation. Although in reality, of course, the consumption of stock precedes its replenishment, we shall record the replenishment first, but only in order to avoid what would otherwise be the absurdity of showing negative stock. The summary transaction representing replenishment requires us to reduce cash by £3,300 and to correspondingly increase the stock (*see* Table 4.4).

Do you recall how your consumption of £3,300-worth of food from your stock should be recorded? Stock is obviously reduced by £3,300, and because the stock has been consumed, used up, your capital must be reduced by the expense of similar amount (*see* Table 4.5). Notice again the fundamental difference between the cost of acquiring the stock, which is simply the conversion of one asset into another, and the expense represented by its consumption, which reduces your capital. Incidentally, suppose that instead of paying cash when you acquired the stock, you bought it on credit, using a credit card or charge card? You would still have acquired the asset "stock of food", but you would have done so by acquiring a corresponding liability – the obligation to pay off the card – rather than using the asset "cash". That is what buying on credit is – acquiring a desired asset now, while delaying the expenditure of cash.

Table 4.4   Personal balance sheet

	Before £	Transaction £	After £
Transaction: cash paid to replenish food stock £3,300			
Assets			
Car	7,500		7,500
Freezer	509		509
Investment (long-term)	41		41
Stock of food	843	3,300	4,143
Debtor (loan to Sam)	249		249
Investment (short-term)	114		114
Cash	14,395	−3,300	11,095
Total assets	23,651		23,651
Liabilities			
Hire purchase loan	6,500		6,500
Loan from Granny	812		812
Capital	1,839		1,839
Profit and loss account	14,500		14,500
Total liabilities	23,651		23,651

Table 4.5   Personal balance sheet

	Before £	Transaction £	After £
Transaction: food consumed £3,300			
Assets			
Car	7,500		7,500
Freezer	509		509
Investment (long-term)	41		41
Stock of food	4143	−3,300	843
Debtor (loan to Sam)	249		249
Investment (short-term)	114		114
Cash	11,095		11,095
Total assets	23,651		20,351
Liabilities			
Hire purchase loan	6,500		6,500
Loan from Granny	812		812
Capital	1,839		1,839
Profit and loss account	14,500	−3,300	11,200
Total liabilities	23,651		20,351

Next, we shall record the remaining rent of £200 per month, summarizing 11 payments into a single transaction of £2,200. Using the short-cut method, rent is regarded as an immediate using up of the asset "right to accommodation", that is as an immediate expense, so we should reduce cash by £2,200 and reduce your capital, via the profit and loss reserve, by the same amount (*see* Table 4.6).

We have not yet taken into account your various other living expenses, such as telephone, car running costs, other travel costs and entertainment. When we come to add them all up they usually have a depressing habit of being quite large. We shall assume that for the whole year these amount to £3,982, and we shall record these expenses also using the short-cut-method. Cash, and your capital, must both be reduced by £3,982 (*see* Table 4.7).

Prompted by the mention of entertainment, and digressing for just a moment to revisit the subject of assets and expenses, if we were using what I described as the long-winded approach to recording expenses rather than the short-cut method, what asset does "entertainment" represent? Well, it depends on the entertainment. If, for example, it consists of a few drinks in a pub, then the asset that you are acquiring is, I suggest, the right to consume drinks in premises that belong to someone else. This asset is quite short-lived, especially if you are very thirsty, so use of the short-cut method, whereby the asset is assumed to be immediately

Table 4.6 Personal balance sheet

	Before £	Transaction £	After £
Transaction: 11 months' rent paid £2,200			
Assets			
Car	7,500		7,500
Freezer	509		509
Investment (long-term)	41		41
Stock of food	843		843
Debtor (loan to Sam)	249		249
Investment (short-term)	114		114
Cash	11,095	−2,200	8,895
Total assets	20,351		18,151
Liabilities			
Hire purchase loan	6,500		6,500
Loan from Granny	812		812
Capital	1,839		1,839
Profit and loss account	11,200	−2,200	9,000
Total liabilities	20,351		18,151

Table 4.7 Personal balance sheet

	Before £	Transaction £	After £
Transaction: paid other living expenses for the year £3,982			
Assets			
Car	7,500		7,500
Freezer	509		509
Investment (long-term)	41		41
Stock of food	843		843
Debtor (loan to Sam)	249		249
Investment (short-term)	114		114
Cash	8,895	−3,982	4,913
Total assets	18,151		14,169
Liabilities			
Hire purchase loan	6,500		6,500
Loan from Granny	812		812
Capital	1,839		1,839
Profit and loss account	9,000	−3,982	5,018
Total liabilities	18,151		14,169

consumed, is not far short of reality. In fact it would be absurd even to consider recording the "right" as an asset at all. Nevertheless, that does not invalidate the rule that an expense is a consumed asset. The principle does not stipulate how long the asset has to last before it is consumed.

From what we already know of "your" financial affairs, there is another quite large item of expenditure that you will also have incurred every month from the beginning of your life "business". You entered into a hire purchase agreement for £6,500 in order to finance the acquisition of your car, and the money borrowed will have to be repaid, with interest. We can use this as an example of how to account for what we might call a composite transaction. We shall suppose that the agreement required payments, monthly in advance, of £258 including interest, based on a compound interest rate of 1% per month, which works out at an annual equivalent rate of approximately 12.7% per year.

Loans of this kind are usually repayable in equal instalments, mainly for the convenience of the borrower. However, the proportion of each payment representing interest is greatest at the beginning of the arrangement, because the amount outstanding is then greatest, becoming progressively smaller as the loan is paid off. Without a financial calculator and a spreadsheet, which is how I did it, the sums would be tiresome. You could work it out for yourself, but you might prefer to take my word for it. The results, which are all that need concern us here, are summarised in Table 4.8. The total cash paid during Year 1 of the loan comes to £258 × 12 = £3,096, of which £2,520 is repayment of principal, and reduces the amount of the loan outstanding. The remaining £576 is interest, which, again using the short-cut method, is an expense – the using up of the right to have the use of someone else's money – which reduces your capital. Table 4.9 shows how this composite transaction is accounted for.

Table 4.8   Hire purchase repayment profiles

	Monthly payment	Total paid in year	Interest	Principal
Interest rate 1% per month, payments at beginning of month				
Debt outstanding at the beginning of Year 1				6,500
Payments during Year 1	258 × 12 =	3,096	576	−2,520
Debt outstanding at the end of Year 1				3,980
Payments during Year 2	258 × 12 =	3,096	329	−2,767
Debt outstanding at the end of Year 2				1,213
Payments during Year 3	258 × 4 =	1,032		
	216 × 1 =	216		
		1,248	35	−1,213
				0

Table 4.9   Personal balance sheet

	Before **£**	**Transaction** **£**	**After** **£**
Transaction: HP instalments paid £3,096, of which interest £576, repayment of principal £2,520			
Assets			
Car	7,500		7,500
Freezer	509		509
Investment (long-term)	41		41
Stock of food	843		843
Debtor (loan to Sam)	249		249
Investment (short-term)	114		114
Cash	4,913	−3,096	1,817
Total assets	14,169		11,073
Liabilities			
Hire purchase loan	6,500	−2,520	3,980
Loan from Granny	812		812
Capital	1,839		1,839
Profit and loss account	5,018	−576	4,442
Total liabilities	14,169		11,073

While not all your good intentions with regard to saving have been followed through, you have nevertheless earned some interest on your modest investments, even if only £8. If interest paid represents the using up of the right to have the use of someone else's money, then interest received is the income earned from letting someone else have the right to use yours. Assuming you have received the interest in cash, rather than letting it accumulate in the investment accounts, your cash has obviously increased by £8 and so has your profit and loss reserve (*see* Table 4.10).

Let us now suppose that, as your cash balance is in reasonable shape, you feel able to pay another £1,100 off the hire purchase loan. Cash is reduced by £1,100, the loan is also reduced by a similar amount (*see* Table 4.11). Table 4.12 shows that, because of the extra payment, the loan will now be paid off within a year, so it is now a short-term loan.

When my children were small, about 5 minutes into any car journey, even one likely to last several hours, the plaintive cry would come from the back seat – "Are we nearly there?" So far as illustrating the kind of transactions that could have led to your personal balance sheet is concerned, we are indeed nearly there. However, are there still any assets that have, at least partly, been used up during this first year of your "business"? If so, we had better record that fact if your balance sheet is to reflect as accurately as possible what is sometimes called a true and fair view of that business.

Table 4.10 Personal balance sheet

	Before £	Transaction £	After £
Transaction: interest received £8			
Assets			
Car	7,500		7,500
Freezer	509		509
Investment (long-term)	41		41
Stock of food	843		843
Debtor (loan to Sam)	249		249
Investment (short-term)	114		114
Cash	1,817	8	1,825
Total assets	11,073		11,081
Liabilities			
Hire purchase loan	3,980		3,980
Loan from Granny	812		812
Capital	1,839		1,839
Profit and loss account	4,442	8	4,450
Total liabilities	11,073		11,081

Table 4.11 Personal balance sheet

	Before £	Transaction £	After £
Transaction: additional payment off the hire purchase loan £1,100			
Assets			
Car	7,500		7,500
Freezer	509		509
Investment (long-term)	41		41
Stock of food	843		843
Debtor (loan to Sam)	249		249
Investment (short-term)	114		114
Cash	1,825	−1,100	725
Total assets	11,081		9,981
Liabilities			
Hire purchase loan	3,980	−1,100	2,880
Loan from Granny	812		812
Capital	1,839		1,839
Profit and loss account	4,450		4,450
Total liabilities	11,081		9,981

Table 4.12 Hire purchase repayment profiles with additional £1,100 paid off at end of Year 1

	Monthly payment	Total paid in year	Interest	Principal
Interest rate 1% per month, payments at beginning of month				
Debt outstanding at the beginning of Year 1				6,500
Payments during Year 1	258 × 12 =	3,096	576	−2,520
Extra payment at end of Month 12				−1,100
Debt outstanding at the end of Year 1				2,880
Payments during Year 2	258 × 11 =	2,838		
	231 × 1 =	231		
		3,069	189	−2,880
				0

Depreciation

What about the car? Well, you may have been lucky and picked up for a song a rare example of a sought-after model. On the other hand, you are probably like the rest of us, for whom the value of a car, whether new or secondhand, drops like a brick the moment we drive it away from the dealer's showroom. Suppose that, a year after you bought the car for £7,500, you estimate that it is now only worth £6,000, with no likelihood whatever that the value will do other than continue on its downward path. You could express it by saying that the car has depreciated in value by £1,500 and, in a rare concession to using everyday terminology, financial people use the same term, depreciation. *Depreciation* is an amount representing approximately the decline in value due to the wearing out or obsolescence of a fixed asset. You could also say that £1,500-worth of the asset has been used up, and has therefore become an expense, in which case you are on what is now familiar territory; you know only too well what should be done about it. The value of the car must be reduced by £1,500, and your capital must be reduced by the same amount, the reduction being shown in the profit and loss reserve.

Exactly the same principle applies to the freezer. It will certainly have gone down in value during the year since you bought it, and your balance sheet should reflect that fact. It is less easy to say what a freezer is worth than what a car is worth, if only because the market in secondhand freezers is much smaller than the market in secondhand cars. However, we'll suppose that you choose an amount of £100 to represent approximately the depreciation of the freezer. After all, rather like the car, you probably expect that it will last you about five years, so it would make sense to depreciate it over its expected useful life. Meanwhile, Table 4.13

Table 4.13   Personal balance sheet

	Before £	Transaction £	After £
Transaction: depreciation of fixed assets £1,600			
Assets			
Car	7,500	−1,500	6,000
Freezer	509	−100	409
Investment (long-term)	41		41
Stock of food	843		843
Debtor (loan to Sam)	249		249
Investment (short-term)	114		114
Cash	725		725
Total assets	9,981		8,381
Liabilities			
Hire purchase loan	2,880		2,880
Loan from Granny	812		812
Capital	1,839		1,839
Profit and loss account	4,450	−1,600	2,850
Total liabilities	9,981		8,381

shows how the depreciation of both the car and the freezer would be reflected in the balance sheet of your "business".

The amount of depreciation charged each year can only be approximate. In practice, what business people usually do is to estimate the life of a fixed asset at the outset, deduct from its cost any expected eventual proceeds of sale, and divide the result by the number of years of life. This gives the amount of depreciation that would be charged each year. Because the amounts are the same each year, this particular method is called "straight line" depreciation. There are other methods of calculating depreciation, but the straight line method predominates.

If, as would be most unlikely, the asset were indeed sold exactly at the estimated time and for the estimated amount, then the asset would be removed from the balance sheet without further adjustment. In reality, however, the proceeds of sale will rarely, if ever, exactly equal the *book value* of the asset, so an adjustment will be made. If the proceeds are less than the book value, then the difference is an expense called loss on sale; the reverse situation results in what is usually called a profit on sale, treated as income in the profit and loss account.

Published Balance Sheets

You will no doubt recognise the balance sheet in the final column of Table 4.13. It is very similar to the statement of assets and liabilities that we produced in Table 2.2 at the beginning of Chapter 2. The only difference is that, in the statement of assets and liabilities, we deducted your total external liabilities from your total assets in order to determine your net worth. A balance sheet, however, also includes the net worth, what the business owes to its proprietor or proprietors, although the name is transformed to "capital". You may recall that net worth is the term usually used when looking at things in the one-sided way, while capital is the term usually used when looking at things in the two-sided way.

As noted then, the numbers that we produced are indeed very similar to the numbers in the J Sainsbury plc balance sheet, shown in Appendix 1 (Figure A1.1), except of course for the little detail of the units in which they are expressed. However, the format is not yet fully similar. We made a start towards converting to a "commercial" format in Table 2.3. Table 4.14 goes a step further, and shows our balance sheet exactly as the J Sainsbury format. In this widely used format, it is not immediately obvious where some of the totals and subtotals come from, or what they comprise. The references are there to make interpretation a little clearer, and the reason for doing all this work at all is, of course, to help you to read and understand *any* published balance sheet. The table also has pointers to the notes in the following paragraphs. These notes provide a brief commentary on the J Sainsbury balance sheet, and describe the few significant differences, apart from the units, between that balance sheet and yours. The notes also explain *why* this particular balance sheet format is widely used, in preference to the simpler one that we have used in building, step by step, your own balance sheet.

One general point remains to be explained before we go any further. Most large businesses consist not of just one company, but of several in what is known as a *group*. Typically, one company, known as the *holding company*, owns all or most of the shares in the others, which are known as *subsidiary companies* or just *subsidiaries*. If the holding company holds 100% of the shares of a subsidiary, then, with impeccable logic, the subsidiary is known as a wholly-owned subsidiary. Subsidiaries within the group may have been acquired by takeover, or formed at various times to perform particular functions, or in different regions or countries in which the business operates.

For reporting purposes, *consolidated* or *group accounts* are produced for the whole group. These are simply the accounts of all the individual companies combined or consolidated into a single balance sheet, and a single version of the other main accounting statements, that we have yet to consider. In published annual reports, it is usually consolidated accounts that you will be looking at. The principles of consolidated

Table 4.14   Personal balance sheet rearranged in typical commercial format

	Ref	Notes*	£
		1	
Fixed assets		2	
Tangible assets	(a)	3	6,409
Investments		4	41
	(b)		6,450
Current assets			
Stocks		5	843
Debtors		6	249
Investments		7,8	114
Cash at bank and in hand			725
	(c)		1,931
Creditors: due within one year		9	
Hire purchase loan			−2,880
	(d)		−2,880
Net current liabilities	(c + d)	10	−949
Total assets less current liabilities	(b + c + d)	(e) 11	5,501
Creditors: due after one year		12	
Loan from Granny	(f)		−812
Total net assets	(e + f)	13	4,689
Capital and reserves			
Proprietor's capital		14,15,16	1,839
Profit and loss account		17,18	2,850
Total capital and reserves		19	4,689

* *The numbers in this column refer to similarly-numbered paragraphs in the main text, which also make reference to the group balance sheet of J Sainsbury plc in Appendix 1.*

accounts are the same as those outlined in this chapter for the accounts of a single business, except that intercompany transactions are eliminated to avoid double counting, and the amount of minority interest, if any, is indicated. *Minority interest* or *minority equity interest* is simply the proportion of the group capital and the group profit attributable to shareholders outside the group, that is other shareholders in subsidiaries that are not wholly owned. If the term refers exclusively to ordinary or equity shareholders, then the term minority equity interest is used, as in the case of J Sainsbury plc.

Notes to Table 4.14

These notes should be read with reference both to Table 4.14 and the group balance sheet of J Sainsbury plc in Appendix 1. Note numbers are as referred to in Table 4.14. In what follows, the explanations are specific to the group balance sheet of J Sainsbury plc, based on information in its published accounts, and the notes attached to them, although the notes are not reproduced here for reasons of space. However, unless stated to the contrary, the explanations would also apply to other companies, obviously with differences of detail.

1. Notice that there are two J Sainsbury balance sheets: one for the group, which is the one that is similar in most respects to your personal balance sheet, the other for the holding company (the "company"). Both, as is required by law, show figures for this year and last year. As you might expect, the main asset of the holding company is long-term investments. These are the shares held in the subsidiary companies.

2. Notice the subdivision of assets into long-term (fixed) and short-term (current), and the similar subdivision of the "external" liabilities – the creditors. These, however, are now called "creditors due within one year" and "creditors due after one year", which is why those terms were introduced in our first attempt at a categorized balance sheet in Table 2.3 in Chapter 2.

3. Company accounts have to be highly summarised. The detail is relegated to many pages of notes. Even in the notes, only broad classifications are given. For example, as you might expect of a company in the retail sector, the notes reveal that the two major classes of tangible asset in the J Sainsbury balance sheet are properties (£5,001m) and fixtures, equipment and vehicles (£1,408m). In your accounts, the tangible fixed assets are the car and the freezer.

4. These long-term investments are mostly significant minority share holdings in other companies – *associated undertakings*. Normally, to qualify as an associated undertaking, the share holding would be at least 20%.

5. From the notes, and not surprisingly, most of the J Sainsbury stocks consist of goods for resale (£702m), the remainder (£141m) being land held for development. The logic here would be that the land is being held short-term en route to being converted into long-term revenue-earning properties.

6. As J Sainsbury is mainly a supermarket business, you would not expect there to be many debtors on the balance sheet. Of the total of £249m, the Notes reveal that only £54m represents *trade debtors*, which means money owed by credit customers. No doubt most of these are related to the Homebase home enhancement part of the business.

7. These are short-term investments, often temporary parking for spare cash.

8. Notice that J Sainsbury has a banking operation. The banking assets of £1,766m are mainly loans to other banks. The banking liabilities of £1,669m are mainly deposits by customers. The only big difference between the J Sainsbury balance sheet and yours, which I arranged to look as much like J Sainsbury as possible, is that, for your balance sheet, I ignored the details of the banking operation. For most of us as individuals, running a bank is not something we tend to do in personal life, although being a parent has close parallels. I have simply added the net banking assets, £1,766m − £1,669m = £97m, to the J Sainsbury investments of £17m to arrive at the figure of £114m, from which is derived the £114 that appears as "investments" in the current asset section of your balance sheet.

9. J Sainsbury's creditors due within one year of £2,880m include £1,084m of *trade creditors*, which means money owed to suppliers for goods and services provided on credit in the ordinary course of trade, short-term borrowings of £665m and accruals of £171m. The remainder is represented by amounts owing for tax and social security, dividends due to shareholders and "other".

10. *Net current liabilities* is the difference between the totals of the short-term assets and the short-term liabilities. Because supermarkets typically buy on credit, turn over their stocks very quickly and sell for cash, and therefore have relatively few debtors, it is common for their short-term liabilities to exceed their short-term assets, depending of course on the relative amounts of cash and short-term borrowings. Subject to the same dependency, in businesses, such as manufacturers, that have large stocks *and* sell on credit, current assets would usually exceed current liabilities.

11. The figure of total assets less current liabilities is a useful one. If you subtract from total assets the total of the *short-term* liabilities, the resulting number (£5,501m) represents the remainder of the assets, that are being financed by long-term money – the money provided by the shareholders and long-term lenders. This is the financial bedrock of a company. In a steadily growing business, this amount would tend to increase steadily over time. You would not expect it to fluctuate much, unless there have been major changes, such as taking over other companies or selling off parts of the business.

12. In contriving the number of £812 representing Granny's loan for your personal balance sheet, I added together the J Sainsbury creditors due after one year (£804m) and their provisions for liabilities and charges (£8m). A *provision* is an amount set aside for a known liability the amount of which cannot be precisely determined. The J Sainsbury provisions of £8m are mainly in respect of tax. It often takes a long time for a large company to determine precisely the final amount of tax payable or refundable in respect of a financial year. As mentioned in paragraph (9) above, amounts that *have* been determined precisely but have not yet

been paid are included in "creditors". Amounts set aside for depreciation are often described as provisions because, by their nature, they cannot be precise.

13. If we subtract from "total assets less current liabilities" the external long-term money being used in the business – long-term loans of various kinds – then the number that we are left with, having already deducted the external short-term money, is the amount of assets being financed by the proprietors. The precise make-up of the proprietors' or share-holders' money is shown in the final section of the balance sheet – capital and reserves.

14. Share capital is the amount paid by the shareholders for the nominal or par value of the original shares in the company and for any that have subsequently been issued. The term "called up" simply means the amount asked for by the company up to this point. Remember that a company will typically not ask shareholders to pay the full amount due for their shares all at once. The nominal or par value of each J Sainsbury share is 25p. The notes to the accounts tell us that all the shares are in fact "fully paid", and that at the accounting date 1,918.2 million shares were in issue.

15. Usually, once decided upon at the beginning, the nominal value of a company's shares does not change. However, the price at which a successful company's shares trade on a stock exchange will tend to increase over time. As new shares are issued by the company in order to finance expansion, those who buy them would obviously expect to pay more than the nominal value. The issue price would bear some resem-blance to the market price of the shares at the time. The difference between the nominal value and the issue price is called the *share premium*. The *share premium account* is a reserve representing the accu-mulated sum of share premiums. Your "business" obviously does not have a share premium account, so I have combined the numbers representing the J Sainsbury share capital in millions (£480) and share premium account (£1,359) to arrive at the £1,839 figure that is the original capital of your "business".

16. The *revaluation reserve* is yet another example of something that is part of the capital of a business but needs to be shown separately. For example, suppose that the car that you bought, although old, was a sought-after model in short supply, and that since you bought it its market value had gone up from £7,500 to £12,000. If you believed that this rise in value was permanent, or at least long-term, you might be justified in reflecting that increase in your balance sheet. How would you record it? As one side of the transaction, you would add £4,500 to the value of the car. Your total capital would increase correspondingly but, for reasons already discussed, you would not change the amount of your original capital. Equally, this increase in capital could not be said to belong in the profit and loss, or earnings, reserve – it is more in the nature of a windfall

profit. You may believe genuinely that the increase in value is long-term, but it may prove not to be. Suppose that at some time the market value of the car fell back to £8,000. What would you do? The obvious answer would be to reduce the value of the car by £4,000 on your balance sheet and to make a corresponding reduction in the revaluation reserve. In commercial companies, revaluation reserves usually only arise from upward revaluations of land and buildings.

17. We have assumed that your "business" has only been running for one year, so it follows that all your "profit" can only have been earned in that year. The J Sainsbury business was founded in 1869, so the total of the profit and loss account (£2,767m) on the balance sheet represents all the profits made, less dividends paid, since that time. (Because your "business" has neither a revaluation reserve nor a minority equity interest, I have made your "profit" a number (£2,850) which, in millions, is the J Sainsbury profit number of £2,767 plus £38 and £45 representing those two items respectively.) After deducting from revenue all the expenses incurred in earning it, *all* the profit that remains belongs to the shareholders. Typically, but not compulsorily, part of it is paid to them each year as a dividend. What is left is retained in the business to finance expansion, and is called *retained profit*. J Sainsbury's retained profit for 1999 is £304m, as we shall see when we come to look at their profit and loss account in more detail. The difference of £2,767 − £304 = £2,463m is the total of all the profits retained from previous years.

18. Refer to the paragraph above, immediately preceding these notes, for an explanation of minority equity interest.

19. The label, if any, given to the bottom line of balance sheets in this format varies from company to company. J Sainsbury call it total capital employed. However, the term *capital employed* is often used in ratio analysis, a topic that we shall consider in a later chapter, to refer to *all* the long-term money used in a business, namely shareholders' capital and long-term loans. Some companies avoid the issue by giving no label at all to that bottom line. Samples from various company annual reports yield the following selection of labels – total funds, shareholders' funds, and total capital and reserves. I have chosen to use the last of those, in order that, later, we may avoid the double meaning, just referred to, of capital employed.

This almost concludes our review of the J Sainsbury balance sheet, the comparison with your own, and indeed the principles applicable to all balance sheets. We have demonstrated, I think you will agree, that every possible kind of transaction is capable of being recorded in a balance sheet. We have also demonstrated that the kind of transactions that might cause a commercial balance sheet to be what it is are much the same as those that might give rise to the very similar personal balance sheet of an individual. The obvious exception, to be addressed in Chapter 5, is that the main income of commercial businesses is derived from selling goods or services, rather than from selling labour, for which wages or a salary are the rewards paid to individuals.

One last thing should be mentioned at this point. Obviously all the numbers in a balance sheet are important, because together they represent the financial state of the business at a particular time. However, can you think of two pieces of information, provided in the balance sheet, that represent things that are so important that all businesses must get them right continually if they are not only to avoid bankruptcy, but to prosper in the longer term? I suggest that they are profit and cash. If these two things are indeed so important, is it not reasonable to suppose that people looking at a balance sheet, and finding just single numbers to represent them, would want to know more about how those numbers are made up, how they came to be what they are? Indeed it is, and they do. The documents that provide the additional information are the profit and loss account and the cash flow statement, and they are the subjects of the next chapter.

5 The Business of Living – Part 4

Profit and Loss Account – Cash Flow Statement

In the previous three chapters, of which this is a continuation, we have looked in some detail at different kinds of transactions, both personal and commercial, and at how they can be recorded in that most fundamental of financial statements, the balance sheet. We also highlighted two items, that appear on any balance sheet, as being of particular importance – profit and cash. In this chapter we shall look at both of these in more detail, continuing with the same example that we have used in the previous three, and starting with profit.

Profit, so far defined, is simply the difference between earnings and expenses, the amount by which a business's net worth or capital has increased over a given period. Given the legal requirement, for reporting and tax purposes, to cut businesses up into periods of one year, profit is generally regarded as the best single measure so far devised of how a business has performed financially during that period. I say *single* measure because many of the judgements that people make about business performance are based not on single numbers but on pairs of numbers, called financial ratios, of some but not all of which profit is a component. Examples are profit compared with sales, and profit compared with capital employed. We shall consider these, and others, in the next chapter.

If, therefore, profit is such an important measure, then it is reasonable to suppose that people reading a balance sheet would want to know something about how the single number representing it was arrived at, especially how much of it has been earned this year. The fact is that they invariably do wish to know, and their wishes are backed by the legal requirement for commercial businesses to publish, along with their annual balance sheet, a summarised account showing how the profit or loss for the year was arrived at.

The Profit and Loss Account

The profit and loss account for a period shows, in summarised form, all those things that have contributed to the profit, or loss, made during the period since the last balance sheet was published or, as with your "business", since the business started. As we have recorded, in Tables 3.2 to 4.13 inclusive, every transaction that has contributed to your final profit and loss account figure of £2,850, it should be a relatively simple matter, by looking through those transactions, to draw up a summarised profit and loss account of your "business", and in a moment I shall suggest that you do so.

First, for most businesses, sales of their products or services are their main source of income. For J Sainsbury it is the sale of goods; for your "business" it is the sale of your labour. So, because it lies at the heart of the business, the income from sales, variously called earnings, *turnover*, revenue or just "sales", would usually be shown first in a profit and loss account. From this, the various expenses would be deducted in order to arrive at the final profit figure. I now suggest that, using Tables 3.2 – 4.13 as a guide, you draw up the profit and loss account of your "business". I also suggest that you use a format similar to that of the statement of your assets and liabilities in Table 2.2 that you produced earlier. In doing so, however, instead of deducting liabilities from assets to arrive at net worth, which is what you did then, you will now be deducting expenses from income to arrive at profit, which you know must come to a figure of £2,850, the same as the profit and loss account figure in the balance sheet. Try it, and if you do not like the application of the word "profit" to personal life, then you could, with equal accuracy, call it a statement of income and expenses rather than a profit and loss account. Your answer will probably look much like Table 5.1.

Earlier, having produced your personal balance sheet, our next step (Table 4.14) was to transform it into a typical format required of a commercial one, just to show the similarity between your personal "business" and a commercial one. We shall shortly do the same with the profit and loss account that you have just produced. Before we do, however, one small change is necessary. Your after-tax earnings for the year totalled £1,250 × 12 = £15,000. Using after-tax earnings was, however, a short-cut. In a real profit and loss account, earnings would always be shown gross, the tax shown as a separate expense. For that reason, and starting to have the J Sainsbury profit and loss account in mind, we shall assume that your gross earnings were £16,433, on which you paid tax of £1,433; a quite low amount, actually – perhaps you found a good tax accountant.

Your transformed profit and loss account appears in Table 5.2. It shows the main elements of any commercial profit and loss account, in the format used *for publication* in the UK. Broadly similar principles apply in other countries. To be more specific, it is the format used by

Table 5.1 Personal profit and loss account or statement of income and expenses

	Ref	£
Income		
Earnings (net)		15,000
Interest received		8
Total income	(a)	15,008
Expenses		
Food		3,600
Rent		2,400
Other - telephone, travel, entertainment		3,982
Depreciation		1,600
Interest paid		576
Total expenses	(b)	12,158
Profit during the period	(a-b)	2,850

Table 5.2 Personal profit and loss account rearranged in typical commercial format

	Notes*	£
Earnings (gross)	1	16,433
Cost of sales	2	
Gross profit	3	
Administrative expenses	4	−11,582
Operating profit	5	4,851
Net interest payable	6	−568
Profit before tax	7	4,283
Tax	8	−1,433
Profit after tax	9	2,850
Dividend	10	
Retained profit	11	2,850

* The numbers in this column refer to similarly-numbered paragraphs in the main text, which also make reference to the group profit and loss account of J Sainsbury plc in Appendix 1.

companies. When used by unincorporated commercial businesses – sole traders or partnerships, the only difference is that, instead of dividends, amounts drawn out of such businesses by their proprietors are called *drawings*. Most of the headings appropriate for a commercial business are also applicable to your personal "business", but not all. The ones that are not are cost of sales, gross profit and dividends, all of which will be explained shortly. In the case of these items I have included the headings, but simply left the amounts blank.

As you can see, in this format, your gross earnings are stated first. Then all your various expenses except interest and tax are lumped together under the heading *administrative expenses.* These are, not surprisingly, the expenses of administering the business. Finally, the interest and tax are deducted to give your profit after tax of £2,850. Above, I stressed the words "for publication". Published accounts are highly summarised. For internal use by the management of a business, however, profit and loss accounts, and indeed balance sheets, can be as detailed as the management likes, and in whatever format it likes.

Now, just as we did with your balance sheet, we shall relate your profit and loss account to the group profit and loss account of J Sainsbury plc, the combined or consolidated profit and loss account of all the companies in the group, reproduced in Appendix 1 (Fig. A1.2). Apart from gross earnings, there can be no further numerical equivalence between the J Sainsbury profit and loss account and your own, because of the obvious differences in reality between a commercial business and the business of living. However, although most of the numbers will be different, the principles will be the same. The approach we shall adopt will be first to look at all the items that are similar to those in Table 5.2, because they are common to all profit and loss accounts. Pointers in Table 5.2 refer to the following notes. Afterwards, we shall look, briefly, at the other items that appear in the J Sainsbury profit and loss account, most of which are also quite common, but may appear or not, depending upon the circumstances of the particular business.

Notes to Table 5.2

These notes should be read with reference both to Table 5.2 and the group profit and loss account of J Sainsbury plc in Appendix 1. Note numbers are as referred to in Table 5.2. In what follows, the explanations are specific to the group profit and loss account of J Sainsbury plc, based on information in its published Accounts and the Notes attached thereto. However, unless stated to the contrary, they would also apply to other companies, although obviously with differences of detail.

1. As already discussed, the selling of goods, services or labour is the central activity in any business, and is the main source of its income, so it makes sense that the income from sales should be the first item in a profit and loss account. Regarding value added tax (VAT) and sales taxes (applicable in the US, in which J Sainsbury also operates), businesses charge VAT and sales taxes to their customers on behalf of the tax authorities and then pay to those authorities the tax so collected. In this respect, businesses act as unpaid tax collectors for the government. Therefore, the true sales of J Sainsbury are the sales excluding VAT and sales taxes.

2. It is self-evident that a company that is in the business of buying and selling goods has to buy the goods for resale. However, having bought them, it then has to get them to the point at which they are capable of being sold, which means on the shelves. *Cost of sales* usually means, in any business, all the costs incurred in getting goods, or services, to the point at which they are capable of being sold to the customer. Although rightly called "cost of sales" up to the point of sale, as goods are actually sold to the customer these costs become expenses according to our earlier definition – the using up of the asset called stock.

3. *Gross profit* is the difference between sales and cost of sales. Especially when expressed as a percentage of sales (called *gross margin*), and compared with past years or with other companies or with industry averages, it is an important financial indicator of how cost-effectively a company is bringing its goods, or services, to market.

4. Administrative expenses are all the other non-financial expenses of administering the business, including selling and delivery expenses; "non-financial" because the financial expenses – interest, tax and dividend – are shown separately, for reasons explained in the next note.

5. *Operating profit* is the result of deducting from sales *all* the non-financial expenses of the business. It, too, may be expressed as a percentage of sales, called *operating margin* or *return on sales*, or as a percentage of capital employed, called *return on capital employed*. For this latter purpose, different people give different meanings to "capital employed". As mentioned in the previous chapter, it is usually taken as meaning all the long-term money used in the business – shareholders' funds and long-term loans, although short-term borrowings net of cash balances are sometimes included.

Precisely because it excludes financial charges, operating profit allows comparison of different businesses at the operational level, regardless of how they are financed. It is also an important number when broken down to the departmental level of a business. Usually only the non-financial expenses of a business are charged out or allocated to departments, such as an IT department. The principle is that departmental managers should only be charged with expenses that they are capable of influencing. Matters such as tax, and the extent to which a company borrows money, are not the responsibility of departmental managers.

6. Net interest is the difference between interest paid and interest received. In the case of J Sainsbury, interest paid exceeds that received by £55m. In one particular kind of business – banking – interest receivable and interest payable are the most important numbers in the profit and loss account, and therefore are shown first. They are a bank's equivalent of sales and cost of sales respectively, and the difference between them, called net interest income is a bank's equivalent of gross profit. No doubt because banking, although important, is not J Sainsbury's main line of business, interest receivable attributed to Sainsbury's Bank (£139m

according to the notes to the accounts) is indeed included in sales, and interest payable attributed to Sainsbury's Bank (£108m) is included in cost of sales.

7. Unlike the case for individuals, almost all the expenses incurred in achieving sales and running a business, including interest, are tax-deductable, which means that they can be deducted from sales in order to arrive at taxable profit. Therefore, *profit before tax* is the number on which, subject usually to some adjustments, tax is payable.

8. Companies in business pay company tax, called corporation tax in the UK. The proprietors of unincorporated businesses – sole traders and partnerships – pay income tax. In most countries the principles of both kinds of tax are much the same, although the rates of tax differ. For example, at the time of writing, in the UK the top rate of personal tax is 40%, whereas the top rate of corporation tax is 30%.

9. Tax is usually the last expense payable by a business in respect of a business year, for the reason that it cannot be worked out until the sales, and all the expenses of achieving them, are known. Once tax has been taken into account, all the expenses of the business, both operational and financial, have been accounted for. What is left is the *profit after tax*, sometimes called the *net profit*. This is what finally belongs to the owners of the business, the shareholders in the case of a company, subject to any adjustment for minority interests – see below.

10. As already mentioned, dividends are not compulsory, but most companies pay a dividend. The amount is typically between 25% and 50% of the profit after tax. The Sainsbury dividend is close to 50% of the profit after tax.

11. Again as mentioned in the context of the balance sheet, retained profit is what is left of profit after any dividend has been taken into account. As a business grows, so does the amount of money which it needs to finance that growth. The best source of additional money, at least for steady year-by-year expansion as distinct from discontinuities such as takeovers or mergers, is that which has been generated internally, namely profit. In deciding upon the amount of dividend, a balance has to be struck between satisfying the expectations of the shareholders and retaining enough of the money represented by profit for expansion.

That completes our description, in the context both of J Sainsbury plc and your "business", of the core items that always appear in a published profit and loss account. Now referring only to J Sainsbury, we shall comment briefly on those other items in their group profit and loss account which are not self-explanatory and which, as already mentioned, depend on circumstances but are also quite commonly encountered. We shall take them in the sequence in which they appear.

Exceptional Items

First, anything described in either a profit and loss account or a balance sheet as an *exceptional item* is something falling within the ordinary activities of the business but which is a "one-off" occurrence or sufficiently unusual to warrant being shown separately. The J Sainsbury "exceptional cost of sales", consequent upon its acquisition of another company, is a typical exceptional item. Year 2000 costs are rather a special case, in that, while exceptional, similar costs would have been incurred by most businesses. J Sainsbury's Year 2000 costs of £30m are shown separately, and described as such. Things called *extraordinary items* also sometimes appear in published accounts. These are material items possessing a high degree of abnormality which arise from events outside the ordinary activities of the business and which are not expected to recur. Examples would be the effect on a business of a natural disaster or a fire at its premises.

Associated Undertakings

An associated undertaking is, broadly, as already mentioned, another company in which a company has a substantial share holding, usually greater than 20% but less than 50%, so that the investing company does not have a controlling interest and the other company is not a subsidiary. In these circumstances the investor company is required to show in its consolidated accounts its share, proportionate to its share holding, of the profit made by the associate company.

The way that profits of associated undertakings are handled, described above, is in contrast with the "minority interest" situation, applicable to subsidiaries. In the case of "minority interest", the full profit of the subsidiary is shown as part of the Group profit, and any minority interest in that profit is then subtracted in order to arrive at the profit attributable just to shareholders of the Group. If, as in the J Sainsbury accounts, the subsidiaries that have a minority interest have made a loss, then the full amount of that loss will have been deducted in arriving at the Group profit. In this case, in order to arrive at the profit attributable just to shareholders of the Group, the minority interest in that loss, £2m in the J Sainsbury case, must be added back.

Equity Dividends

Equity dividends are what the words imply – dividends on ordinary or "equity" shares. As already mentioned (Chapter 1), some companies have other kinds of shares in addition to ordinary shares. Most common among these are preference shares, which usually carry a right to a fixed rate of interest rather than a variable dividend. They may also give their holders preferential rights over ordinary shareholders if the company were to be wound up.

Earnings per Share

Because the number of shares in issue by a company varies from time to time, an additional view of the company's profit performance, over and above the absolute number representing profit is given by *earnings per share*. This is the profit after tax attributable to ordinary shareholders (for J Sainsbury £598m) divided by the weighted average number of shares in circulation during the year (1,904.5 million), hence the earnings per share of 31.4 pence. A second figure (29.2 pence) is shown, which excludes the effects of exceptional items, and which would exclude the effects of extraordinary items had there been any.

Diluted Earnings per Share

In addition to shares actually in circulation during the year, there may be additional shares that could have been issued if certain events had taken place or if certain rights had been exercised. For example, a company may grant employees options to buy its shares at a price less than the market price. At the accounting date, the company will calculate how many shares would be in circulation had all employees exercised their options to the fullest extent. Obviously, the greater the number of shares in circulation, the less the earnings per share. One could say that the earnings per share would have been diluted to a smaller number had these additional shares actually been issued, hence the term *diluted earnings per share*.

In summary, a profit and loss account can be thought of as an explanation of the amount by which the profit and loss reserve shown in the balance sheet has increased (profit) or decreased (loss) during the period since the previous balance sheet or, in the case of a new business, since the start of the business. Alternatively, it can be thought of as a summary of the income and expenses of a business during a period, and the resulting profit or loss made during that period. Whether concerning a commercial business or the personal "business" of living, the principles are the same. "Income" means income earned, whether or not it has yet been received in cash. "Expenses" means expenses incurred, whether or not they have yet been paid in cash.

A business must make adequate profits. Profit is the only fund out of which dividends can legally be paid; it represents the most important source of additional money for expanding the business. Profit is the most important single measure by which a business is judged and it is the basis for taxation of a business. It is also used as a basis for measuring the performance of divisions and departments, and as a basis for rewarding managers. However, the most spectacular profit performance will not prevent a business from going bankrupt if it runs out of both cash and the capacity to borrow. A mountain of profit does not of itself pay the bills. If you doubt it, then try writing a cheque designated in profit rather than cash next time you have to pay a bill. If insufficient of a business's assets are in the form of cash, and if it cannot borrow any more, then the business may fail through inability to pay its bills as they fall due. The same applies also, of course, to an individual's "business" of living. We shall now, therefore, turn our attention to cash, and do something very similar to what we have just done, but with respect to cash rather than profit.

The Cash Flow Statement

"Where did all the money go?" Unless you are a very well-organized person, that is a question that you probably ask yourself from time to time, usually just after your bank statement or credit card statement has arrived. Even though businesses are required by law to be well-organized, at least where accounting is concerned, managers, investors, lenders, suppliers and any other people with an interest in the business, ask the same question. And because the cash had to come from somewhere before it could disappear, the complete question is this: where did the money come from and where did it go to? In this context, "money" means cash.

The answer is provided by the third of the three main accounting documents of a business – the cash flow statement. A *cash flow statement* is just a list showing, under various headings, where indeed the cash came from during the year, and where it went to. Earlier, we looked at the profit and loss account as an explanation of how the profit number in the balance sheet was arrived at or, to be more precise, how the change in the profit number from one year to the next was arrived at. Now we shall be looking at the cash flow statement as an explanation of how the change in the cash number in the balance sheet from one year to the next was arrived at. We shall use the same methods that we have used hitherto, even though, at the end, there will be a slight sting in the tail.

The cash flow statement shows, in summarised form, all those things that have caused the cash figure in the balance sheet to change from one year to the next. As we have recorded, between Tables 2.4 and 4.11 inclusive of the previous three chapters, every transaction that has contributed to your final cash figure of £725, it should be a relatively simple matter, by looking through those transactions, to draw up a detailed cash flow statement of your personal "business", and I should like to suggest that you do so. The question is simply: which of your transactions caused a cash inflow, and which of them caused a cash outflow? In doing this task, in order to be consistent with the way we did things last time, I suggest that, at this stage, you keep to recording your *net* salary as a cash receipt.

When, as by now you will be anticipating, we come to transform your statement into a commercial format, and then to compare it with the J Sainsbury cash flow statement, we shall once again suppose that your gross salary amounted to £16,433, on which you paid tax of £1,433.

I suggest that you use a format similar to that of the statement of your income and expenses in Table 5.1 that you produced earlier. However, instead of deducting expenses from income to arrive at your profit figure, which is what you did then, this time you will be deducting your cash payments from your cash receipts in order to arrive at your final cash figure of £725. If you prefer, then you could with equal accuracy, call your answer a statement of receipts and payments rather than a cash flow statement. Remember, that because yours is a new "business", it started with nothing, so you will have to include everything that has had an effect on the "business's" cash, right from the very first item, the receipt of Granny 1's loan. Your statement will probably look much like that in Table 5.3.

Table 5.3   Personal cash flow statement or statement of receipts and payments

	Ref	£
Cash receipts		
Long-term loan from Granny 1		812
Proprietor's capital paid into the "business"		1,839
Loan from hire purchase company		6,500
Loan repayment from Sam		251
Earnings (net)		15,000
Interest received		8
Total receipts	(a)	24,410
Cash payments		
Paid for car		7,500
Paid for freezer		509
Paid into long-term investment		41
Loan to Sam		500
Net payments into short-term investment		114
HP loan repayments – principal, including extra payment of £1,100		3,620
– interest		576
Initial stock of food		843
Replenishment of food stock		3,600
Rent		2,400
Other - telephone, travel, entertainment		3,982
Total payments	(b)	23,685
Increase in cash during the period	(a–b)	725

In looking at profit and loss, our next step, in Table 5.2 was to transform your personal profit and loss account into commercial format, which we did in order to continue emphasizing the similarity between a personal "business" and a commercial one. We shall now do the same with the cash flow statement. However, as noted above, in doing so we shall show your gross earnings of £16,433 as a cash receipt, and tax of £1,433 as a cash payment.

In looking at the commercial format of the profit and loss account, it was relatively straightforward to think of a logical sequence in which to set out the various items. Indeed, the sequence almost suggested itself: start with sales, the most important activity in the business, then deduct the various expenses, starting with those most directly connected with sales and finishing with those least directly connected – the financial expenses. It is less easy to hit upon a logical sequence for the commercial format of the cash flow statement, although it does start in much the same way as the profit and loss account – with the net cash inflow from operating activities. As the main activity of any business is sales, it follows that the main source of cash for a business, at least once it is established, is payments received in respect of sales. However, the expenses incurred in achieving the sales and in running the business have to be paid for, also of course in cash. The difference between these two is the net cash inflow from operating activities, which is the first line in the cash flow statement.

Table 5.4 represents your transformed cash flow statement. It shows the main elements of any commercial cash flow statement, in the format used by companies for publication in the UK. Broadly similar principles apply in other countries. As with the profit and loss account, amounts drawn out of unincorporated businesses by their proprietors – sole traders or partners – are called drawings, not dividends. Most of the headings appropriate for a commercial business are also applicable to your personal "business", but not all. The ones that are not are acquisitions and disposals of other companies, and dividends. For these, I have included the headings, for the sake of completeness, but simply left the amounts blank. Not all the headings in Table 5.4 are self-explanatory. Where the meaning is not obvious, I have appended in italics a brief explanation of the headings used.

Now, just as we did with your balance sheet and profit and loss account, we shall relate your cash flow statement to the group cash flow statement of J Sainsbury plc, the combined or consolidated cash flow statement of all the companies in the group, reproduced in Appendix 1 (Fig. A1.3). As with the profit and loss account, there can be no further numerical equivalence between the J Sainsbury cash flow statement and your own, because of the obvious differences in reality between a commercial business and the business of living. However, once again, although the numbers will be different, the principles will be the same. In fact, after

Table 5.4 Personal cash flow statement rearranged in typical commercial format

	Notes*	£
Net cash inflow from operating activities	12,13	5,608
(cash received from earnings less cash paid for goods and services)		
Returns on investments and servicing of finance	14	−568
(interest received and paid)		
Taxation		−1,433
(tax paid or refunded)		
Capital expenditure and financial investment		−8,050
(mainly cash paid or received re the purchase or sale of fixed assets)		
Acquisitions and disposals		
(mainly cash paid or received re the purchase or sale of other companies)		
Equity dividends paid		
Management of liquid resources		−114
(mainly withdrawals from or payments into short-term deposits)		
Financing		5,282
(mainly cash from the injection of proprietor's capital, or from loans taken out or repaid)		
Increase in cash in the period	15	725

* The numbers in this column refer to similarly-numbered paragraphs in the main text, which also make reference to the group cash flow statement of J Sainsbury plc in Appendix 1.

what we have done so far, the Sainsbury cash flow statement is largely self-explanatory. Pointers in Table 5.4 refer to the following notes.

Notes to Table 5.4

These notes should be read with reference both to Table 5.4 and the group cash flow statement of J Sainsbury plc in Appendix 1. Paragraph numbers are as referred to in Table 5.4. In what follows, the explanations so far as they relate to J Sainsbury, are specific to the Group cash flow statement of J Sainsbury plc, based on information in its published accounts and the notes attached thereto. However, unless stated to the contrary, they would also apply to other companies, although obviously with differences of detail.

12. As you see at the beginning of Table 5.4, the net cash inflow from your "operating activities" is £5,608. This represents the cash inflows resulting from earnings, less the cash outflows representing all the non-financial expenses of achieving those earnings. Table 5.5 shows how this is made up. Exactly the same principle lies behind the J Sainsbury figure of £1,322m. That figure represents the cash inflows resulting from sales, less the cash outflows that paid for goods and non-financial services.

13. Note that, in the J Sainsbury group profit and loss account, it was the proportion attributable to the group of *profit* made by associated

Table 5.5 Detail of net cash inflow from operating activities

	£
Gross salary	16,433
Food	−4,443
Rent	−2,400
Other living expenses	−3,982
Net cash inflow from operating activities	5,608

undertakings that was shown. In the cash flow statement, what is shown is that part of the profit actually received in *cash* by the group as dividends.

14. The term *finance lease*, used under this heading in the J Sainsbury statement and also under the later heading "financing", will be defined and explained in Chapter 8, which looks at the various methods and principles of financing, particularly those applicable to IT. Briefly, here, a finance lease is a method of financing the acquisition of medium-term assets that is, for most practical purposes, similar to hire purchase. The main difference between the two lies in their tax effects.

15. In Table 5.4, because your "business" is new and therefore started with nothing, the increase in cash shown by the cash flow statement is the same (£725) as the cash figure in the balance sheet. It is the difference between the cash figure this year (£725) and the cash figure last year (£0). By the same logic, you might reasonably suppose that the increase in cash shown by the J Sainsbury cash flow statement (£568m) would equal the difference between the cash figures in *their* 1999 and 1998 balance sheets, of £725m and £270m respectively. But it does not, and it rarely does in published accounts. This is because of differences between the requirements of the accounting rules for balance sheets and those for cash flow statements. This is the sting in the tail that I referred to earlier.

The rules for balance sheets require cash, short-term investments (which category includes any deposits, such as bank deposits, repayable on demand) and creditors due within one year (which category includes any overdrafts, which are also usually repayable on demand) to be shown separately. In the rules for cash flow statements, however, "cash" is defined as cash plus deposits repayable on demand, less overdrafts. Using figures from the J Sainsbury accounts as an example, Table 5.6 shows how these two different approaches can be reconciled. Usually, however, as with J Sainsbury, this can only be done by reference to the detail in some of the notes to the accounts.

I believe you will agree that all three accounting documents that we have covered up to this point – the balance sheet, the profit and loss account and the cash flow statement – have been relatively logical and straightforward. It is a pity that the straightforwardness has been slightly

Table 5.6 Reconciliation of J Sainsbury plc Group Cash Flow Statement with Balance Sheet

	Ref	£m
J Sainsbury plc group balance sheet 1999		
Cash at bank and in hand		725
Investment (current asset investments)		17
Total cash and investments 1999	(a)	742
J Sainsbury plc group balance sheet 1998		
Cash at bank and in hand		270
Investments (current asset investments)		14
Total cash and investments 1998	(b)	284
Increase in cash and investments during 1999	(a–b)	458
Decrease in overdrafts*		110
Increase in cash in the period shown in the cash flow statement		568

* *This figure is derived from information in the Notes to the Accounts. These are not reproduced in this book.*

diminished by those differences in the rules that we have just encountered. In fact, however, that little difficulty makes this a good place to stop. The last line in the cash flow statement that we considered, the increase in cash in the period, is in fact the bottom line of the cash flow statement, both your own and J Sainsbury's. The few lines that follow in the J Sainsbury accounts are really a separate statement, one of several more required by the accounting rules, which we shall not consider. They too involve the kind of difficulties that we have just encountered, and a need to refer to the detailed Notes, and they are not essential to the understanding of business and finance.

There are further references to J Sainsbury plc at the beginning of Chapter 7. The purpose of Chapter 7 is to compare and contrast the financial characteristics of various different kinds of business. The four kinds of business referred to in that chapter are: supermarkets (represented by J Sainsbury plc); manufacturing (Glynwed International plc); a water company (Severn Trent plc), and an IT solutions company (Logica plc). Since it is primarily in the balance sheet that the main financial differences between such diverse businesses can be discerned, only the balance sheets of Glynwed, Severn Trent and Logica have been reproduced, also with permission. They appear as, respectively, Figures 7.1, 7.2 and 7.3 in Chapter 7.

We now know what kind of information is conveyed by the three main financial statements of a business, and we understand something of the accounting methods by which it gets there. We now need to consider how it is used, and by whom. That is the subject of Chapter 6.

6 The Numbers Game – Ratio Analysis

Shareholder's View – Lender's View – Management View

We have spent some time learning about the three main financial statements – the balance sheet, the profit and loss account and the cash flow statement – and how the information that they contain gets there. But what is the reader to make of the Annual Report and Accounts of J Sainsbury plc, or of any other company? Perhaps we should start by asking who the readers are likely to be. For whom is the annual report, whether Sainsbury's or any other company's, intended? To whom is the annual report of a company reporting? The answer is – to the shareholders. So, what are the shareholders interested in? What would they turn to first in an annual report?

Most shareholders, indeed most people, if asked what was the key measure of a company's success, would answer: profit. In previous chapters we have already discussed how important profit is, although we have also discussed reasons why cash is at least equally, and in some ways more important. A mountain of cash but no profit is slow death for a business; a mountain of profit but no cash is a quick death. Yes, profit is important, but which profit? In your profit and loss account in Table 5.2 there were five different headings containing the word profit – gross profit, operating profit, profit before tax, profit after tax and retained profit. In the J Sainsbury profit and loss account there are eight. I suggest that the key questions are: which profit, and profit in relation to what? The answer will depend to some extent upon who you are. Since the annual report and accounts are indeed produced primarily for the shareholders, let us start with them. However, before we do so, the following paragraph explains how we shall proceed.

In looking at what people usually call *financial analysis* or *ratio analysis*, which is what this chapter is about, we shall not be referring specifically to the Accounts of J Sainsbury plc, or to any of the other companies, whose balance sheets we shall examine in Chapter 7, although there is nothing to stop you doing so. The reason is simple. These companies have kindly given permission for the inclusion in this book of their accounts, or extracts from them, for the sole purpose of illustrating current good practice in setting out the three main financial statements, and as examples of accounts from various industry sectors.

We shall be using a sample balance sheet and profit and loss account – the accounts of EAG Ltd – for our exploration of the fundamentals of financial analysis. There are two particular advantages to be had from adopting this approach. First, we can choose to concentrate on the core items of any balance sheet and profit and loss account, thus avoiding unnecessary complications and allowing us to see more clearly the principles involved. A second advantage is that we can choose numbers that are easy to work with. You will find our sample balance sheet and profit and loss account in Table 6.1, and we shall refer to them often in this chapter. The accounts in Table 6.1 follow exactly the commercial formats of the balance sheet (Table 4.14) and the profit and loss account (Table 5.2) that we developed earlier. All unnecessary detail for our purpose has been eliminated but, as is done in practice, I have included prior year numbers.

The Shareholder's View

If you are a shareholder of EAG Limited, which of those five profit numbers reviewed above actually *belongs* to you, in proportion to your share holding? The answer is profit after tax (and after minority interest if any), or "profit for the financial year", or "net profit", or simply "earnings". How much of that did EAG Ltd make this year? From the profit and loss account we find that it was £3m. This means, since there are 20 million shares, that earnings per share (EPS) were 15 pence, shown at the bottom of Table 6.1. That may have a nice ring to it, but the first and obvious question is: how did the company do in the previous year? Has it done better or worse this year? The profit and loss account tells us that, too. Last year the company made a profit after tax of £4m, so that earnings per share came to 20 pence. That represents a decrease this year of 33.3% in both numbers, which is not good news.

In a real situation, the next step would be to see if there were anything specific that might have contributed to making this year look worse, or indeed better, than it really was for the underlying, ongoing business. Were there any extraordinary or exceptional items that would explain the fall in profit after tax? That is why such items are required to be shown separately. Has there been a change in the accounting date that would mean that this year and last year do not represent a true comparison?

You would also read the annual report in detail, not just the accounts, to find the factors that, in the opinion of the directors, have contributed

Table 6.1   Sample balance sheet and profit and loss account – EAG Ltd

	This year £m	Last year £m
Fixed assets	32	30
Current assets		
Stocks	18	21
Debtors	13	12
Cash at bank and in hand	1	2
	32	35
Creditors due within one year		
Trade creditors	12	11
Other creditors	2	3
	14	14
Net current assets	18	21
Total assets less current liabilities	50	51
Creditors due after one year		
Long-term loans	20	23
Total net assets	30	28
Capital and reserves		
Share capital – 20 million £1 shares	20	20
Profit and loss account	10	8
Total capital and reserves	30	28
Profit and loss account for the period ended . . .		
Sales	90	88
Cost of sales	75	72
Gross Profit	15	16
Administrative expenses	8	7
Operating profit	7	9
Net interest payable	2	2
Profit before tax	5	7
Tax	2	3
Profit after tax	3	4
Dividend	1	1
Retained profit	2	3
Earnings per share	15p	20p
Dividend per share	5p	5p
Assume share price at end of year	*200p*	*300p*

to the year's results. Such factors might include an increase in the price of raw materials, adverse movements in currency exchange rates or in interest rates, a falling off in demand for one or more of the company's products or services, or general economic doldrums. The more you understand about the conditions in which the company has been trading, the better are you able to interpret what the numbers are telling you. In this sense the numbers are a bit like musical notation. The more you understand about the conditions during the period in which the music was written, and the life of the composer, the better are you able to interpret and understand it. The above remarks apply to everything that we shall be discussing in this chapter.

Where might we go from here? Profit after tax represents the profit that finally belongs to the ordinary shareholders after all the expenses of the business have been taken into account. What kind of return does that represent on the shareholders' investment? Well, how do we measure whether the amount of interest that we have received on money invested in, for example, a deposit account is good or bad? The answer is by comparing it with the amount invested and expressing the answer as a percentage. It would appear to make sense to use the same method to evaluate the return on money invested in a company.

By reference to Table 6.1, how much of the money in EAG Ltd belongs to the shareholders? It is tempting to say £20 million, but this is only the original capital, the equivalent of the original amount paid into the deposit account. Remember that interest that has been added to the deposit, less any part of it drawn out, also belongs to the depositor. In the same way, a company's retained profits, the balance on the profit and loss account after dividends paid, also belong to the shareholders, together with other reserves, if any. The *return on equity* (ROE) is the profit that belongs to the shareholders compared with the capital or equity that belongs to them, expressed as a percentage. For EAG Ltd this year it is $3 / 30 \times 100 = 10\%$. Whether this is a better return that would have been obtained by having the same amount of money on deposit depends on prevailing interest rates. It is certainly less good than the $4 / 28 \times 100 = 14.3\%$ of last year.

However, you will recall that while profit after tax in a year all *belongs* to the shareholders, it would not usually all be paid to them. How have the shareholders fared in terms of the dividend that they have received? Even though the profit after tax has declined from £4m to £3m the dividend of £1m, which represents 5 pence per £1 share, has been maintained. As human beings, the people who run companies try to make the best of bad news, and maintaining the dividend in a bad year is a way of trying to signal to the market – which means everybody interested or potentially interested in the company – that the bad news is just a blip, a temporary setback.

So, again expressed in percentage terms, what return in terms of dividend have the shareholders received? The possible temptation here is to compare the dividend with what the shareholders originally paid for their shares. However, the method is in fact to compare the dividend per share with the *current* share price – what someone buying that share today, or in this case on the accounting date, would have to pay for it – and to express the answer as a percentage of that. This answer is called the *dividend yield*. The reason behind the method is that shareholders are always free to sell their shares. If they did so, the question is: what would be the return on their investment if they chose to buy them back again at today's price? Dividend yields are often quite low, as in this case. Remember, however, that dividends are only one way in which shareholders expect to receive a return on their shares, the other being capital growth, as represented by an increase in the share price. Provided the expectation of capital growth is sufficiently high, then many investors will be willing to accept low dividend yields – bread today in the expectation of jam tomorrow. The reverse is, of course, also true.

Dividend yield and earnings per share are both measures that reflect the past. EPS reflects profit after tax already earned, divided by the number of shares, while dividend yield represents the dividend per share already paid, or at least declared (decided upon) as a percentage of the current share price. People invest in shares, or in anything else, because they have an expectation of *future* performance of a company. Is there some measure that reflects the market's expectation of future performance? Yes, there is, and it is called the *price/earnings* (PE) *ratio*, which is the relationship between the current market price of the share and the latest earnings per share. The argument can be described as follows.

If investors want a virtually risk-free investment, then they can invest in government bonds, often called *gilt-edged securities* or *gilts* in the UK, or in bank deposit accounts. What is the nature of the return from investing in government bonds or bank deposits? It is the regular payment of interest, usually at a fixed rate. If investors want a higher return, then they must be prepared to take higher risks, and the commonest way of doing so is to invest in ordinary shares. Wherein lies the risk in shares? As already discussed, ordinary shareholders get their return in one or both of two ways – dividends and capital growth, but neither of these is certain. At any time, there will be an expectation of an average future rate of return on shares in companies of a particular kind in a particular industry, and that expected rate will tend to determine the market prices of the shares in those companies. Depending upon factors such as prevailing interest rates, investors are willing to pay a particular price today for an expectation of future returns, just as they are when putting money into a bank deposit account.

If it is believed that one particular company will provide better than average returns for a company of its kind in its industry, then demand for its shares will increase and the share price will rise, and vice versa. As already stated, ordinary shareholders get their return by a combination of dividends and capital growth. Both of these depend upon profit, and specifically profit after tax. Dividends can only legally be paid out of profit, and future increases in the share price will depend upon continuing market expectations of profits in this company exceeding the average.

There is thus a link between the market price of a share and the profits or earnings of the company. It is this link that is expressed by comparing the two in the price/earnings (PE) ratio. Now we can see why the earnings per share (EPS) in the profit and loss account is such an important number. It enables us to compare the price per share with the profit or earnings per share. The EPS is historical and the share price is current, but comparison of the two tells us something about the market's expectation for the future. In general, the higher the PE ratio, the higher the expectation of future earnings, and vice versa. The higher the expectation of future earnings, the higher the price investors will pay today for a share in those earnings. EAG Ltd's PE ratio last year was 300p/20p = 15, which says that investors were then willing to pay a price for its shares equal to 15 times its current earnings. This year the PE ratio, often also called the *multiple* for this reason, has declined to 200p/15p = 13.3. This relatively small decrease may suggest that, perhaps encouraged by the maintenance of the dividend, the market tends to believe that this year's decline is indeed a temporary blip.

In summary then, there are three ratios that are of particular interest to shareholders. They are return on equity, the dividend yield and the price/earnings ratio. That is not to say that shareholders will not be interested in other measures of their company's performance; nor is it to say that other interested parties will be uninterested in the ratios that we have just discussed. Ideally, all parties interested in the fortunes of a company will examine all the available measures in order to get as comprehensive an understanding as possible of what is happening in the company and how it got to where it is. Having started by looking at the shareholder's view, we shall now turn to the other main external providers of a company's money – the lenders.

The Lender's and Creditor's View

While you cannot have a company without shareholders, you can certainly have a company without lenders. You may even, just possibly, have a company without creditors. Borrowing is not compulsory, any more than it is for individuals, but there are two ways in which it can be very useful, one of them long-term and the other short-term. First, the long-term use. Suppose that you have inherited £120,000 (£120k), and that you wish to start your own business, for example a small manufacturing business. You set up a company, with you as the only shareholder. In fact, there must be a minimum of two shareholders to form a company, but we shall ignore that for the purpose of example. You invest your £120k by buying 120,000 £1 shares in the company. However, you work out that in order to get started – to buy equipment, rent premises and pay the initial costs of the business – you actually need a total of £300k.

Where are you going to get the little matter of the remaining £180k? Suppose you believe that you could persuade various friends and relations to become additional shareholders, and that you invite them to invest cash in exchange for shares. Would you be wise to raise the full £180k in that way? I think not, because companies are democracies – one share one vote. If you had 120,000 shares and the others had 180,000 between them, then they could outvote you; you would have lost control of the business. Indeed, you could find yourself fired before the business had even started. Also, although dividends are not compulsory, the profits belong to all shareholders, in proportion to the number of shares that they hold. You may not wish to spread the profits around to that extent. What you might do, in these circumstances, would be to raise, for example, a further £100k by issuing more shares, and then to borrow the remaining £80k. That way, you would retain control of the company.

This kind of borrowing can only sensibly be long-term. It must be money that you can rely on for a long period as part of the fundamental financial resources of the business. You could, in theory, finance the purchase of a house using a bank overdraft, but you would be very unwise to do so, and a bank would be very foolish to let you. Why? Because an overdraft is intended as short-term finance. It is usually more expensive than long-term borrowing and, most importantly, it can be called in, a euphemism for withdrawn, at any time. So, the main advantage to a company of long-term borrowing is that it is a way of raising more money without diluting the control of the existing shareholders.

The main disadvantage of all borrowing is that interest on loans, unlike dividends on shares, is compulsory. Try telling your bank manager that you have decided not to pay interest on your overdraft this year. Interest is an expense. It therefore reduces profit, and so the shareholders lose some of their profit anyway. It also tends to be true that the greater the amount of borrowing, the greater the say that the lender has in how the business is run, so in practice the shareholders may lose some control as well. It is all a question of balance; too much borrowing can impose an interest burden so great that it eats up all the profits, and it may lead to effective loss of control and even to bankruptcy.

An analogy is often drawn between the effects of borrowing on a business and the effects of gearing on a bicycle or in a car. What happens on a bicycle when you change to a higher gear? The answer is that, for one turn of the pedals, you travel further along the road. The price that you pay is the expenditure of extra effort in turning the pedals. When a company borrows, it is like changing to a higher gear. For the same amount of shareholders' money the business is able to do more; to press the analogy, it is able to travel further along the business road. The price that the company pays is the expenditure of extra money on the interest it has to bear. What happens on a bicycle when you change to a gear that is too high for the prevailing conditions? You come to a stop. What happens when a business borrows more than it should? The answer is the same: it comes to a stop, financially, and it may go bankrupt. The term *gearing* is often used to describe the relationship between the amount of borrowed money relative to shareholders' money in a company. The American equivalent term is leverage, suggesting a similar analogy.

The second use of borrowing for a company is short-term, and it is usually done through the mechanism of overdrafts. The purpose of over-drafts for businesses, as for individuals, is to tide them over short-term shortages of money. Such shortages might be predictable, such as those caused by seasonal or cyclical factors, or unpredictable, such as may be caused by a fire or the sudden failure of a major customer.

A typical example of a seasonal business is the toy manufacturing business. Toy companies spend much of the year stocking up for the Christmas trade. So, much of their expenditure occurs in the first nine months of the year, while much of their income occurs in the last three months. It might be considered unnecessary to have permanent finance in the company sufficient to meet the needs of, say, the third quarter of the year, likely to be the time of greatest cash shortage. The level of permanent finance regarded as prudent might be sufficient for perhaps the average requirements of the nine-month stocking up period, while shortfalls in the latter part of that period would be covered by overdraft facilities.

This chapter is about ratio analysis, and that really only has meaning in an established company. So we shall now look at four commonly used financial ratios which are of particular interest to institutions being asked to lend to an established company, such as EAG Ltd. The first two ratios are directly related to the two key questions which a potential lender would ask, probably before any others. The first is – how much borrowed money does this company already have relative to shareholders' money? The second is – if they borrow from us, can they afford to pay the interest? There is, of course, a third question – can they afford to repay the prin-cipal on the due date? For the answer to that question, the lender would probably look at the latest cash flow statement and the latest cash projec-tions of the business, and make estimates about its likely future cash-generating capability over the period of the loan.

The first consideration above – how much borrowed money the company already has relative to shareholders' money – is addressed by what is variously known as the *debt/equity ratio* or *gearing ratio*. Once again, why have only one name when two will do? Be aware that with this, as with many other ratios, there is no universal agreement on its name or even its components. This is very much the territory of art rather than science. In this chapter I am following what I believe to be the majority preference, both in names and components. "Debt" in this ratio is usually taken to mean all interest-bearing debt. In practice, this usually means the total of long-term borrowings and bank overdrafts. This is the figure that we shall use. Some people would subtract from that total any positive cash balances. The argument against doing so is that there are presumably good reasons why there are some overdrafts as well as some positive cash balances, often due to different bank accounts in different regions in which the company operates. The existence of the cash balances, probably earning little or no interest, does not prevent interest being payable on the overdrafts. "Equity", usually the denominator of the debt/equity ratio, means the equity shareholders' capital and reserves.

In EAG Ltd, as there are no overdrafts, the debt/equity ratio is there-fore the long-term loans compared with the equity shareholders' capital and reserves. Expressed as a ratio this would be 20:30. More usually, expressed as a percentage it is $20/30 \times 100 = 66.7\%$, as against $23/28 \times 100 = 82.1\%$ last year. A look at the balance sheet shows that this reduction was due to two factors. The first is that £3m of long-term loans has been repaid during the year, the second is that equity shareholders' capital and reserves have increased by £2m, the amount of this year's retained profit. Cash at bank and in-hand has gone down from £2m to £1m, so it may be questioned whether the higher level of cash last year was indeed surplus to requirements, or whether the repayment of some of the long-term debt has caused a potential cash shortage. Perhaps the interested lender is indeed a bank being asked either for an overdraft facility or for a replace-ment of the long-term loans that had become due for repayment.

Some people make the denominator of the debt/equity ratio the sum of the equity shareholders' funds and the long-term loans, namely all of the long-term money being used in the business. If this were done here, then the ratio this year would be $20/50 \times 100 = 40\%$, compared with $23/51 \times 100 = 45.1\%$ last year. Because of differences in the ways in which various ratios can be expressed, and because different people include different components, it is always important to ensure that like is being compared with like, especially when comparing ratios of different companies. Remember also that different companies give different names to some items in the balance sheet. Most confusing, as already mentioned, can be the various names given to the last line in the balance sheet, the line that in EAG Ltd I have called total capital and reserves.

The second ratio of particular interest to lenders is the amount of inter-est expense already being incurred on borrowings compared with the oper-ating profit against which it is charged. This comparison, called *interest cover*, will help to answer the question: could they afford the additional interest if we were to lend them more money? In EAG Ltd's case, the inter-est cover this year is down to $7/2 = 3.5$, having been $9/2 = 4.5$ last year. Because the same amount of interest has been incurred as last year, but on lower borrowings, that suggests that interest rates have been higher this year. Suppose, despite its own optimism, the company were to have another bad year next year and interest rates were to rise again. Would a potential lender regard their interest cover as adequate? The answer is, perhaps not. The level of interest cover required by a lender would also depend on the stability or volatility of the industry in which the company operates.

The remaining two ratios of particular interest to lenders, and to other providers of finance such as suppliers of goods or services on credit, are those that concern the *liquidity* of the business, its likely ability to be able to pay its bills as they fall due. Liquidity means the ease with which an asset can be turned into cash. Just as we, as individuals, need to have the means of paying our bills more or less on the due dates, so does a business. If you had to sell your house in order to be able to pay the fuel bills, you would have a slight problem. If a manufacturing business had to sell its factory in order to pay the wages, the business would have a slight problem. Fixed assets, such as a house or a factory, or major items of IT equipment, are the lest "liquid" assets, mainly because, even if it is wished to sell them, it is usually a long time before the sale can be concluded and the cash received.

In a business, there are only two broad classifications of assets – fixed assets and current assets. So, if the fixed assets are not suitable for the payment of bills, then the current assets had better be. The next question is: what are these "bills" that have to be paid? They obviously come from people, or organisations, to whom we owe money, so they are liabilities. There are two broad classifications of external liabilities in a business – the long-term liabilities and the current liabilities. Loans from long-term lenders will certainly have to be repaid on their due dates, but that is not exactly an everyday occurrence. That leaves the current liabilities – the suppliers – people to whom we owe money for goods or services provided and other short-term lenders. These are the bills that have to be paid on a day-to-day basis.

So the first, rather broad, question is: what is the relationship between the current liabilities and the current assets – the bills that have to be paid, and the only part of the company's resources that is normally available for paying them? In EAG's case, the total of the current assets is £32m; the total of the current liabilities, the "creditors due within one year", is £14m. These two numbers are often linked in what is called the *current ratio*, which is current assets divided by current liabilities. In our case, the current ratio this year is £32m/£14m = 2.3.

Of all the ratios that we have discussed, this one is probably the most dependent on trends and comparisons for any real meaning. For example, manufacturing companies typically carry a lot of stock and sell on credit, so their stock and debtors will usually exceed their current liabilities, as do EAG's. Supermarkets, as we have seen with J Sainsbury plc, carry a lot of stock, which they turn over quickly, but do not sell much on credit, although they do buy on credit, so they would typically have a current ratio of less than one, current liabilities exceeding current assets.

Remember that current liabilities, excluding overdrafts, usually represent free credit. When current assets exceed current liabilities, the excess must be being financed by long-term money; where current liabilities exceed current assets the excess represents the extent to which long-term assets are being financed by short-term money, much of which, trade creditors, may be free.

The current ratio tells us about the relationship between current assets and current liabilities, but it does not tell us about the ability of the business to pay its bills immediately, should it be called upon to do so. We have already agreed, I think, that you can't write a cheque designated in profit. Neither can you write a cheque designated in stock or debtors. Cash is the only thing that counts when it comes to paying the bills. In general, EAG Ltd is probably not in bad shape financially, but let us suppose that, for some reason, its creditors became worried about its viability, and all of them demanded payment immediately.

In those circumstances, which of the current assets other than cash could be converted into cash quickly? Could stock? It would depend on the nature of the stock. Finished goods could be shifted rather faster than usual by having a sale, or otherwise selling them at a discount, but that would take time. Stocks of raw materials may have an intrinsic value that would enable them to be sold, although almost certainly much more cheaply than they were bought, and that too would take time. Furthermore, it would depend on the nature of the stock. There may not be too much demand for secondhand sulphuric acid, for example, even at knockdown prices. As for work in progress, that has no value until it is completed. So, in general, stock is likely to be a dead loss as a liquid asset.

What about debtors? At first glance, the idea of selling debtors for an immediate cash sum sounds strange, but that is exactly what some businesses increasingly do. There are specialist companies, called *invoice discounters* or *factors*, who buy other companies' debtors in return for a discounted lump sum. For example, debts totalling £1m might be traded for a cash sum, typically between £800k and £850k. The amount of the discount will depend upon the quality of the debts and the nature of the service provided. In general, invoice discounters provide the upfront money while leaving the trader to manage and collect the debts, while factors, in addition to that, also take over the management and collection of debts, providing what is, in effect, an outsourcing service for that particular business function. Debts due from large, well-known companies would be more favourably looked upon than those on a customer list of small businesses that few people have ever heard of. What the discount is paying for is the privilege of cash today instead of cash in some months' time, the risk that some of the debts will be paid late or not at all, and the service provided. The point is that debtors can be highly liquid assets; if of good quality, they are convertible into cash relatively easily.

So, the next ratio that we shall consider is a fine-tuned version of the current ratio that takes into account the liquidity of the various current assets. It is called the *quick ratio* or the *acid test ratio*, and it is generally taken as the sum of all the current assets except stocks, divided by the current liabilities. In EAG's case this would be $(32 - 18)/14 = 1.0$. Last year's equivalent value would be $((35 - 21)/14)$, which also equals 1.0. A quick ratio of 1.0 says that, in theory, the company could just pay all its bills immediately if called upon to do so. But, of course, this is very approximate and, probably more than with any other ratio, the significance of this one depends almost entirely upon the nature of the business and its overall financial health. Again it is trends and comparisons that are more important than a single ratio for one year.

You may have spotted that, in working out the ratio, no account is taken of the discount that would be charged on discounting or factoring the debts. True, it is not taken into account, but then neither is any assumption made about the realizable value of any of the stocks. Even secondhand sulphuric acid must have some value, while the stock in a retail store would have substantial value. For the purpose of the ratio, stock is assumed to have a knockdown value that equals the factoring discount. As you will have gathered, ratios should be treated as very approximate tools – yet another example of finance in general, and ratio analysis in particular, as being an art rather more than a science. Ratio analysis can provide useful insights into the state of a business, but it should be accompanied by liberal quantities of commonsense.

The Management View

We have now looked at several financial ratios that are likely to be relevant to anyone interested in a company, including of course its directors and managers, but of particular relevance to, respectively, shareholders and lenders or potential lenders. These ratios have been concerned with what are often called "below the line" items in the profit and loss account, which means "below the line called operating profit" and, in the balance sheet, with the long-term money being used in the business. All the ratios have been concerned with the financial state of the company, and have had little, if anything, to do with its operations – the activities that led to that financial state being what it is. Business operations are the particular province of the directors and managers of the business. However, it would be surprising if the two providers of the company's long-term money were not also interested in the operational reasons that lie behind the financial results. The ratios that follow give some insight into the operations of the business.

There is one particular ratio, usually called return on capital employed (ROCE), and already mentioned briefly, that can be thought of as representing a link between the ratios just covered and the ones about to be covered. ROCE is certainly about the finances of the business, but it also moves higher up the profit and loss account and uses operating profit, as the numerator of the expression. The denominator is the capital employed, which is usually taken as meaning *all* the long-term money being used in the company. In the case of EAG Ltd, this means the equity shareholders' capital and reserves (£30m) plus the long-term loans (£20m). Also, as in EAG Ltd, it is the same number (£50m) as that described as total assets less current liabilities.

Return on equity (ROE) only measured the return on part of the long-term money being used in the business, that part belonging to the equity shareholders. It told us nothing about the return on all the long-term money being used. But this is just as important a measure of the company's performance. Let us, for this purpose, forget where the money came from. During the year the company has been using a total supply of long-term money of £50m. Or has it? Would it not be more accurate to take the *average* capital employed during the year, in this case £50.5m? Yes, it would. However, in practice this is often not done, for two reasons. One is that, in order to be able to compare this year with last year, it would be necessary to know the capital employed for the year before last, in order to work out last year's average for comparison. The second reason is that, precisely because the real usefulness of ratios is in terms of comparison – this year with previous years, this company with other companies and with industry averages – the same trends are almost certain to emerge, whether average values are used or the simpler approach of using numbers all from the same year.

So, what is the return on capital employed of EAG Ltd? The operating profit is £7m and the capital employed or long-term money used is £50m, so the ROCE is $7/50 \times 100 = 14\%$. Last year it was $9/51 \times 100 = 17.6\%$. This, not surprisingly, tells the same story as the return on equity did and suggests a decline, perhaps temporary, in the company's fortunes.

In the eyes of some people, return on capital employed is the ultimate measure of business performance. The question it purports to answer is: what long-term money is being used in the business, and what return has it made? In our case the answer has confirmed a decline in EAG's fortunes during the year. However, does the answer give us any idea what has led to the decline, and what we might do about it? The answer is, unfortunately, no. To find that out, we must dig a little deeper.

What is any business actually doing? What is the "capital employed" being employed to do? The answer is: via the assets in which it is invested, to generate sales that make a profit. There are two quite separate things here. The first is to generate sales of goods or services; the second is to make a profit out of those sales. Two questions now suggest themselves. The first is: for the capital that we are employing, how much sales are we generating? The second question is: for the sales that we are generating, how much profit are we making? Notice how we have broken return on capital employed down into two component parts. We could very easily put it back together again by eliminating the term "sales we are generating" from both of those two questions and recombining them into a single question: for the capital that we are employing, how much profit are we making? We wanted more information about why the ROCE had declined. There seems a reasonable chance that the answers to those two subsidiary questions might tell us. We shall take them in order.

First, for the capital that we are employing, how much sales are we generating? The answer is that sales of £90m are being generated by assets (less current liabilities) of £50m, a ratio of 9:5 or, as it would more usually be expressed, 9 / 5 = 1.8. EAG would be said to have an *asset turnover* of 1.8. Alternatively, expressing it in terms of the capital which is financing the assets, EAG might be said to have *capital productivity* of 1.8. These are simply two ways of expressing the same thing. What was the asset turnover last year? The answer is 88 / 51 = 1.73. This means that the effectiveness with which capital is being invested in assets to generate sales would seem to have improved, a piece of good news. That in turn would suggest that the problem must lie in the other half of the equation, our ability to make profit out of sales. Notice, incidentally, that where a financial ratio, as conventionally expressed, would usually come to a number greater than one, then it is expressed as a number; when the ratio, as conventionally expressed, would usually come to a number less than one, then it is expressed as a percentage. Rarely are any of these "ratios" actually expressed as ratios.

What then of our second question? For the sales that we are generating, how much profit are we making? The answer is that an operating profit of £7m is being made on sales of £90m, a ratio of 7:90 or, as it would more usually be expressed, 7/90 × 100 = 7.8%. EAG would be said to have achieved an *operating margin* or a *return on sales* of 7.8%. Last year's equivalent was 9 / 88 × 100 = 10.2%. So it is indeed our ability to make profit out of sales that has declined.

Before determining the possible reasons for this decline, just to prove that asset turnover or capital productivity and operating margin are indeed the two components of return on capital employed, try multiplying asset turnover by operating margin, and see what answer you get. It will, of course, be the return on capital employed. For this year, the calculation is 7.8% × 1.8 = 14%; for last year: 10.2% × 1.73 = 17.6%. Figure 6.1 shows these relationships diagrammatically. Figure 6.2 is the same, but shows EAG Ltd's particular numbers. From the diagrams it is perhaps understandable that return on capital employed is sometimes called the primary ratio, while its two components are called the secondary ratios. The diagrams also show operating margin as the key to analyzing the profit and loss account, and asset turnover or capital productivity as the key to analyzing the balance sheet. Finally, sales is

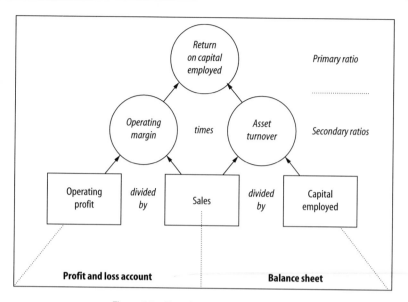

Figure 6.1 The primary and secondary ratios

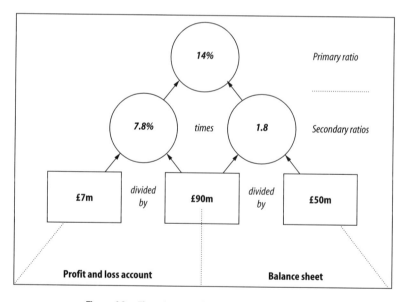

Figure 6.2 The primary and secondary ratios of EAG Ltd

shown as occupying the central place in the finances of a business, and as the link between the balance sheet and the profit and loss account.

As we have seen, there is good news and bad news from our analysis so far. The good news is the increase in asset turnover or capital productivity – the effectiveness with which capital is being invested in assets to generate sales. Asset turnover is on the balance sheet side of the diagram, so if we want to find out more about how the increase arose, then we must look more deeply into the balance sheet. The bad news is the decline in operating margin. Operating margin is on the profit and loss account side of the diagram, so if we want to find out more about how the decline happened, then we must look more deeply into the profit and loss account. Let's take the bad news first.

From the profit and loss account we can see that sales have increased, so why might our operating margin have declined? At the highly summarised level at which published accounts allow us to work, there is one further test that we can do. Just as it was useful to compare operating profit with sales, so it can be useful to compare gross profit with sales. Recall that gross profit is what is left after deducting from sales the costs of getting the goods or services sold to the point of sale. This year, a gross profit of £15m was made on sales of £90m, a ratio of 15:90, more usually expressed as $15 / 90 \times 100 = 16.7\%$. Last year's equivalent was $16/88 \times 100 = 18.2$, indicating a decline this year of 1.5 percentage points. So that accounts for part of the decline. The rest of it must be due to the increase in administrative expenses and, from the profit and loss account, we can see that these have indeed increased from £7m to £8m, an increase of 14%.

Without further information we cannot explain the reasons for this increase in administrative expenses. Because of the highly summarised nature of *published* accounts, the ability of an analyst without inside information to explain the results of analysis is limited. However, you can be sure that it will be analysed to a much greater level of detail by the directors and managers within the company. They have an obvious advantage over us in that, in most companies, detailed profit and loss accounts and balance sheets are available monthly or with greater frequency, or even on demand, depending upon the sophistication of the accounting systems. By the time that you and I might read the published accounts, the causes of the increase in expenses should have been determined, and action taken to reverse the trend.

Of course, you may *have* inside information. If, for example, you were a salesperson working for an IT company, an important part of your job would be, by building working relationships with key people in your customer companies, to find out the weaknesses, financial or otherwise, to which your products or services may represent potential solutions. Analysis at the level at which we are currently discussing it may at least help you to understand broadly where the weaknesses lie, and therefore whom you should be talking to in order to find out more. Furthermore, demonstrating an understanding of the customer's business is an excellent way for a salesperson positively to differentiate themselves from their competitors. People in companies appreciate salespeople who take the trouble not only to understand their business problems, but to express that understanding in their terms, which usually means financial terms.

Why has the gross margin declined? Once again, in order to know more we would need more detail. However, we can speculate on the possible causes. Gross margin is gross profit as a percentage of sales; gross profit is sales less cost of sales. The profit and loss account tells us that the monetary value of sales has increased, from £88m to £90m, but that the cost of sales has increased even more. Has the company sold a slightly higher *quantity* of goods, or services, at the same prices as last year? Or a lower quantity at higher prices? Or a considerably higher quantity at lower prices? Has the unit cost of things sold remained constant? If so, then the higher cost of sales, coupled with the decrease in stocks shown by the balance sheet, might suggest the third of those three possibilities. If so, then it would seem that the increase in sales resulting from the lower prices was not as great as had been hoped. An increase in sales quantities could also explain the increase in administrative expenses, part of which would be the expenses of selling and delivery. Finally, of course, it could be that the unit cost of sale of things sold has increased. Most likely is that a combination of some of these factors has contributed to the decline in gross margin.

Now let us return to the good news – the balance sheet side of Figure 6.2 and the increase in asset turnover or capital productivity. Last year, for every £1 of capital employed we generated, via the assets in which it was invested, £1.73 of sales. This year, we generated £1.80 of sales; a modest increase, but an increase nevertheless. Let us concentrate on the phrase "assets in which it (the capital) was invested". With asset turnover, we are looking at all the assets that are financed by long-term money – the capital employed. We could, of course, also do the calculation using *total* assets, regardless of how they are financed. However, we could also carry the principal to a more detailed level by doing the same calculations for various *classes* of asset; for example, fixed assets, stocks and debtors. These latter two in particular can provide useful insight. We shall look first at stocks, and then at debtors.

Stocks

For those businesses that hold stocks, the heading "stocks" in a balance sheet refers to the total of any or all of three things – stock of raw materials, work in progress and stock of finished goods. With each of these, the smaller the quantity the better. Small is beautiful. Why? Very simply, because a stock of anything only earns money for a business when it comes to be sold or, in the case of raw materials and work in progress, when it is transformed into something that in turn is sold. Until then, stocks *cost* money, often a lot money. Think of stocks of raw materials in a store, waiting to be used in a production process; or stocks of finished products in a warehouse, waiting to be sold. Think of the costs involved; for example: interest on the money spent on buying or producing them, the cost of the storage space and the people to administer it, insurance and, depending on the nature of the stock, deterioration, obsolescence and pilferage. Work in progress is even more useless than the other kinds of stocks in one sense; they might at least have an intrinsic resale value, whereas work in progress would usually have none. Who wants a half-built car?

Stocks are held in order to facilitate sales, so a useful yardstick might be the comparison of the amount of stocks held with the amount of sales achieved. In our case, sales of £90m are being facilitated by stocks of £18m, a ratio of 90:18 or, as it would more usually be expressed, 90/18 = 5. EAG would be said to have a *stock turnover* or *stockturn* of 5. Last year, the equivalent calculation was 88/21 = 4.2. Such an increase in stock turnover would be regarded as good provided, of course, the relative reduction in stock has not been such as to delay production through lack of materials, or to lose customers through inability to supply products on time.

Now suppose that the average stock turnover for companies in this industry, or of our major competitor, were 6. Then, by comparison with the industry average, we would still have some way to go. Let us pursue this point. Our stock turnover is currently 5, stock of £18m facilitating sales of £90m. Suppose that, perhaps by installing more sophisticated information systems, we were able, by having lower stocks, to achieve per-manently the industry average stock turnover of 6. For sales of £90m, what would our stock level then be? The answer is £90m/6 = £15m. This would represent a further reduction in stocks of £3m from our current level of £18m. Suppose that, on average, the total of our stock holding costs – the kind of costs we listed above – were, say, 20% of the value of stocks held, a not unusual proportion. How much money would we save *each year* in stock holding costs as a result? The answer is 20% × £3m = £600k.

Suppose that you were indeed an IT salesperson, and that on rough cal-culations you believed that you could deliver a solution that would enable your customer to achieve that target stock turnover, that would cost, say, £350k per year? If the expected results were indeed achieved, then the net savings per annum would be £250k. Where would these savings be reflected in the accounts? In a reduction in expenses, and therefore a con-sequent increase in profit. It looks like a good deal. At least you would have the basis for opening a conversation with your customer.

Debtors

The word "debtor" could be thought of as a polite way of referring to money in someone else's bank account that should be in yours. The sooner you can get the money transferred to its rightful place the better. When you receive it and pay it into the bank, the higher your bank balance, on which you can earn interest, or the lower your overdraft, so reducing the amount on which you pay interest. Like stock control, debtor control is a common candidate for improvement by information systems. It is a question of proper credit checking before taking on a new customer, keeping track of amounts due and from whom, the due dates for payment and, if overdue, then by how much, generating letters of appropriate levels of severity, and so on.

While stocks are held in order to facilitate sales, debtors occur as a result of sales, so once again there is a connection with sales. Therefore, another useful yardstick might be the comparison of the amount of debtors with the amount of sales that gave rise to them. In our case, assuming all sales to be on credit, sales of £90m have resulted in debtors of £13m, a ratio of 90:13 or, as it could be expressed, 90/13 = 6.9. EAG could be said to have a debtor turnover of 6.9. Last year, the equivalent calculation was 88/12 = 7.3. With stock, the more frequently we "turn it over" the better, and this is reflected in number terms by preferring a higher stock turnover to a lower. "Stock turnover" is a useful term because it summons up a picture of stock being taken from a store, used or sold and then replenished, and the quicker the better. There is a catchphrase associated with supermarkets: pile it high and sell it cheap. Why does this accurately reflect what supermarkets try to do? They pile it high and sell it cheap in order to "turn over" their stock as quickly as possible. The faster they turn over their stock, the more sales they are making. This is the origin of the word turnover as meaning sales.

Similar principles apply to debtors, which are simply another current asset. However, is there a more useful way of expressing it? The important thing about a debt is how long it has been outstanding, so is there a way in which we can express the numbers that will tell us, at least on average, how long debtors are taking to pay their bills? Indeed there is. EAG Ltd's sales this year are £90m, which we have assumed are all credit sales. On average, therefore, what are the sales per day? The answer is, of course, £90m/365 = £246.6k. If total debtors are £13m and sales per day are £246.6k, then how many days' worth of sales are not yet paid for? The answer is £13m/£246.6k = 53. This is the number of days which customers are taking, on average, to pay their bills. The equivalent number last year was 50, so there has been a small but significant deterioration in the time that customers are taking to pay.

The above two calculations were taken separately in order to explain the principle. Usually, as you might expect, they are combined into a single calculation as follows: *debtor days* = (trade debtors/credit sales × 365). So our debtor days are £13m/£90m × 365 = 53 days. Last year's debtor days were £12m/88 × 365 = 50 days. In order to find out how much of "debtors" in a set of published accounts represents trade debtors you would usually have to refer to the notes. As to how much of "sales" represents credit sales, managers within a company would, of course, have precise information. Without inside information you would probably have to make an estimate, based on any knowledge you might have of the particular industry.

Suppose that EAG's terms of trade, the terms under which we are prepared to offer credit, are payment within 30 days. Judged against that, our customers are pretty bad payers on average. What is that costing us? Our current debtor days are 53, while if all customers kept to the agreed terms, then debtor days would be 30. So, 23 days' worth of sales that should have been paid for have not been paid for. That works out at £246.6 × 23 = £5.7m. Suppose that, because of our deteriorating cash position, we have just negotiated the availability of an overdraft facility with the bank that, at today's rates, would cost us 8% per annum. Clearly, if all our customers were to pay on their due dates, then the overdraft would be unnecessary, so we could say that late payment is costing us £5.7m × 8% = £456k per annum on average. In the real world, customers often do not pay strictly according to the terms of trade and, while the situation can often be improved with better systems, to some extent it is a problem that businesses have to live with. You could send in the bouncers to sort them out, and by doing so you might achieve a temporary improvement in your bank balance but, longer-term, you might just possibly lose customers.

We have just looked at debtor days, a way of working out how long, on average, our customers are taking to pay their bills. The other side of the coin is "creditor days": how long are we taking, on average, to pay our suppliers? From a financial point of view, we want our customers to pay us by the due date. Equally, we should pay our suppliers on the due date, but not before, unless there are discounts that make it financially attractive to do so. If the requisite information is available, and usually it is not in published accounts, then the calculation of creditor days is similar to that of debtor days: creditor days = (trade creditors/credit purchases × 365).

If we were to take cost of sales as an approximation to credit purchases, which might be reasonable for a retail company but not for, say, a manufacturing company, then EAG's creditor days would be £12m/£75m × 365 = 58 days. If that were indeed the situation, and if our suppliers' terms of trade were also, on average, 30 days, then we would clearly be causing our suppliers a problem similar to the one that our customers are causing us. Late paying does not make for good trading relations, on either side. Even more of an approximation sometimes used is to compare trade creditors with sales, simply because the sales figure is more accessible. However, such a comparison would only make any sense as a possible indicator of a trend.

There is one other class of ratio that is commonly used. It refers to those important assets that do not usually appear on company balance sheets, namely people. The most widely used such ratios are probably sales per employee and operating profit per employee, but many others are, of course, possible. Finally, we might ask where, if at all, does the cash flow statement feature in ratio analysis? The answer is that usually it does not – directly, although, as already discussed, people interested in the accounts of a company, especially potential lenders, will certainly pay close attention to the cash flow statement and to any cash forecasts.

The more you know about the company whose accounts you are analysing, the less likely are you to draw wrong conclusions from your analysis. To illustrate this point, we shall refer again to the toy manufacturing business. We have already discussed the fact that toy manufacturers might spend much of the year making and stocking toys that will be sold during the weeks before Christmas. Suppose that you are comparing and analysing the accounts of two similarly sized toy-manufacturing companies, and that you find them similar in most respects. However, in looking at their balance sheets you note that one company has a very high level of stocks relative to its sales, while the other has a very low level of stocks relative to its sales.

You might be tempted to conclude from this that the company with a high stock level, and therefore an apparently low stock turnover, must be substantially less efficient in its use of stock than the other company, which appears to have a high stock turnover. You are about to reach for the telephone to sell your shares in the apparently inefficient company when, taking a last look at its accounts, you notice the small print right at the top which tells you that its financial year ends on the 30 September.

You are prompted by this to look at the other company, and having done so find that its financial year ends on 31 December. You decide that the high level of stock in the first company could well indicate prudent stocking up in readiness for the Christmas trade, while the low level of stock in the second company could show that it got its forecasts right and made about the right amount of toys during the year, most of which were sold prior to Christmas. You put the telephone down, and decide to keep your shares in both companies.

Finally, Table 6.2 shows the accounts of EAG Ltd with, appended to them, all the financial ratios that we have discussed with the exception of creditor days and, for each ratio, references to the items in the accounts from which it was derived.

Table 6.2   Sample balance sheet and profit and loss account – EAG Ltd, with typical ratios

	Ref	This year £m	Last year £m	Ratios (in sequence covered in text)	Ref	This year	Last year
Fixed assets		32	30	Return on equity	p/h	10%	14.3%
				Dividend yield	r/s	2.5%	1.7%
Current assets				Price/earnings	s/q	13.3	15
Stocks	(a)	18	21				
Debtors	(b)	13	12	Debt/equity	(g + d)/h	66.7%	82.1%
Cash at bank and in hand		1	2	Interest cover	m/n	3.5	4.5
	(c)	32	35				
				Current	c/e	2.3	2.5
Creditors due within one year				Quick or acid test	(c–a)/e	1	1
Overdrafts	(d)	0	0				
Trade creditors		12	11	Return on capital	m/f	14%	17.6%
Other creditors		2	3	Asset turnover or			
	(e)	14	14	capital productivity	j/f	1.8	1.73
Net current assets		18	21	Operating margin			
				or return on sales	m/j	7.8%	10.2%
Total assets less current liabilities	(f)	50	51				
Creditors due after one year				Gross margin	k/j	16.7%	18.2%
Long-term loans	(g)	20	23	Stock turnover	j/a	5	4.2
Total net assets		30	28	Debtor days	365(b/j)	53	50
Capital and reserves							
Share capital – 20 million £1 shares		20	20				
Profit and loss account		10	8				
Total capital and reserves	(h)	30	28				
Profit and loss account for the period ended . . .							
Sales	(j)	90	88				
Cost of sales		75	72				
Gross profit	(k)	15	16				
Administrative expenses		8	7				
Operating profit	(m)	7	9				
Net interest payable	(n)	2	2				
Profit before tax		5	7				
Tax		2	3				
Profit after tax	(p)	3	4				
Dividend		1	1				
Retained profit		2	3				
Earnings per share	(q)	15p	20p				
Dividend per share	(r)	5p	5p				
Assume share price at end of year	(s)	200p	300p				

7 Other Kinds of Business

Buying and Selling – Manufacturing – Utilities – IT Solutions

Thus far in this book we have made extensive use, as a learning tool, of the published accounts of J Sainsbury plc, the well-known UK retailer, as reproduced in Appendix 1. It will also be helpful to look at some other kinds of businesses, commenting on their different characteristics and financial requirements, and seeing how the principles that we have discussed are applied in their particular circumstances.

There are many possible ways in which businesses could be categorized. In this chapter, I shall follow Horngren, Foster and Datar (1997) in suggesting three main categories of business that have contrasting financial characteristics and requirements: manufacturing businesses, buying and selling businesses, and service businesses. Manufacturing businesses sell products that have been converted into a different form from those that they bought. Buying and selling businesses, whether retail or wholesale, sell products that are, generally, unchanged from those that they bought, while service businesses do not sell tangible products at all; they sell . . . services, of many different kinds.

It follows from the distinguishing characteristic of those three main categories that there are probably very few businesses that exist in those "pure" forms. The doctor and the TV engineer are examples of service providers. However, the doctor may also have a dispensary from which you can buy medicines. The TV engineer will come to see to your TV, but may also sell you a new aerial if that is what is necessary to improve the fuzzy picture. The department store will sell you a vacuum cleaner, but will also offer to provide, or arrange for, service and maintenance facilities. The car maker will make cars, but it will also provide support services to its dealers, and it will sell accessories, many of which it will have bought in from other suppliers.

We might think that the service-provider who comes closest to offering a pure service, untainted by goods, whether transformed or otherwise, is a member of one of the artistic professions – the musician, for example, or the painter. However, the musician will gladly sell you a programme or CD of the concert, the artist a catalogue of the exhibition. The point is that our threefold classification is only a useful starting point for describing certain characteristics of business, especially their financial characteristics. We shall consider the three kinds of business in turn, again using as examples the accounts of some companies typical of each category. In considering the very broad category of service businesses we shall refer to two contrasting examples – a water company and an IT solutions company. However, since we have spent much of our time so far in the retail world, we shall start with buying and selling.

Buying and Selling Businesses

In the process of working through the published accounts of J Sainsbury plc, reproduced with introductory comments in Appendix 1, you will, I believe, have learned quite a lot about their particular kind of business – mainly supermarkets. All that we need do here, therefore, is to summarise the main characteristics that we have already noted.

As exemplified by J Sainsbury, characteristics usually associated with supermarkets are these: they have a substantial requirement for fixed assets – mainly properties, fixtures, equipment and vehicles; they carry substantial stocks of goods for resale, which they turn over rapidly, and which would usually be bought on credit; most of their sales are for cash, so they have few trade debtors, and finally, depending on the relative quantities, which of course vary over time, of cash held, overdrafts and other short-term loans, their current liabilities typically exceed their current assets.

Other buying and selling businesses – wholesalers in general, and some kinds of retailer, for example department stores – sell wholly or partly on credit, the obvious result being that they carry debtors. This, together with the fact that they would typically turn their stocks over rather less rapidly than supermarkets, would mean a greater likelihood of current assets exceeding current liabilities.

Manufacturing Businesses

Manufacturing businesses usually, but not necessarily, have the following characteristics: they too have a substantial requirement for fixed assets, such as buildings, plant and machinery; they also carry substantial holdings of stocks, of three main kinds: raw materials or bought-in parts, work in progress and finished goods; most or all of what they sell is sold on credit, so they usually carry substantial debtors. Finally, they also buy on credit, as do most businesses, but because of their often high levels of stocks and debtors their current assets would usually exceed their current liabilities, subject, as above, to the relative amounts of cash and short-term borrowings.

As a focus for discussing these characteristics in a little more detail, we shall refer to the 1999 group balance sheet of Glynwed International plc, reproduced in Figure 7.1, although notice that, as with J Sainsbury plc, the

As at 31st December

		Group		Company	
	Notes	1999 £m	1998 £m	1999 £m	1998 £m
Fixed assets					
Goodwill	12	272.6	130.7	-	-
Tangible assets	13	272.1	265.4	-	-
Investments	14	1.2	1.9	495.5	326.0
Total fixed assets		545.9	398.0	495.5	326.0
Current assets					
Stocks	15	166.6	163.6	-	-
Debtors	16	181.0	208.5	619.1	517.1
Businesses held with a view to resale	14	-	17.7	-	-
Cash at bank and in hand	18	34.7	62.3	7.3	0.9
Total current assets		382.3	452.1	626.4	518.0
Creditors – amounts falling due within one year					
Operating creditors	17	(158.4)	(232.3)	(426.1)	(265.9)
Borrowings	18	(25.4)	(47.1)	(30.2)	(48.8)
Tax and dividends payable	17	(27.9)	(30.4)	(21.3)	(29.2)
Total amounts falling due within one year		(211.7)	(309.8)	(477.6)	(343.9)
Net current assets		170.6	142.3	148.8	174.1
Total assets less current liabilities		716.5	540.3	644.3	500.1
Creditors – amounts falling due after more than one year					
Borrowings	18	(251.1)	(173.7)	(230.6)	(165.6)
Exchangeables	18 & 21	(32.1)	-	-	-
Provisions for liabilities and charges	20	(37.1)	(32.1)	-	-
Total net assets employed		396.2	334.5	413.7	334.5
Capital and reserves					
Ordinary shares	21	60.6	60.6	60.6	60.6
Preference shares	21	-	1.3	-	1.3
Called up share capital		60.6	61.9	60.6	61.9
Share premium account	22	25.8	25.6	25.8	25.6
Revaluation reserve	22	7.6	16.0	-	-
Capital redemption reserve	22	2.3	1.0	2.3	1.0
Profit and loss account	22	298.5	221.1	325.0	246.0
Total shareholders' funds (1998 including non-equity interests)		394.8	325.6	413.7	334.5
Equity minority interests	23	1.4	8.9	-	-
Total funds		396.2	334.5	413.7	334.5

The accounts on pages 28 to 52 were approved by the Board of Directors on 21st March 2000 and were signed on its behalf by:

ECS Macpherson   Chairman
WB McGrath   Finance Director

Notes to the accounts are on pages 33 to 52.

Figure 7.1   Balance sheets of Glynwed International plc as at 31 December 1999

balance sheet of the holding company (the "Company") is shown as well. As stated in its Annual Report 1999, Glynwed is a long-established British manufacturing company having two main lines of business. It is Europe's largest pipe systems manufacturer with a product range serving industrial, utility and construction markets. It is also a UK market leader in domestic cookers and in sales to commercial kitchens of cookers and refrigerators. Its brands include the well-known Aga and Rayburn ranges. Its total turnover in 1999 was £878 million.

We shall refer to the Glynwed balance sheet for three purposes. First, it illustrates the typical financial characteristics of a manufacturing company, outlined above; second, it contains several items that were not present in the balance sheet of J Sainsbury plc, to which we have already given detailed consideration; third, the manufacturing context provides additional insights into some items, especially stocks, that we have only considered so far in the rather simpler retail context. The following paragraphs refer to selected items in the Glynwed balance sheet in Figure 7.1. They are in the same sequence as the items to which they refer.

Goodwill

Goodwill is the term used to describe the amount by which the price paid for a business exceeds the market value of the assets less liabilities acquired. It therefore only arises where a company has taken over one or more other businesses, as did Glynwed during 1999. By way of illustration, think about your local corner shop. Let us assume that it has been there for many years, that it has a good reputation and that its loyal customers travel some distance to it because they appreciate the personal service that it has always provided. If you wanted to buy the shop as a going concern, then you would, I think, expect the purchase price to be more than just the total of the values of the shop and its stock less any bills outstanding. You would expect to have to pay something extra for its loyal customer base and its reputation, built up over many years. That "something extra" is what would be called the goodwill of the business.

Goodwill may be an intangible asset, but it is an asset nevertheless, and like most other assets except land it depreciates over time. Five or ten years from now, the reputation of the shop is going to be largely down to you, for better or worse. Your predecessor will be forgotten. Like other fixed assets, the depreciation of goodwill has to be recorded over its expected useful life. If, like Glynwed, you were buying, not the corner shop, but a large company, then, in addition to the customer base and the reputation, you might also be buying such valuable intangible assets as a foothold in a different country, brands, trademarks and patents well established in that country, a loyal and trained labour force and intellectual property. Of the total goodwill of £272m on Glynwed's balance sheet, the notes to the accounts tell us that £165m arose from acquisitions made during the year.

Tangible Fixed Assets

As you might expect, Glynwed's tangible fixed assets consist almost entirely of land and buildings, plant, machinery and equipment.

Stocks

A manufacturing company such as Glynwed provides us with additional insights into the matter of stocks. The notes to the Glynwed Accounts, not reproduced here, tell us that the total stocks of £166m do indeed consist of the three elements outlined above: raw materials and consumables £38m, work in progress £18m and finished goods and goods for resale £110m. "Consumables" are things such as tools and spare parts. You will recall that stocks, far from earning money for a business, cost money until they are sold or are transformed into goods that are sold. Optimally, therefore, raw materials and finished goods are held in the minimum quantities necessary to ensure, respectively, that production is not held up for want of materials, and sales are not lost for want of finished products. However, at least these two kinds of stock are deliberately acquired.

Because the manufacturing process is not instantaneous, it follows that at any particular time there will be a quantity of partly finished goods on hand. It is this that is meant by the term *work in progress*. Work in progress, like stock of finished goods, will be valued at the total of the costs that have been incurred in producing it – usually a combination of raw materials, labour costs, machine usage costs and *manufacturing overheads* – less any necessary allowance for obsolescence or deterioration.

Raw materials, labour costs and machine usage costs can usually be traced to a particular unit of cost – such as a product, a batch of products or a process – in an economically feasible way, and when this is the case they are called *direct costs*. Manufacturing overheads, also called *indirect production costs*, are those costs of manufacture that cannot so be traced directly to particular units of cost. Examples of manufacturing overheads would be the costs of insuring, heating and cleaning a factory building. These have to be allocated to products or batches in an estimated way in order that, eventually, all the costs of manufacture are allocated to all the products manufactured. Recall our earlier definition of "cost of sales" as being the costs incurred in getting goods (or services) to the point at which they are capable of being sold to the customer. These costs become expenses – cost of sales – when the goods are sold.

Does the inclusion of materials, labour and machine usage costs in the value of work in progress and finished goods not offend against the principle, discussed earlier, that expenses are used up assets? Have not

the assets "raw materials" and "right to labour" been used up in the manufacturing process? Furthermore, what does "machine usage cost" mean if
not depreciation – the partial using up of the asset "machine"? For the
answer to this perfectly reasonable objection, let us refer back to the last
occasion where we encountered a stock of something – your personal
stock of freezer food. When you bought the food, we noted that what
you had done was to convert one kind of asset called cash into another
kind of asset called food.

The word "stock" implies something being held temporarily pending
the use for which it is was intended. It is only "used up" when it is put
to that purpose. The purpose for which the asset "stock of food" is held
is, eventually, to be eaten. When the food is eaten, but not before, it is
used up. It is then that it becomes an expense. The purpose for which
the asset "finished goods" is held by a company is, eventually, to be sold,
in order to earn revenue. When goods are sold, but not before, they are
used up. It is then that they become an expense, called cost of sales.

Only one asset – cash – needed to be converted in order to obtain your
stock of food, so the food stock was valued at whatever amount of cash
that you spent on it. The same would be true of the stock that J Sainsbury
plc buys for its supermarket shelves. Only one asset – cash – needs to be
converted in order to obtain a stock raw materials, so Glynwed's raw materials would also be valued at whatever amount of cash was spent on them,
subject to any adjustments described above. However, to produce an asset
called "finished goods" is a much more complex process. It involves the
conversion of not just one asset – raw material being the obvious one –
but several others as well: the (contractual) right to use employed labour,
part of the value of a machine, and part of the (contractual) rights to have
the factory insured, lit, heated and cleaned. These are all first converted
into the asset "work in progress", and as goods are completed there is
another conversion; work in progress becomes finished goods.

Above are summarised the financial and accounting reasons why
stocks are valued at the cost of *all* the assets from the conversion of which
they were produced. Ultimately, however, the most important reason why
all the costs attributable to finished goods – products – must be so attributed concerns *pricing*. If you do not know how much your products cost
to make, then how can you know what prices to charge for them? We
have already discussed at considerable length the implications of the fact
that profit is earnings less expenses. If you are a manufacturer, then your
earnings come from selling the products that you make. So, your total
earnings had better be enough to cover all the expenses of the business
and produce the profit that you wish to make. If that is true of the business as a whole, then it had better be true in respect of individual
products, because your total earnings are derived from a very simple
piece of arithmetic: total earnings are the total numbers of products sold
times their various selling prices.

One of the most difficult things in any business, but especially in manufacturing, is to determine just what is the cost of an individual product. We have already noted that the indirect costs of manufacture have to be allocated to products in an estimated way. In order to determine the total costs of products, all the indirect costs of the business as a whole – the administrative expenses – have to be allocated as well. This too can only be done in an estimated way. It can never be a precise process, although advances in information systems are helping to make the task a little easier. For more information on the topics of costing and pricing, see Chapter 12.

Net Current Assets

Glynwed did indeed have current assets substantially in excess of its current liabilities, both in 1999 and 1998.

Exchangeables

The notes to the accounts tell us that these are shares issued by a subsidiary of the Glynwed Group as part of the consideration for the acquisition of a foreign company. At the option of the holders, these shares may, within specified times, be converted either into Glynwed shares or into cash. This is a good example of an item, arising out of a particular set of circumstances, that you would not expect to find in every balance sheet that you might look at.

Capital Redemption Reserve

When preference shares are "redeemed" or cancelled, their nominal value being repaid to their holders, an amount equivalent to that nominal value must be transferred from the profit and loss reserve to a "capital redemption reserve", which is not available for the payment of dividends This is an accounting technicality that need not concern us further.

Utilities

Companies such as water, electricity and transport undertakings, often called utilities, usually but not necessarily have the following characteristics. These businesses, like the others so far considered, have a substantial requirement for fixed assets. In addition to buildings, plant and equipment, they also carry large amounts of fixed assets relevant to their particular business. A water company, for example, would have substantial "infrastructure assets" – mains and sewers, reservoirs and dams, while a transport company would have vehicles, such as buses, trains or aircraft, relevant to the business.

By contrast with the other kinds of business so far considered, utilities usually have quite small amounts of stocks, which might be, for example, spare parts or fuel. The amount of debtors depends on the kind of business. For example, gas, electricity and telephone bills are usually payable in arrears, but with an option to pay monthly, while water charges, at least unmetered charges, are usually payable in advance, but with an option to pay monthly. Payments for transport are either made in cash at the time of travel, or in advance. To the extent that payment is made in advance, for any service, you will no doubt recall that the company has a corresponding liability, called deferred income or deferred revenue, to provide the service paid for. This will be contained within one or other of the items called "creditors", depending upon the period within which the obligation has to be fulfilled.

The 1999 group balance sheet of Severn Trent plc is shown, together with that of the holding company (the "Company"), in Figure 7.2. As stated in its Annual Report 1999, Severn Trent's principal business is the provision of water and sewerage services in central England and parts of Wales. Through a subsidiary, it is also one of the leading integrated waste management companies in the UK and in Belgium. Through other subsidiaries, Severn Trent also supplies products, processes and services associated with water and waste water, including contract operations and consultancy, to industrial and municipal markets and provides software solutions and IT services to water and other utilities. Its turnover in 1999 was £1,364 million.

The Severn Trent balance sheet illustrates typical financial characteristics of a utility, especially of course a water utility. Once again, we shall refer only to items that have not appeared in earlier balance sheets or that call for special comment. The following paragraphs should be read with reference to the Severn Trent balance sheet in Figure 7.2. They are in the same sequence as the items to which they refer.

Tangible Fixed Assets

These do indeed comprise the three main kinds of asset described above. Of the total of £4,237m, the infrastructure assets – water mains and sewers, reservoirs, dams and pipelines – account for £1,784m, land and buildings £1,266m, and plant and equipment £1,287m. Net additions to these assets during 1999 were, respectively, £208m, £108m and £257m, a total net investment during the year of £573m.

Joint Ventures

A *Joint Venture* is defined as an undertaking by which its participants expect to achieve some common purpose or benefit, controlled jointly by two or more parties or "venturers".

Balance sheets
At 31 March 1999

	Notes	Group 1999 £m	Group 1998* £m	Company 1999 £m	Company 1998 £m
Fixed assets					
Intangible assets – goodwill	9	56.6	–	–	–
Tangible assets	10	4,237.9	3,873.8	7.2	7.4
Investments in joint ventures					
Share of gross assets		5.9	7.9	–	–
Share of gross liabilities		(6.2)	(8.6)	–	–
Loans to joint ventures		4.7	9.0	0.1	–
		4.4	8.3	0.1	–
Investments in associates		17.2	16.3	–	–
Investments in subsidiaries		–	–	1,618.7	1,725.9
Other investments		3.1	1.3	2.2	1.1
Total Investments	11	24.7	25.9	1,621.0	1,727.0
		4,319.2	3,899.7	1,628.2	1,734.4
Current assets					
Stocks	12	82.2	82.1	–	–
Debtors	13	284.9	234.0	94.3	92.1
Short-term deposits		22.9	32.7	–	–
Cash at bank and in hand		9.3	14.7	396.8	226.3
		399.3	363.5	491.1	318.4
Creditors: amounts falling due within one year	14	(923.4)	(754.1)	(478.4)	(235.2)
Net current (liabilities)/assets		(524.1)	(390.6)	12.7	83.2
Total assets less current liabilities		3,795.1	3,509.1	1,640.9	1,817.6
Creditors: amounts falling due after more than one year	15	(1,306.2)	(1,179.5)	(125.4)	(376.9)
Provisions for liabilities and charges	17	(42.7)	(48.9)	–	–
Net assets		2,446.2	2,280.7	1,515.5	1,440.7
Capital and reserves					
Called up share capital	18	231.1	230.3	231.1	230.3
Share premium account	19	5.4	3.3	5.4	3.3
Capital redemption reserve	19	147.0	147.0	147.0	147.0
Profit and loss account	19	2,062.4	1,899.8	1,132.0	1,060.1
Total shareholders' funds		2,445.9	2,280.4	1,515.5	1,440.7
Equity shareholders' funds		2,436.8	2,271.3	1,506.4	1,431.6
Non-equity shareholders' funds		9.1	9.1	9.1	9.1
Minority shareholders' interest (equity)		0.3	0.3	–	–
		2,446.2	2,280.7	1,515.5	1,440.7

* Group 1998 comparative figures for Tangible assets and Provisions for liabilities and charges have been restated following the adoption of Financial Reporting Standard 12, 'Provisions, Contingent Liabilities and Contingent Assets'. (Note 1d)i)).

Signed on behalf of the Board who approved the accounts on 7 June 1999.

David Arculus Chairman   **Alan Costin** Group Finance Director

Figure 7.2   Balance sheets of Severn Trent plc as at 31 March 1999

Stocks

The notes to the accounts show that stocks consist of "stocks and work in progress" £18m and development land and properties £64m.

Creditors: amounts falling due within one year

These do indeed include £263m of deferred income, no doubt reflecting the fact many consumers pay their water charges in advance. This represents the company's obligation to provide the services that have been paid for. The creditors also include dividends payable of £247m. Only £38m represents trade creditors. Most of the remainder represents short-term borrowings.

Net Current Liabilities

Here is another example of a company whose current liabilities exceed its current assets, at least in 1999 and 1998.

IT Solutions

Businesses providing "know-how", such as consultancies, usually have the following characteristics: their requirements for fixed assets are often limited primarily to IT and communications equipment, and premises; they carry negligible stocks; their services are sold on credit, but in the case of long contracts their clients may be required to make stage payments, some of them in advance, so that they may have substantial amounts of both accrued revenue or accrued income – work done but not yet invoiced, and deferred revenue or deferred income – work paid for but not yet done.

The 1999 consolidated or group balance sheet of Logica plc is shown in Figure 7.3. Its holding company balance sheet is shown on a separate page of its Annual Report, and is not reproduced here. As stated in its Annual Report 1999, Logica is a leading supplier of global solutions to companies around the world. It is dedicated to helping "blue chip" organisations transform their businesses through the innovative use of information technology. Its turnover in 1999 was £659 million.

The balance sheet illustrates typical financial characteristics of a services company, especially of course an IT consultancy. As before, we shall refer only to items that have not appeared in earlier balance sheets or that call for special comment. The following paragraphs should be read with reference to the Logica balance sheet in Figure 7.3. They are in the same sequence as the items to which they refer.

Intangible Assets

The Notes to the Accounts tell us that these consist entirely of goodwill. Notice how, although the form and content of published Accounts are prescribed in considerable detail by company law, different companies may, in some cases, describe the same item in different ways. As previously stated, published Accounts should always be read together with the detailed Notes. That is what they are there for.

Tangible Assets

These comprise freehold and leasehold land and buildings £16m, equipment and plant £30m. No doubt much of the latter would be computer and communications equipment.

Consolidated Balance Sheet

At 30 June	Note	£'000	**1999** **£'000**	£'000	1998 £'000
Fixed assets					
Intangible assets	10		190,980		–
Tangible assets	11		46,834		33,005
Investments	12	17,832		6,423	
Investment in associate	12	2,158	19,990	2,014	8,437
			257,804		**41,442**
Current assets					
Debtors	14	155,596		117,466	
Cash at bank and in hand and deposits	26	129,659		77,455	
		285,255		194,921	
Creditors – amounts falling due within one year					
Borrowings	15	(41,029)		(18,448)	
Other creditors	16	(200,778)		(126,930)	
		(241,807)		(145,378)	
Net current assets			**43,448**		**49,543**
Total assets less current liabilities			**301,252**		**90,985**
Creditors – amounts falling due after more than one year					
Borrowings	17	(1,289)		(5,021)	
Other creditors	18	(1,191)	(2,480)	(2,979)	(8,000)
Provisions for liabilities and charges	20		(680)		(110)
Net assets			**298,092**		**82,875**
Capital and reserves					
Share capital	23		39,495		7,380
Share premium account	24		191,863		71,451
Shares to be issued	24		35,677		–
Special reserve	24		159		158
Other reserves	24		2,487		2,484
Profit and loss account	24		28,411		1,402
Shareholders' funds – equity			**298,092**		**82,875**

The financial statements on pages 45 to 75 were approved by the board on 7 September 1999 and were signed on its behalf by:

Dr M P Read
A F Given
Directors

Figure 7.3   Consolidated balance sheet of Logica plc as at 30 June 1999

Debtors

£97m of these are trade debtors, which you will recall represent work which has been invoiced to clients but not yet paid for. Prepayments and accrued income are grouped together at £16m. Also included is an item described as "amount recoverable on contracts" £28m. This concerns long-term contracts and represents the excess of the value of work carried out to date over cumulative payments on account received. It, too, therefore represents accrued income, but with specific reference to long-term contracts which extend beyond the current year.

Creditors – Amounts Falling Due Within One Year

These include "payment received on account" £23m. This represents the obligation to do work that has been paid for. It is what, elsewhere, I have described as "deferred revenue" or "deferred income".

Net Current Assets

As previously discussed, whether current assets exceed current liabilities or vice versa depends to some extent on the mix of stock, trade debtors and trade and other creditors. It also depends on the relative amounts of cash and short-term borrowings. Reference to the notes is always necessary.

The purpose of this chapter has been to show how the characteristics of very different businesses are represented in their published Accounts using the same fundamental principles that we have considered hitherto. If you have given some study to the exposition of those principles, then, with a little understanding of the nature of the particular business, and with reference to the notes to the accounts, you should be able to understand much of what any set of published Accounts is telling you, with a few possible exceptions. Some businesses, for example banks and insurance businesses, are so specialised that anyone uninitiated in the particular business and its jargon would be able to understand rather less of their Accounts than those of other companies. We shall not consider them here; nevertheless, the principles on which they are based remain the same.

Mention of banks should serve to remind us that they are foremost among the providers of finance for other businesses. Finance, to remind you, simply means money resources, and financing means the process of obtaining those resources. In Chapter 8, we shall look at some of the principles of financing in general and of one kind of finance in particular – leasing.

8 Financing and Leasing

To Buy or Not To Buy – Rental – Operating Leases – Hire Purchase – Finance Leases – Service and Project Finance – Outsourcing

Financing means acquiring the money resources for something. Earlier in the book, we discussed the idea that assets should, in general, be financed over their expected useful lives. By way of illustration, we contrasted the reasonably sensible practice of using a 25-year loan to finance the purchase of a long-term asset such as a house, with the slightly less sensible idea of using a 5-year loan to finance a 3-week holiday. In this chapter we shall, primarily, be discussing a method of financing that is of particular importance for medium-term assets, such as IT assets, namely leasing. First, however, we shall consider financing in general in the context of the purpose of business.

To Buy or Not To Buy?

Suppose that, rather than renting accommodation, you do indeed wish to buy a house, and are fortunate enough to have sufficient cash with which to buy one, and still have enough for your day-to-day needs. Should you use the cash, simply transforming the asset "cash" into the asset "house" or should you take a loan? What is the main financial factor that you should take into account? The question is: what else could you do with the money? If you believed that, by investing it in something else, you could earn a higher percentage rate of return than would be charged by the lender, then the rational choice would be to take the loan. For you, the "something else" might be, for example, starting a business or buying shares in someone else's.

Businesses look at things in the same way, and for the same reasons. In general, a business will try to ensure that its long-term assets are financed with long-term money – shareholders' money or long-term loans. If the business has sufficient cash with which to purchase a particular asset outright and still have enough for its day-to-day needs, the question should be the same – could we earn a higher return by taking a long-term loan, and investing the cash in something else? For a company too the "something else" might be a new business – perhaps diversifying into a new product or a new market, or buying shares in another company. Like us, a company might buy a minority holding of shares; usually unlike us, a company could buy a majority or controlling interest of more than 50%, in which case it would be said to have effected a take over of the other company. The company taken over would then be called a subsidiary. If the controlling interest is 100%, then it would be called a wholly-owned subsidiary.

In theory, the principle of matching the length of the finance to the expected life of the asset is just as applicable to short-term assets, those assets with a life of less than one year, such as stocks and debtors. In almost all businesses to some extent, and in some businesses to a considerable extent or totally, the finance for these assets is indeed the kind of finance that also lasts for less than one year – credit from suppliers, possibly supplemented by overdrafts. In practice, as we have seen, short-term assets and short-term liabilities are rarely in balance, the imbalance being dictated to a large extent by the nature of the business. For example, supermarkets typically have short-term liabilities that exceed their short-term assets. This is because they buy on credit, sell for cash and turn over their stocks faster than they have to pay their bills. Manufacturing companies, on the other hand, typically have an excess of current assets over current liabilities. This is because, while they too buy on credit, they sell on credit also, and turn their stocks over rather more slowly than does a supermarket. To the extent of the difference, an equivalent amount of current assets is being financed by long-term money.

Remember, however, that the total of current assets includes cash, and the total of current liabilities includes overdrafts, so in any particular company the balance of current assets and current liabilities could be distorted by a preponderance of cash on the one hand or of overdrafts on the other. Cash is shown as a separate item on the face of the balance sheet, whereas overdrafts are usually included with other liabilities under the heading "Creditors due within one year". Always look at the detailed notes to a set of published accounts to determine precisely what has given rise to the figure of either net current assets or net current liabilities.

What, however, about the financing of medium-term assets – those, including IT equipment, that are classed as fixed assets but have expected lives of, say, 3–5 years? Here, the availability of choice reasserts itself, as does the principle of financing assets over their expected useful lives. Here, as with long-term assets, companies can pay cash upfront if they wish and if they have it, but the question should still be: Is this the best use we can make of our cash at this particular time? Obviously, from a purely financial viewpoint, the scale of the proposed acquisition in the context of the size of the company is relevant; the greater the amount, the more consideration should be given to the question. However, it is equally true that a large number of small acquisitions may involve more cash than one large one.

For the acquisition of, for example, IT equipment, what choices are available to companies, besides outright purchase for cash – the conversion of the asset "cash" into the asset "IT equipment"? One choice would be for the company to finance them with additional bank borrowing. However, if the term of the loan does indeed coincide more or less with the expected life of the asset or assets, then it would be classed as long-term borrowing, and it would therefore increase the total of the long-term money used or "capital employed" in the business. Does this matter? For the answer to this question let us return briefly to our financial analysis of EAG Ltd in Chapter 6, and specially to Table 6.2, with its summary of EAG Ltd's accounts and the financial ratios that we derived from them.

Suppose that the IT equipment referred to above costs £4m, and that it were indeed to be financed with additional bank borrowing. To keep the arguments simple, we shall assume that the loan is arranged, and the equipment purchased, on the last day of EAG's financial year or accounting year. This means that in the few hours until the books are closed for the year, neither of the additional assets associated with these transactions – the equipment, and the right to use an extra £4m of borrowed money – could reasonably be regarded as having been used up to any significant extent. Therefore, no additional expenses will have arisen, and therefore the profit and loss account will not change. However, three of the fourteen financial ratios shown in Table 6.2 would change as a result of these transactions. Which are they, and are the changes for the better or the worse? I suggest that you work out the answers for yourself, as revision of the work we did on financial ratios. When you have done so, check your numbers against the revised EAG Ltd accounts in Table 8.1, which shows the ratios both before and after the change.

As for the interpretation of the numbers, are the changes for better or worse? The answer is that in most circumstances they would be regarded as for the worse. The return on capital employed has gone down from 14% to 13%, the asset turnover has decreased from 1.8 to 1.67 and the debt/equity or gearing ratio has risen from 66.7% to 80%, taking the company nearer to the point at which it might become significantly more difficult to obtain further borrowing. You could of course argue that all this is rather artificial, and I would agree. I chose a non-trivial amount of £4m precisely in order to show significant effects on the financial ratios. You might also think that no company would undertake such a major transaction on the last day of its accounting year, knowing that some of the measures by which it will be judged would be so adversely affected. Here, I would not agree so readily.

Table 8.1   Revised accounts of EAG Ltd, reflecting additional fixed assets and loans of £4m

	Ref	Before £m	After £m	Ratios (in sequence covered in text)	Ref	Before	After
Fixed assets		32	*36*	Return on equity	p/h	10%	10%
				Dividend yield	t/s	2.5%	2.5%
Current assets				Price/earnings	s/q	13.3	13.3
Stocks	(a)	18	18				
Debtors	(b)	13	13	*Debt/equity*	*(g+d)/h*	*66.7%*	*80%*
Cash at bank and in hand		1	1	Interest cover	m/n	3.5	3.5
	(c)	32	32				
				Current	c/e	2.3	2.3
Creditors due within one year				Quick or acid test	(c−a)/e	1	1
Overdrafts	(d)	0	0				
Trade creditors		12	12	*Return on capital*	*m/f*	*14%*	*13%*
Other creditors		2	2	*Asset turnover or*	*j/f*	*1.8*	*1.67*
	(e)	14	14	*capital productivity*			
Net current assets		18	18	Operating margin or	m/j	7.8%	7.8%
Total assets less current liabilities	(f)	50	54	return on sales			
Creditors due after one year				Gross margin	k/j	16.7%	16.7%
Long-term loans	(g)	20	*24*	Stock turnover	j/a	5	5
Total net assets		30	30	Debtor days	365(b/j)	53	53
Capital and reserves							
Share capital – 20 million £1 shares		20	20				
Profit and loss account		10	10				
Total capital and reserves	(h)	30	30				
Profit and loss account for the period ended . . .							
Sales	(j)	90	90				
Cost of sales		75	75				
Gross profit	(k)	15	15				
Administrative expenses		8	8				
Operating profit	(m)	7	7				
Net interest payable	(n)	2	2				
Profit before tax		5	5				
Tax		2	2				
Profit after tax	(p)	3	3				
Dividend		1	1				
Retained profit		2	2				
Earnings per share	(q)	15p	15p				
Dividend per share	(r)	5p	5p				
Assume share price at end of year	(s)	200p	200p				

What are the pressures that in practice might indeed cause a company to undertake just such a transaction as the one above near the end of its financial year? First, there is the question of need. The acquisition would only be contemplated if the company had already decided that it would be beneficial to undertake it, that the benefits would sufficiently exceed the costs for it to be a worthwhile investment and better than all the alternatives available at that time. If so, the sooner it is undertaken, the sooner the benefits will start to accrue. Second is the question of budgets. Budgets are, broadly, authorisations to individual managers to spend money up to a given amount. The people concerned know that, in busy companies, in which budgets are often applied rigidly, if money authorised this year is not spent, then the amount authorised next year will probably be reduced – not a pleasing thought if you are a budget-holding manager and you have ambitious plans for your department next year. Third, although we are largely ignoring taxation in this book, there may be tax advantages to a business from investing in equipment now rather than later. Finally, do not underestimate the persuasiveness of a good salesperson, especially one who has a good relationship with their customer and who may be armed with special offers that happen only to apply until the end of the customer's financial year. Salespeople too have a strong interest in making sure that their customers' budgets get spent.

For all these reasons, major acquisitions may occur at any time, including at or near a company's year-end. The question then becomes – do such transactions have to be financed in a way that causes both an immediate cash outflow and those disadvantageous effects to financial ratios that we have just seen? Those effects arose because the company bought the assets with additional borrowings, thereby acquiring ownership of them. But does the company need to *own* the assets? Could it not, for example, rent them? If we want a TV, then we, as individuals, have the choice of buying and owning one, or of renting one. Our actual interest in the matter is the wish to be able to receive TV transmissions. Provided we are convinced that either financial option would give us that facility, why indeed not rent?

Rental

Unless, for some reason, ownership gives us as individuals some nice warm feeling, renting the TV might be a better option. First, from a cash viewpoint, we would be exchanging the obligation to pay a quite large amount today, for the obligation to pay small amounts every month for as long as we keep the TV, thereby conserving our cash for other things. Second, a typical rental contract allows for termination after a stated period and on giving a required amount of notice; we can just hand back the TV to the rental company and have no further obligation. Third, other services are usually included in a rental agreement, including repair or replacement should the TV go wrong. Fourth, express or implied in the ability to hand the TV back to the supplier is an exchange option – hand back the old TV and replace it with a more up-to-date model, usually for a relatively small increase in rent. Precisely because it *is* usually for a small increase in already small periodic payments, we would have little problem in affording such an upgrade out of our personal "budget".

For "TV" in the preceding paragraphs read "IT equipment" or indeed many other things including vehicles, and in principle the arguments for rental in relation to businesses are the same as those for individuals, although nowadays the mechanism for achieving the desired end is rather different, as we shall see. Rented equipment belongs to the supplier or the finance company. The accounting effects of this are that neither the rented asset nor the obligation to make periodic payments for using it appear on the balance sheet of the user company. So, by renting instead of purchasing, EAG Ltd would still have the unfettered right to use the £4m of equipment for an agreed period, but without the detrimental effects on their financial ratios.

Until about 1980 almost *all* IT equipment was rented, together, at a single all-in "bundled" price, with the associated software and services. This was a situation that user companies seemed to find quite accept-able, although they would no doubt have wished for lower prices and more choice. Most equipment was, in practice if not in theory, simply not available for purchase. However, several things caused that situation to change at about that time, for IT in particular, of which three can suffice for explanation. First was a series of US legal decisions that required the "unbundling" and separate pricing of hardware, software and services; second, the increasing pace of technological change, including the emergence of the personal computer; third was the ensuing rapid proliferation of IT companies of all kinds – software, services and hardware.

These three things combined to make the continuation of rental too high a business risk for the then established major IT suppliers. The main reason was the possibility that the rental price of their equipment might at any time be substantially undercut by software-compatible equipment from any of an increasing number of new companies, with the result that their equipment might be returned in large quantities. Within a short space of time, true rental of hardware was dead, except for very short-term requirements, and outright purchase from the manufacturer became the only option for the customer.

Nevertheless, we have seen above how obviously attractive rental was to many businesses: it conserved cash, it provided budget flexibility, it did not cause unfavourable movements in financial ratios, it relieved the user to some extent of concerns about obsolescence and it was a conve-nient mechanism for exchanging old equipment for new. Furthermore, rental made for simpler accounting than did outright purchase. If an asset does not appear on a company's balance sheet, then it does not have to be depreciated, thus avoiding awkward decisions about expected useful life and the depreciation method to be used. Rental payments are payments for the right to use equipment that belongs to someone else. Using what has earlier been referred to as the short cut method, these payments are simply charged straight to the profit and loss account as expenses, as they are made.

Where there is a demand for such obvious benefits, there will soon be companies ready to seize the opportunity of satisfying it, and that was the beginning of the leasing industry as we know it today. The main reason why leasing has become such an important method of financing IT is that it provides much the same benefits to user companies as renting used to provide, but at acceptable risk to the finance provider – the lessor, and therefore at acceptable cost to the user company, the lessee. Leasing is today a very widely used method of financing medium-term assets, including, but certainly not limited to, IT assets.

Leasing

A *lease* is a contract that confers on the lessee the right to use assets belonging to the lessor in return for periodic payments that include interest. Payments are usually of fixed amount at regular intervals, but other payment profiles are quite common, including holidays and steps. A holiday lease is the equivalent of the "buy now, pay later" idea that is a common feature of advertisements for consumer goods; there is a period at the beginning before payments are required to start. Step payments allow the lessee to start with small payments and progress to bigger ones, in line with expected cash availability or budget availability, or perhaps in line with increasing benefits expected to be delivered by the asset.

A lease is a particular variation on the theme of lending money on security, subject to creditworthiness. Since the lessor is the owner of a leased asset, the security is very strong, at least if the asset concerned is hardware. If the lessee defaults in payment, then the lessor can repossess the asset. It follows that hardware represents the greatest security for lessors, precisely because it could be repossessed and is likely to have some market value in that event. In some countries, including the United Kingdom, licence payments for software can also be leased. However, a software licence could not be repossessed, neither does it have a market value, so it does not provide any security for a lessor. Despite that, to meet customer demand, lessors will usually be prepared to write software-only leases, but they prefer financing arrangements that include a substantial hardware element as well.

The third element in IT – services – can also usually be written into a financing arrangement. However, in this case, what the user company requires is not finance for the use of an asset or a licence, it is finance for the rearrangement of payments due at particular times for the service. Because of the different characteristics of hardware, software and services, they usually require different kinds of financing contract, and in what follows we shall look at these in turn. However, at least for payment purposes, these differences are usually made transparent, the user company simply being required to make a single stream of regular payments for the whole deal, with holidays or steps if required.

Operating Leases

The name *operating lease* means, literally, a lease that allows the lessee to use or operate equipment that belongs to the lessor. It is the kind of lease that was originally designed to provide as closely as possible the kind of features, described above, earlier provided by rental, but at acceptable risk to the lessor and therefore at acceptable cost to the lessee. Strictly, an operating lease only applies to equipment, but the term is sometimes used more loosely to apply to financing arrangements that also include services and software. As already stated, "equipment" means any equipment or machine – for example vehicles, aircraft, manufacturing plant, medical equipment – not just IT equipment.

We might ask how finance companies – lessors – come to own in the first place the equipment that they lease. They do not buy equipment speculatively. What happens is that when a company, or any other organisation, wishes to acquire use of equipment, they first enter into the usual contract of sale with the supplier. If they wish to acquire ownership, then they pay for the goods, and title – the right to ownership – passes to the buyer. If, on the other hand, they wish to lease, then by a legal process known as novation, by agreement of all the parties, the finance company pays for the goods and title passes instead to them.

In constructing an operating lease, the lessor deducts from the value of the equipment – usually the purchase price – an amount, called the *residual value*, based on the equipment's expected market value at the end of the lease. During the primary period of the lease – usually for IT equipment no longer than about three or four years – the lessee only pays the difference, plus interest, in periodic payments. How are these payments accounted for? Shorn of some detail, the accounting rules currently in force in most countries, including the United Kingdom, are as follows. If the present value of the minimum payments due under the lease is less than 90% of the fair value (usually purchase price) of the leased asset, then the lease will usually qualify to be *off balance sheet* so far as the lessee is concerned. See chapter 10 for an explanation of "present value".

This means that, for accounting purposes, the lease is indeed treated just like rental, the periodic payments being charged direct to the profit and loss account as an expense. As already described, this expense represents the using up of the right to use equipment that belongs to somebody else. This "90% rule" is one, but only one, of the criteria that define a lease as an operating lease. Although obviously arbitrary, it conveys the idea that the lessee is not paying for all of the value in the asset, but only for part of it. That is the justification for treating the payments as payments for using the asset rather than as payments for acquiring it.

Note that the lessor normally pays the supplier the purchase price of the equipment at the outset of the lease, but that by the end of the lease the lessor might only have received from the lessee, say, 80% of that purchase price, plus interest. The need of the lessor to recoup *all* its expenditure defines the two main things that a lessee may do at the end of an operating lease – hand back the equipment or extend the lease. The payments required for extension will reflect the further amount of value that will be taken out of the equipment by use during the extension period. If, at the end of the extension period, the expected market value is nil, then the amount charged for the extension will be at least the original residual value. If the equipment is returned to the lessor, then they will either sell it, obviously hoping to receive at least the residual value and preferably more, or re-lease it secondhand.

As did rental, the right of the lessee to hand equipment back at the end of an operating lease provides an obvious mechanism, express or implied, for exchanging old equipment for new. Thus, operating leases do indeed provide for lessees most of the benefits – cash conservation, budget management, preservation of financial ratios, and exchange, that we saw as the benefits of rental. As with "pure" rental, however, "pure" operating leases do not always provide the lessee with an option to take ownership. In the United Kingdom, for example, such an option is not usually permitted. However, companies that wish to spread the payment for equipment and eventually take ownership of it have another financial mechanism available to them. It is the commercial version of a financing method common in personal life, namely hire purchase.

Hire Purchase

Hire purchase is a lease with a purchase option. Although we may well be familiar with it in personal life, the rates charged for commercial hire purchase are substantially less than you and I might pay. As with the operating lease described above, a hire purchased asset is owned initially by the finance company. However, title passes to the lessee on making the last payment, which may be a nominal amount of, say, £1. Although the purchase option is just that, an option, it is almost invariably exercised by the lessee, and in certain key respects – accounting and taxation – eventual exercise of the option is assumed from the outset.

Looking at the accounting aspects, the leased asset is shown on the balance sheet of the lessee from the outset, even though the lessee does not actually own it until the purchase option is exercised. On the other side of the balance sheet is shown the obligation eventually to pay for it. As payments are made, this obligation is reduced by the principal element of the payment, the interest element being charged to the profit and loss account as an expense, as we saw in Tables 4.8 and 4.12. Sometimes there may be an option either to make the last payment or to return the asset. In such a case, in its practical effect the hire purchase arrangement takes on some of the characteristics of an operating lease, although it remains very different from an accounting and taxation viewpoint. However, this kind of option is more common with hire purchase of assets such as cars; much less so with IT.

Why is commercial hire purchase necessary? We have already asked whether companies need to own assets at all, and we decided that for most companies unfettered use of assets is what they are actually concerned about, ownership being of secondary importance or even a disadvantage. However, for some companies that may wish to spread payments, ownership *is* important. For example, a requirement of owner-ship might be imposed by a foreign parent company as a matter of worldwide policy, perhaps for tax reasons in the foreign country.

It should be clear from the above that hire purchase of equipment is very different from an operating lease, and usually only delivers the one benefit to the lessee that all leases provide – the ability to spread the payments – while also providing ultimate ownership as an option. It certainly does not represent off balance sheet finance for the lessee.

We have now looked at two very different kinds of lease – the oper-ating lease and hire purchase. Unfortunately, neither of them is suitable for leasing one-time payments for software licences, an increasingly common requirement. Why are these leases not suitable, starting with the operating lease? Well, what is the essential characteristic of an oper-ating lease? It is the residual value. Can a software licence have a residual value? No it cannot, at least not in the sense of a value at which the licence could be "sold" or re-leased. So, operating leases cannot be used for leasing software.

Where hire purchase is used for IT, the customer is usually paying to *buy* the equipment, albeit in instalments and, on making the last payment, becomes the owner. Does the owner of some proprietary software want its ownership passed to the customer of a finance company through the mechanism of a hire purchase contract? The answer is probably not. So, neither hire purchase nor operating leases are suitable vehicles for leasing software. Some other kind of lease is required, one that neither builds in a residual value nor passes title to the lessee. Such a lease is the *finance lease*, or more specifically a *full payout finance lease*. For the reason just given, it is therefore easier these days to think of this as a mechanism for financing software. However, finance leases have been around for a long time and were originally used as a tax-efficient method of financing hardware. They are still used to finance equipment, especially equipment that, because it is already secondhand or because a long lease is required, has little or no expected residual value.

Finance or Full Payout Finance Leases

To the lessee, for accounting purposes, a full payout lease is like hire purchase. The leased asset – software licence or hardware – is shown on the balance sheet of the lessee from the outset, even though in this case the lessee can never own it. Strange, you might think, but the reasoning is based on the economic substance of the transaction rather than its legal form. As with hire purchase, the lessee is paying for all the value in the asset, not part of it. Therefore, the argument goes, it should be accounted for in the same way as hire purchase. Increasingly in accounting, precedence is given to the economic substance of certain transactions rather than their legal form. On the other side of the balance sheet is shown the obligation eventually to make the payments, these being treated broadly the same as for hire purchase.

Given the economic similarity between hire purchase and full payout finance leases, where, as is quite common, the latter are used to finance equipment, such contracts usually contain terms that seek to put the lessee company in the same economic position, so far as possible, as they would have been in with hire purchase. At the end of the primary term, the lessee may either extend into a secondary term, for a nominal payment called a peppercorn rent, or sell the equipment, acting as the lessor's agent, and keep most of the proceeds.

Given the practical similarity of hire purchase and full payout finance leases, but that hire purchase bestows ownership while finance leases usually do not, why would any company wishing to finance equipment, as distinct from software, choose the full payout finance lease? In the United Kingdom the reason is, at least partly, the historical one mentioned above. From the tax viewpoint of the lessee, there is now usually very little financial difference between the two forms of finance. Originally, however, there were big differences between the two that substantially favoured finance leases. Although the tax differences between them have been eroded, the two forms of finance have continued to coexist, and will no doubt continue to do so.

Services and Project Finance

Services of one kind or another represent an increasing proportion of what businesses spend on what is broadly called IT. The term "services" includes many different activities; for example maintenance, training, help desk, disaster recovery, project management, and the range of activities usually described as installation services – those activities concerned with ensuring that all elements of an information system actually work when installed in a particular environment.

Strictly, you cannot lease a service, but what you can do with the help of a financer is to rearrange the times when payments are made for the service, usually via the mechanism of a loan. For example, a company may be entering into a maintenance contract that requires 36 monthly payments of £10,000 or, as an alternative, a single upfront payment of, say, £320,000, the sump sum being obviously less than the sum of the monthly payments because the service provider is getting its money sooner. The company may already be arranging leases for hardware and software that include a 6-month initial holiday because of a temporary cash shortage. The financer might pay the £320,000 lump sum due to the service provider, in addition to sums due to the providers of hardware and software, and arrange a single payment stream in respect of the total system, the first payment from the company being due at the end of the holiday period.

The actual construction of the total arrangement might be quite complex. For example, the different items of hardware might be financed with operating leases, each having different residual values depending on the type of hardware; one-time charges for software would usually, in the United Kingdom especially, be financed with full payout finance leases; the maintenance contract, other services and possibly other things, such as the initial costs of setting up a project, or charges incurred by terminating existing leases, would be financed by means of a loan. All these elements can be packaged into a single convenient payment stream, whose detailed complexities are not visible to the lessee.

Who provides leasing and related finance? There are three main kinds of organisation: banks, independent leasing companies and equipment manufacturers. For banks, leasing is simply another mechanism for lending money on the security of assets. Banks generally have no interest in trading equipment so, although with some exceptions involving specialist subsidiary companies, they do not usually offer operating leases. Their main offerings are hire purchase and full payout finance leases. Independent leasing companies are traders, as well as being lessors. They offer mainly operating leases, and may also offer related services such as project finance. For equipment manufacturers, financing is a sales aid and a service to their customers. They may offer the whole range of leasing and hire purchase facilities.

Outsourcing

While not, at least primarily, a method of financing, mention can usefully be made at this point of *outsourcing*. Leasing is evidence of the recognition by an organisation that it is not necessary to have ownership of assets in order to be able to use them. An extension of this idea is to recognize that it is not necessary to have a particular application or business function performed in-house or by one's own people in order to obtain its benefits. Particular business functions might be contracted out to specialist companies.

Outsourcing is the arranging of work previously done within an organisation to be done by an outside contractor. It is often done by organisations trying to restrict their internal activities to what they regard as their core business. Early examples of outsourcing occurred in the United Kingdom when local authorities were allowed to contract out functions such as refuse collection and maintenance of open spaces, previously done by themselves, to outside contractors. In IT, early examples of outsourced functions were payroll and data entry.

If you can outsource one function, then you can outsource others, so some organisations, for example, outsource their whole accounting function, while others outsource a major part, or the whole, of their IT function. All combinations are possible, from the contractor using the organisation's own equipment and people to the contractor using its own equipment and people. The latter could be said to represent a kind of "off balance sheet" financing, to the extent that the previously in-house function used assets that were on the company's balance sheet, whether they were owned, hire purchased or finance leased.

In this chapter we have considered some general principles of financing and then looked in some detail at some specific methods of providing medium-term finance, especially those with particular relevance to IT. In principle, businesses have much the same choice of financing methods for the goods and services they need as individuals have, although the precise mechanisms may differ. For long-term assets, if they could afford the cash, the question is: is this factory or this manufacturing plant the best thing on which to spend cash at this time, or could we get a better return by financing those assets and conserving the cash for something else? The same principle holds good for medium-term assets.

However, there is an additional dimension to be considered in the financing of medium-term assets, and especially those concerned with IT. Leasing, depending on the kind of lease, can help businesses conserve cash, preserve financial ratios, and facilitate the exchange of old equipment for new. It may also help budget-holders to better manage their budgets, depending upon the degree of flexibility that they are allowed, and leasing can often be shown to be, financially, the best way of financing the medium term assets in which a company has decided to invest its money. Finally, we considered how outsourcing can be thought of in some ways as an extension of the principles upon which decisions to lease are usually based.

If leasing is indeed a way of financing assets in which a company has decided to invest, the question then arises: how do companies determine what is the best investment in the first place? With almost limitless opportunities for spending limited amounts of money, how do business people decide, financially, between the alternatives available? This is the main theme of the following three chapters of this book.

9 Is It a Good Investment?

Benefits and Costs – Cash or Profit – Opportunity Cost – Decision Criteria – Cost/Benefit Analysis Example

When we are buying something we usually try to get the best deal – the best value for the lowest price or, one could say, the best return on the money invested. So do businesses. Throughout this book I have demonstrated the similarities between business and personal finance, and here is another obvious parallel. There is, however, also an important difference. We as individuals, spending our own money, can include emotional factors as benefits in our calculations. For example, if we can afford it, we can choose to buy a smarter or more powerful car than we actually need, simply because it might make us feel good. Businesses cannot, or at least should not afford themselves this luxury, because businesses are always spending other people's money.

Every penny that a business spends belongs to someone else, someone who has provided that money for one reason only – to maximise their personal wealth; someone who, for the time being at least, believes that investing in that particular business rather than any other is the best way of achieving that objective. When they cease to believe that, rational investors will withdraw their money and put it somewhere else.

Benefits and Costs

IT people get used to thinking in terms of projects. In business, "a project" may be anything from launching a new product, entering a new market or taking over a competitor, to replacing old IT technology with new or outsourcing all or part of an in-house IT function. A project involves investing money today in order to achieve benefits tomorrow. But wait a minute – is that not what business as a whole is all about too? It is indeed; in fact, one way of thinking about a business is to regard it as a series of projects, some long, some short, some big, some small, and not of course all concerning IT, each of which involves the expenditure of part of the business's limited supply of money in order to gain future benefits. If this is so, and if the purpose of the business as a whole is to maximize the wealth of its owners – its shareholders, if a company – then that had better be the purpose of every project in which the business engages. And if the effectiveness of the business is ultimately measured in terms of benefits delivered compared with costs incurred, then so should the effectiveness of projects.

This is not to say that every single "project" that a business invests in is capable of delivering benefits, at least not directly. There are many things that businesses have to do for legal reasons. These include keeping accounts, obeying data protection regulations and satisfying health and safety requirements. These are obviously not profitable, or at least not directly so. Other projects that businesses undertake are enabling projects, also not profitable in themselves but providing the basis for other projects that *will* be. An example is installing a network – this may cost a lot of money, but the network itself does not deliver benefits; they come from the subsequent uses that will be made of it as a medium of communication. Other projects are undertaken to protect against possible loss. For example, it happens that this book is being written during the transition from the previous millennium to this one, a period during which very large sums of money were expended trying to ensure that computers and other machines were capable of handling the date change. Projects such as these are not profitable; at best they may help to avoid or reduce losses.

So perhaps we should narrow and refine our definition. *Discretionary* projects in which businesses invest should deliver a return on the money invested sufficient to contribute to the aim of maximising shareholders' wealth. To achieve this aim, the benefits of any business investment must exceed its costs by the maximum possible amount. The question then arises: what do we mean by benefits and what do we mean by costs? One might be tempted to ask what the problem is. Surely "benefits" means money received and "costs" means money paid? Unfortunately it is not always that simple, and to illustrate the difficulties, we shall work through an example. It happens to relate to IT, but the principles that it illustrates are applicable to any investment decision. Before doing so, however, we shall work through a much simpler example from everyday life in order to derive some rules for guiding us through the difficulties in cost/benefit analysis and helping to avoid them in any future real situations.

Cash or Profit?

Cost/benefit analysis is a method for helping to decide whether or not a particular project or investment should be undertaken by comparing its relevant likely costs and benefits over its estimated lifetime. Earlier, we discussed the differences between cash and profit, and I suggested that these two things are arguably the most important measures of business activity. They are certainly the two things that people running a business must get right continually if the business is to succeed and prosper. Of these two, cash is a matter of fact; you've either got it or you haven't, you have received it or you have paid it. You may not like the bright red colour in which the final balance on your bank statement is printed, but except in the unlikely event that the bank has made a mistake, you cannot argue with it.

Profit, however, is to some extent a matter of opinion. There are at least two things, often major items in a business's accounts, that are, at least to some extent, either a matter of opinion or left to the discretion of the business person. One is the valuation of stocks, the other is depreciation. There are others, but these two will suffice to make the point. Think again of the small corner shop near to where you live. In order to produce a balance sheet and a profit and loss account, the stock has to be counted and valued. But what is the value of the stock in a shop? Well, a starting point is to know what it cost. But stock that has been on the shelves for different amounts of time will have been bought at different prices. The stocktaker will certainly not look back in the records to see what each individual tin of beans cost, and faithfully record it. They will do an approximate count of the total number of tins, and assign the same price to all of them. This may be the price of the earliest purchases or the latest, or it may be the average price over a period, and there are arguments in favour of all of these approaches. Furthermore, allowance should be made for deterioration and obsolescence of some kinds of stock. Ask ten different people to value the stock in a shop, and you will get ten different answers. The point is that the valuation of stock is a matter of judgement.

Also a matter of judgement is how the depreciation of assets is recorded, as you will recall from the earlier mention of the subject. The only rule is that an asset should be depreciated over its expected useful economic life. But what is that? Different people would make different estimates of useful life. The longer the expected life, the lower the per annum charge for depreciation; the shorter the expected life, the higher the annual charge. Almost every aspect of depreciation is left to the judgement of the business person, including the method to be used. The reducing balance method – under which a fixed percentage of depreciation is charged each year on the reducing balance, as distinct from a fixed amount – will result in a higher charge in early years and a lower charge in later years than will the straight line method. Whatever the method, the total amount of depreciation will be reduced by any expected proceeds of sale at end of life, but that too can only be an estimate.

So, both stock values and depreciation – both possibly major items in a business's accounts – are matters of judgement. The question is – is our primary basis for measuring the effectiveness of an investment of part of the company's money going to be its effect on profit – something that is a matter of opinion, or its effect on cash – something that is a matter of fact? The answer is, of course, its effect on cash, and there is almost universal agreement among the authorities that it is indeed cash flow, not profit, that should be the primary basis for measuring the effectiveness of a business investment. Lumby (1999) observes that "to use the accounting profit concept in financial decision making would be to use an entirely inappropriate concept – a concept specially developed for reporting the outcome of decisions and not developed for helping to take the actual decision itself." Furthermore, concentrating on cash in financial decision making fits in with the fact that the purpose of business is to maximize the wealth of the proprietors. If that means anything, ultimately it means their cash wealth, because that is the only thing with which the bills can be paid and luxuries bought.

That is not to deny the importance of profit or the importance to business people of estimating what the *effect* on profit would be of an investment once decided upon. Because of the requirement quite artificially to chop businesses up into one-year chunks for reporting and taxation purposes, profit is a very important measure indeed, and for this purpose the best method yet devised. Furthermore, quite apart from those external reporting requirements, divisional and departmental managers, including IT managers, may well be measured and bonused on the profit attributed to their business units. However, for the reasons given, profit should not be the *primary* basis for investment decision-making, for all its usefulness for other purposes.

Opportunity Cost

One concept, important in cost/benefit analysis, and that we need to understand, is opportunity cost. *Opportunity cost* is defined as the benefit lost by not employing an economic resource in the most profitable alternative activity. A simple example will illustrate the concept. We may be thinking about trading in the old car for a newer one, but having reflected on the state of our finances, decide that we must wait for a year before doing so. Suppose that, were we to trade in now, we might reasonably expect to get £1,000 for the old car, but that if we wait for a year we would only get £400. By delaying the trade-in, we would have incurred an opportunity cost of £1,000 − £400 = £600. Another example is that you may choose to be self-employed. If you do, then the opportunity cost to you is the highest salary that you might reasonably have expected to get had you instead chosen to work as an employee.

The previous paragraph contained two examples of binary decisions: to keep the old car or to trade it in, to have a job or to be self-employed. Many business investment decisions, including IT decisions, are also binary. Should we continue as we are, or should we make a change and do something else? Should we keep existing equipment or exchange it for something more up-to-date? Should we continue with our existing methods or move towards computer-integrated manufacturing? In order to decide which is the best course of action in financial terms it is necessary to determine the expected benefits and the expected costs of each course of action, and to compare them.

Gathering the data on likely costs and benefits for such decisions is often a complex and time-consuming task, and methods of doing so are outside the scope of this book. However, once gathered, there is a long way of summarising and setting out the data, and there is a shorter way. Take as an example the decision whether to keep the old car or to trade it in. The long way of setting out the data would be to list all the running costs of the old car and the eventual proceeds of sale at the end of a chosen period, say three years, then to list all the running costs of the newer car, its initial cost and *its* eventual sale proceeds at the end of the same period, and then to compare the results of the two to determine which is the best deal, in this case the deal involving the lowest net costs.

Decision Criteria

Table 9.1 shows that, using the numbers given, trading in the old care for new would appear to be the lowest-cost option by £8,931–£8,625 = £306. However, the approach adopted in Table 9.1 involves making two separate lists, and it also involves some repetition. For example, including road tax on both lists would usually be a waste of time because the amounts would be the same for both cars, and so do not differ among the alternatives. When comparing two alternative courses of action, it is generally preferable to draw up a single list, of the *incremental* costs and benefits of one course of action *vis-à-vis* the other. If the alternatives are to stay as we are or to do something new, then the cost/benefit analysis should show the *incremental* costs and benefits of the new course of action relative to the current state of affairs.

For example, relative to staying as we are and keeping the old car, we would expect the incremental costs of trading it in for a newer one to include, obviously, the cost of the new car and, perhaps, an increase in insurance premium. We would expect the incremental benefits to include the trade-in value of the old car and the greater eventual sale value of the new car over that of the old, plus the expected reduction in maintenance costs and, perhaps, a reduction in fuel costs because of greater fuel efficiency. *See* Table 9.2. Why should the eventual sale value of the new car be included, as well as the sale of the old one? The answer is to ensure that we are comparing like with like. In both situations we end up with no car at the end of our chosen evaluation period.

Table 9.1   Keep the old car or trade it in?

Assume costs increase by 5% per year	Year 0 £	Year 1 £	Year 2 £	Year 3 £	Total £
Keep the old car					
Fuel		−1,500	−1,575	−1,654	−4,729
Maintenance		−900	−945	−992	−2,837
Road tax		−160	−168	−176	−504
Insurance		−400	−420	−441	−1,261
Sell after three years				400	400
Net cashflows		−2,960	−3,108	−2,863	−8,931
Trade in for new					
Cost of newer car now	−5,000				−5,000
Sell old car now	1,300				1,300
Fuel		−1,000	−1,050	−1,103	−3,153
Maintenance		−600	−630	−662	−1,892
Road tax		−160	−168	−176	−504
Insurance		−500	−525	−551	−1,576
Sell after three years				2,200	2,200
Net cashflows	−3,700	−2,260	−2,373	−292	−8,625

Table 9.2   Keep the old car or trade it in – the fully incremental approach

Assume costs increase by 5% per year	Year 0 £	Year 1 £	Year 2 £	Year 3 £	Total £
Incremental cash flows arising from trading in old car for new					
Cost of new, less trade-in	−3,700				−3,700
Fuel		500	525	551	1,576
Maintenance		300	315	330	945
Insurance		−100	−105	−110	−315
Sell after three years				1,800	1,800
Net incremental cashflows	−3,700	700	735	2,571	306

Incidentally, the term "Year 0" is conventionally used to mean the first day of the project being evaluated. In our example this would be the day on which the old car would be traded in for the new. "Year 1" is deemed to begin on the following day. Noting *when* cash flows occur is a very important part of financial decision-making. This is partly to make the calculations easier, by dividing the amounts up into manageable chunks. However, it is mainly for the very important reason, that we shall pursue in the next chapter, that the value of money changes, depending upon when it is received or paid, an effect often called the *time value of money*, and it is vital that those changes in value are taken into account.

Why in the above example have we not included the original cost some years ago of the old car? There are two reasons. One is that, like the road tax, the amount would of course be the same in both scenarios, so that there would be no difference between the alternatives, but there is another reason. Why are we doing the cost/benefit analysis at all? It is to help us to decide whether, at least from a financial viewpoint, to keep the old car or to trade it in. Can we make decisions about the past? Should we allow things that have happened in the past *and cannot be changed*, to affect decisions about the future? The answer is, of course, no. Nothing can change the earlier decision to buy the old car and certainly nothing can bring back the money that we spent on it. Therefore it should be excluded from our decision-making, as should all other costs already incurred. The term often used to describe costs already incurred that cannot be recouped is *sunk costs*.

Sometimes, in IT and in other projects, decisions have to be taken on whether to continue with a project, once begun. In that case, then "Year 0" is taken to mean the point of decision and, for decision-making purposes, all costs incurred up to the point of the decision have become sunk costs. I imagine that, during the building of the tunnel under the channel between England and France, as it became increasingly difficult to finance costs that proved substantially higher than the original estimates, there were a number of times at which meetings were held to decide whether to continue the project or abandon it. Would the future revenues to be generated by the tunnel, when completed, ever be sufficient to recoup the costs incurred? If not, would the future costs of abandonment result in even greater losses? In this example, costs incurred up to the date of the decision, to the extent that they could not be recouped, were sunk costs, in this case literally as well as metaphorically, and would not have featured in the decision-making.

Referring again to Table 9.2, another point to note is that, in the incremental way of looking at costs and benefits, the avoidance of a cash outflow, for example the expected reduction in fuel costs, is shown as a positive number, as though it were a cash inflow. The reason for this is that the avoidance of a cash outflow is just as much a benefit as is an increase in cash inflow. A reduction of £100 in the rent due to your landlord is just as much a benefit to you as would be an after-tax salary increase of the same amount.

Let us now summarize the points made so far in this chapter. In business, investment decisions have consequences both for cash flow and profit. Profit is, to some extent, a matter of opinion, while cash is a matter of fact. The purpose of a business is to maximize the wealth of its owner or owners; ultimately this means maximizing their cash wealth. For these reasons, for discretionary investments, cash flow is generally regarded as the primary financial basis for deciding whether or not to proceed, although it is usually desirable also to estimate the *effect* on profit were the investment to be made. Sunk costs should be excluded, as should any other cash flows that do not differ among the alternatives. Finally, the avoidance of a cash outflow is just as much a benefit as is an increase in cash inflow of the same amount. Horngren, Foster and Datar (1997) summarize the above into a single rule, as follows. "Relevant cash flows (for decision-making purposes) are expected future cash flows that differ among the alternatives."

We can now embark on a detailed consideration of the factors often involved in making decisions about business investments, or indeed personal ones, using a proposed IT investment as an example. In the following example I have tried to include as many as possible of the things that often cause difficulty, in particular in answering the question: is this a benefit, or a cost, that is attributable to the proposed investment? Because of this, some aspects of the example may be thought rather artificial, and in some cases the numbers used are trivial. However, since any artificiality or triviality is only there to assist understanding, I trust that you will regard it as a justified means to the end of understanding a very important, and often ill-understood, aspect of finance. We shall work through the example step by step, and I shall explain each step as we proceed. However, you may well gain benefit from first working through the whole example yourself, ignoring the explanations until you have got to the end.

Cost/Benefit Analysis Example

JPB Ltd is a manufacturing company. Some time ago a small team was appointed to collect data on the likely benefits and costs to the company of an IT project to improve various aspects of the company's operations. Imagine that you are a member of this team, and that you have been asked by the team leader, who is not financially trained, to produce a list of the relevant cash flows from the following data.

The proposed project is to be evaluated over four years. Solely to make subsequent calculations easier, all cash flows are assumed to arise on the last day of the year to which they relate. Except where otherwise stated, prices and wage rates will increase at an annual compound rate of 5% per annum. All current prices and wage rates will remain the same until the end of Year 1, before increasing as stated. Taxation will be ignored. Some of the following paragraphs are numbered for subsequent reference.

1. The increases in net cash inflow attributable to the project, a combination of increased cash inflows and reduced cash outflows, *before* taking into account the items described in the following paragraphs, are expected to be as follows in Years 1 to 4 respectively: £620k, £844k, £772k, £474k. These are simply the totals of amounts that do not have

any characteristics needing particular comment or likely to cause difficulty. They might include incremental cash inflows expected to result
from increased sales less the incremental cash outflows to be expended
in achieving them. They might also include reductions in cash outflows
associated with various administrative expenses.

Table 9.3 shows these as positive cash flows, the first items in what
will eventually be the full cost/benefit analysis. Note that the amounts
are shown in columns representing the years in which it is expected that
they will be received. The amounts shown, on this and on all the subsequent lines, are the expected incremental cash flows. Usually, as we shall
see in the next chapter, unless the differences are significant, the same
numbers would be used if it was the estimated impact on the profit and
loss account, rather than the cash flow, that we were trying to determine.
Timing differences between the earning of revenues and their receipt in
cash, and between incurring expenses and paying them in cash, would
usually be ignored.

In the following paragraphs concerning items that *do* call for special
comment, each item will be treated in the same way: a numbered paragraph containing the given data, a reference to a table, similar to Table
9.3, which shows how the item should be treated, followed by comments
on the item and why it has been treated in that particular way. At the
end of the example, Table 9.14 will show the complete cost/benefit cash
flow analysis. This we shall then use in the following two chapters as the
basis for a study of the time value of money and of the various investment evaluation methods typically used by company financial people.

2. The project will require the replacement of some existing equipment, which has zero book value. It has been fully depreciated or "written
off", and we shall assume that, but for this project it would have been
kept for the foreseeable future. Its estimated resale value on Day 1 of the
project, Year 0, is also nil. Assume that, if *not* replaced now, maintenance
and power costs of the existing equipment would be £30k in Year 1, then
increasing at an annual compound rate of 10% for the next four years.

Table 9.4 shows a nil cash flow for proceeds of sale in Year 0, followed
by positive numbers in Years 1 to 4 representing the avoidance of future
cash outflows on maintenance. The reason why no maintenance cash flow
is shown in Year 0 is that "Year 0" is defined as the first day of the project.
Year 1 begins on the following day. Any costs incurred before Year 0 are

Table 9.3   Incremental cashflows arising from changes if new investment is undertaken

	Year 0 £000	Year 1 £000	Year 2 £000	Year 3 £000	Year 4 £000	Total £000
Various net cash inflows		620	844	772	474	2,710
Totals		620	844	772	474	2,710

Table 9.4 Incremental cashflows arising from changes if new investment is undertaken

	Year 0 £000	Year 1 £000	Year 2 £000	Year 3 £000	Year 4 £000	Total £000
Existing equipment:						
Proceeds of sale	0					0
Old running costs avoided		30	33	36	40	139
Totals	0	30	33	36	40	139

sunk costs, and therefore do not differ between the alternatives. As you may recall from earlier discussions of depreciation, any book value remaining after deducting proceeds of sale, nil in this case, is an expense – loss on sale – that must be charged to the profit and loss account. It simply represents inadequate depreciation charged in the past and, like depreciation, is not a cash item. The only cash flow resulting from this transaction would be any proceeds of sale, also nil in this case.

3. The new equipment will cost £700k if purchased outright on Day 1 of the project, Year 0. It will run all systems required by the new project and will also incorporate all work currently being done on the existing equipment. Estimated resale value after four years – nil; straight line depreciation will be £175k per year. Maintenance and power of the new equipment will cost £10k in Year 1 (maintenance will be free because of a one-year warranty), £21k in Year 2, and will then increase at an annual compound rate of 5% over the life of the project.

Table 9.5 illustrates that, as always in a cash flow analysis, it is the incremental cash flows that are shown here, in this case cash outflows – the purchase price and the running costs. Depreciation is not a cash item, so it is ignored. When, however, in the next chapter we come to look at the impact of the project on the profit and loss account of the company, then the situation will be reversed. The depreciation will then be shown, because that is what affects the profit and loss account, while the cash payment would be ignored.

If the equipment were to be leased instead of being purchased then the cash payments under the lease would be shown, in their appropriate

Table 9.5 Incremental cashflows arising from changes if new investment is undertaken

	Year 0 £000	Year 1 £000	Year 2 £000	Year 3 £000	Year 4 £000	Total £000
New equipment:						
Purchase price	−700					−700
New running costs incurred		−10	−21	−22	−23	−76
Totals	−700	−10	−21	−22	−23	−776

columns, rather than the purchase price. However, an alternative approach would be to evaluate the project initially assuming outright purchase of equipment, then to do separate evaluations of alternative methods of financing, such as lease versus purchase. Many companies keep what they would call the investment decision quite separate from the financing decision.

4. Additional software licences will be required. These will cost £300k in total. Ignore software maintenance or "subscription" charges. In the UK, but not in all countries, one-time payments for software licences longer than two years are treated for accounting, and tax, purposes the same as payments for hardware. The payment is capitalized, which means that the licence is shown as a fixed asset on the balance sheet and depreciated over its expected life. For this reason, payments for software licences can be leased just as can payments for hardware. In our example, like the equipment, the cash cost of £300k would be shown as a cash outflow in Year 0, and the depreciation ignored, just like the purchase price of the hardware in Table 9.5

5. Assume that, among other kinds, two particular kinds of computer stationery, Type 1 and Type 2, are currently used by JPB Ltd. Facts about this stationery are given in Table 9.6. Type 1 stationery is used regularly in many applications. Type 2 is now rarely used, and if this particular project is not undertaken, then the remaining stock will be sold during Year 1 as scrap. Assume that the quantities of both Type 1 and Type 2 supplies used by the project would be replaced and paid for at the end of each year during which they have been used by the project, except that the stock of Type 2 supplies would be allowed to run down to zero by the end of Year 4. Replacement costs and resale values for all supplies are expected to rise at an annual compound rate of 5% per year over the life of the project.

Tables 9.7 and 9.8 show the relevant cash flows. These items were included to show how to deal with the costs attributable to a project of using resources, usually materials, that the business already has in stock. The three possible "costs" are original price, current replacement cost and resale value. Of these, original cost is never relevant, because it is a *sunk cost*. It represents money already spent that cannot be brought back. It

Table 9.6 Facts about computer stationery (JPB Ltd)

	Unit	Type 1	Type 2
Quantity per year required by the proposed project	Boxes	4,000	2,000
Quantity in stock now	Boxes	7,000	3,000
Original cost per box	£ per box	11	9
Current purchase price per box	£ per box	12	10
Current scrap value per box	£ per box	1	1

Table 9.7 Incremental cashflows arising from changes if new investment is undertaken

	Year 0 £000	Year 1 £000	Year 2 £000	Year 3 £000	Year 4 £000	Total £000
Type 1 supplies:						
Replenishment costs		−48	−50	−53	−56	−207
Totals		−48	−50	−53	−56	−207

Table 9.8 Incremental cashflows arising from changes if new investment is undertaken

	Year 0 £000	Year 1 £000	Year 2 £000	Year 3 £000	Year 4 £000	Total £000
Type 2 supplies:						
Opportunity cost		−3				−3
Replenishment costs		−20	−21	−11	0	−52
Totals		−23	−21	−11	0	−55

is futile to make decisions about the past. If resources are used elsewhere in the business, as with Type 1, then the cost attributable to the project of using them is their replacement cost, because if they are to continue being used elsewhere, then they would have to be replaced. So, replacement cost is the cost of their use.

If the resources already in stock have no other use (Type 2), then they would only need to be replaced in sufficient quantities for the proposed project. However, if used by this project, then the business loses the opportunity of making a little money by selling them as scrap. So the costs attributable to the project are the costs of replenishing the stocks up to the point at which they can be run down to zero, and the opportunity cost represented by the loss of the sale proceeds of £3k.

There is obviously an element of artificiality here, in two respects. First, to be evaluated at all, projects are assumed to have a finite life, and for IT projects this is typically four or five years. However, many innovations that start out as projects become established parts of the way a company does business. For example, a project to introduce computer aided manufacturing may be initially evaluated over, say, five years, but it is most unlikely that at the end of that period the company would revert to the old way of doing things. It may be that the particular technology with which it was first implemented might need replacing, but in that case the "project" for doing so would be evaluated for what it would then be – a technology replacement project, not a new application project. If this were so, then the stock of many kinds of supplies would almost certainly *not* be run down to zero by the end of the first evaluation period. With our particular example of stationery, it is probably arguable that after four years the design may need to be changed anyway. The point is that here is another example of the need to apply judgement, and to try to reflect the reality of the particular situation.

6. Assume that each year the proposed project will require 4,000 hours of specialist programming skills, the equivalent of two people full-time, at a cost of £25 per hour each in salary and benefits. Salary and benefit costs of these programmers are expected to increase at an annual compound rate of 5% per year over the life of the project. The IT department, which does external revenue-earning work as well as serving JPB Ltd, anticipates a shortage of the specialist programmers during the first year only, and that approval for the project would make it necessary during that period to give up other, external, work on which it is estimated that revenue of £60 per specialist hour would have been earned.

See Table 9.9 for the relevant cash flows. This item concerns the attributable costs of scarce resources, especially people. Because of the shortage in Year 1 of specialist programmers, they can only be used at the expense of other work. The cash flow that would be forfeited if the project goes ahead would be the revenue from the other work, £60k × 4,000 = £240k. So it is this – the lost revenue – that is the opportunity cost of diverting the scarce resource to this project. Because, after Year 1, the resource is no longer scarce, it is assumed, because we are not told otherwise, that it can be hired. So, the attributable cash flows then are only the salaries and the overheads of the additional people hired.

Suppose that, during Year 1, the specialists would otherwise be employed, not on external revenue-earning work, but on other *internal* work. Would there still then be an opportunity cost of diverting them on to our proposed project for that year? The answer is yes, but that the amount of the cost would depend on the benefits expected to accrue to the company from that particular project, and the cost of delaying those benefits by one year. In practice, based on its accumulated experience of the benefits achieved by projects of that particular type relative to their labour costs, a company might apply a percentage uplift on those costs to represent an approximate, average opportunity cost. In this example, an uplift of, say, 40% would result in an internal opportunity cost in Year 1 of £10 × 4,000 = £40k.

Table 9.9 Incremental cashflows arising from changes if new investment is undertaken

	Year 0 £000	Year 1 £000	Year 2 £000	Year 3 £000	Year 4 £000	Total £000
Specialist IT personnel:						
Opportunity cost		−240				−240
Salaries and benefits			−105	−110	−116	−331
Totals		−240	−105	−110	−116	−571

In this example, we have considered the case of resources which are genuinely scarce, and it has been assumed that the IT department is free to hire non-scarce resources for the project when they become available. However, this may not be the case; the company may have a freeze on hiring. In this situation, resources may not actually be scarce, but they *are* limited, and so the "scarce resource" arguments would then apply to all personnel and all projects. What some companies do in these circumstances is to apply an average opportunity cost, described above, to all project evaluations, based usually on the labour costs associated with them. That could be said, however, to be a significant shift away from the original simple concept of attributable cash flows. Some companies only include actual incremental labour costs – resulting from hiring or firing – in such cost/benefit analyses. They exclude costs associated with existing labour, especially where all internal projects undertaken are of at least roughly similar size, use similar amounts of resources and are known or believed to deliver roughly similar benefits relative to their costs.

7. Assume that the project would also require 8,000 hours of non-specialist IT skills, the equivalent of four people full-time at a cost of £20 per hour each in salary and benefits. Salary and benefit costs of these programmers are expected to increase at an annual compound rate of 5% per year over the life of the project. Also assume that, in the first year only, the IT department expects, unless they are used on this project, to have 8000 surplus non-specialist staff hours. Assume, finally, that JPB Ltd has an agreement with staff for whom there is temporarily no work, whereby it lays them off and pays them one-half of their normal salary and benefits during the layoff period.

Table 9.10 shows the attributable cash flows. The attributable cost of the non-specialists in Year 1 is the *incremental* cost; half of their salaries and benefits would, owing to the agreement, be paid anyway. After Year 1, the required resource is no longer available, so it is again assumed, because we are not told otherwise, that it can be hired. If not, then similar considerations to those discussed above with respect to the specialists would apply.

8. Assume that JPB Ltd's stores personnel will each cost £18k in salary and benefits per year during Year 1 and that these costs are expected to

Table 9.10 Incremental cashflows arising from changes if new investment is undertaken

	Year 0 £000	Year 1 £000	Year 2 £000	Year 3 £000	Year 4 £000	Total £000
Non-specialist IT personnel:						
Year 1		−80				−80
Subsequent years			−168	−176	−185	−529
Totals		−80	−168	−176	−185	−609

increase at an annual compound rate of 5% per year over the life of the project. If the project goes ahead, one such person would be surplus to requirements from the beginning of Year 1, and would not need to be replaced. As an alternative to being made redundant, at a cost to the company of £30k, payable at the beginning of Year 1, he has agreed to be transferred to another job within JPB Ltd as from the beginning of Year 1 at his existing rate of pay. Unknown to him, the job to which he would transfer is currently being advertised externally, at a salary which, including benefits, represents a cost to the company of £22k. This is also expected to increase at an annual compound rate of 5%. If it is decided to undertake the project, the advertisement will be withdrawn, and this person transferred to the new job immediately.

There are two separate situations here. First, if the project goes ahead, then the company would incur a termination charge of £30k, but would save the employee's salary over Years 1 to 4. If it were not for the other job being available, then those would be the attributable cash flows. However, the second situation is that, quite independently of the project, another job happens to be available, and is already being advertised, for which the company would be paying £22k, increasing at 5% per annum. Again only if the project goes ahead, this job can be filled by the storeman, at his existing salary. The effects of this are to cancel out both the termination charge and the avoidance of the storeman's salary. The net result is the avoidance by the company of the cash outflows that would have resulted from the externally advertised job, as shown in Table 9.11.

9. Also if the project goes ahead, another stores person will become surplus to requirements at the *end* of Year 1, and would not need to be replaced. This person is, however, due to retire at the end of Year 2. It has been agreed that she would be prepared to retire one year early on payment of a lump sum of £15k at the end of Year 1 in lieu of her Year 2 salary.

Table 9.12 shows the relevant cash flows. There are two cash flows attributable to the person taking early retirement – the lump sum payment of £15k in Year 1 and the avoidance of that person's salary in Year 2. However, if the project is not undertaken, then the retiring person would have to be replaced at the beginning of Year 3. The avoidance of the cash outflows representing the costs of this replacement in Years 3 and 4 is therefore also attributable to the project.

Table 9.11 Incremental cashflows arising from changes if new investment is undertaken

	Year 0 £000	Year 1 £000	Year 2 £000	Year 3 £000	Year 4 £000	Total £000
Stores personnel (1):						
Costs of advertised job avoided		22	23	24	25	94
Totals		22	23	24	25	94

Table 9.12 Incremental cashflows arising from changes if new investment is undertaken

	Year 0 £000	Year 1 £000	Year 2 £000	Year 3 £000	Year 4 £000	Total £000
Stores personnel (2):						
Early retirement cost incurred		−15				−15
Salary and benefits avoided			19	20	21	60
Totals		−15	19	20	21	45

10. Some consultancy work has already been done on the project, at a cost of £30k. Of this, £20k represents work already completed and paid for, £10k represents work completed and invoiced but not yet paid for, and it is estimated that a further £50k of work would be done in Year 1 if the project is approved.

See Table 9.13. We cannot make decisions about the past. The cash already paid is a sunk cost. The cash cannot be recovered. The invoice representing the obligation to pay £10k cannot be torn up. It will have to be paid whether the project goes ahead or not, so the £10k does not differ among the alternatives. For decision-making purposes, therefore, both these amounts are ignored. Of course they cannot be ignored for total project costing and pricing purposes, but here we are only concerned with decision-making, and decisions can only concern the future. The only cash flow attributable to the project is the £50k, which will only occur if the project goes ahead.

11. Assume that the rent of one of JPB Ltd's locations, payable to an external landlord, is £200k per annum, fixed for ten years by a contract signed last year. One effect of undertaking the proposed project would be that one-quarter of this space would become surplus to requirements from the beginning of Year 2. Another department would move into the vacated space to relieve overcrowding in the space that they currently occupy. One-quarter of the rent would be cross-charged to the other department for the remainder of the lease.

A cross-charge is simply an internal accounting transaction, transferring a notional charge from one manager's budget to another's. The

Table 9.13 Incremental cashflows arising from changes if new investment is undertaken

	Year 0 £000	Year 1 £000	Year 2 £000	Year 3 £000	Year 4 £000	Total £000
Consultancy fees:						
Paid for and invoiced						0
Future		−50				−50
Totals		−50				−50

question therefore is: would there be any incremental effect on *cash flow* from the cross-charge? Given the only information available, the answer is no. The only cash outflow is the rent. That is fixed for ten years and must be paid whether or not this project goes ahead. If, however, for example, the other department had already decided to rent additional external space in order to relieve their overcrowding, it might be a different matter. If the contract for additional space had not yet been signed, so that the decision could be rescinded, then the avoidance of the additional cash outflow would be a benefit attributable to the project.

This is the end of this part of our example. There are a couple of other problem areas in cost/benefit analysis that could also have been illustrated, but for particular reasons I have left these in abeyance until chapter 11. Table 9.14 shows, with references to the above numbered paragraphs, the complete list of attributable cash flows that we have produced, totalled by column, and showing a grand total. What information does this table convey? Well, it is a list of the cash flows that are estimated to occur if the proposed project is undertaken and that would not occur otherwise. Positive numbers represent cash inflows or the avoidance of cash outflows, while negative numbers represent cash outflows. So, the first question has to be: what is the sign of the grand total, the number in the bottom right-hand corner? If it were negative, it would mean that by undertaking the project the business would be worse off in cash terms

Table 9.14   Summary of estimated incremental cash flows – JPB Ltd

	Ref* para	Year 0 £000	Year 1 £000	Year 2 £000	Year 3 £000	Year 4 £000	Total £000
Incremental cash flows arising from changes if new investment is undertaken:							
Items are listed in the sequence given in the example							
Various net cash inflows	1		620	844	772	474	2,710
Old equipment	2	0	30	33	36	40	139
New equipment purchase	3	−700	−10	−21	−22	−23	−776
New software licences	4	−300					−300
Type 1 supplies	5		−48	−50	−53	−56	−207
Type 2 supplies	5		−23	−21	−11	0	−55
IT specialists – Years 2 to 4	6		−240	−105	−110	−116	−571
IT non-specialists	7		−80	−168	−176	−185	−609
Stores personnel (1)	8		22	23	24	25	94
Stores personnel (2)	9		−15	19	20	21	45
Consultancy	10		−50				−50
Space cross-charge	11						0
References to paragraphs in the text.							
Totals		−1,000	206	554	480	180	420

that it was before, and *if* the main decision-making criterion were financial, then the proposed project would of course be rejected.

If the grand total is positive, and if the main decision-making criterion is financial, then the question is: how big is the grand total relative to the net investment? In many projects, the net investment is the total of the "Year 0" column, because any project usually involves spending money today – an investment – in order to achieve benefits in the future – the return. Even if the investment cash flows do not all occur on one day – Year 0 – it is usually convenient to assume, for evaluation purposes, that they do. That is one reason why the financing method that will be used for the investment is often ignored at this stage. By financing method I mean, for example, outright purchase of equipment, or leasing; up-front payment for software licences, or leasing; rescheduling of initial payments due under contracts for services, and so on. Those matters are usually the subject of a quite separate decision – the financing decision – which was alluded to in Chapter 8. Here we are concerned with the investment decision.

As so often, it is much the same as in personal life. For example, first you decide whether to acquire a car, or to change your car, then you decide whether you will pay for it outright, enter into a hire purchase contract or rent it. It is true that your investment decision may be influenced by the availability of suitable and affordable finance. That, too, is true in business, but the decisions are still best kept separate.

Returning to Table 9.14, what does the bottom line actually tell us? It is this: invest £1 million and, over a four-year period, *if* all our estimates prove accurate, we shall get our money back plus £420k. That certainly looks like a better return than would be achieved by putting the £1 million in the bank for four years – unless interest rates make a spectacular leap quite soon.

However, talking of interest, is there something we have forgotten to include in our analysis of cash flows? If the company intends to borrow money in order to be able to undertake the project, will that borrowing not incur interest? It certainly will. If so, then should this interest not be shown as a cash outflow? The answer would be yes, were it not for the existence of a much simpler and more effective mechanism for achieving the same thing. This mechanism is called *discounted cash flow*, and we shall be considering it in some detail in the next chapter. Meanwhile, suffice it to say that all of what we might call "financial cash flows" are ignored in cost/benefit analysis of the kind we have just done. As well as interest, that term includes the cash inflow represented by money being borrowed, and the cash outflow when it is repaid.

One last thought for this chapter: suppose that the company has sufficient cash to make the initial project investments without borrowing? Could interest then be ignored? No, we could not ignore it, any more than you could if we refer back to your car-buying decision. The interest on borrowed money is obvious, because it is highly visible; it has to be actually paid. However, *all* money has an interest cost, whether it is borrowed or not. Using your own money to buy the car incurs an interest cost, but it is less visible, and therefore less obvious. The cost to you of using your own money to buy the car is the opportunity cost of the interest that you would forego by spending the money rather than investing it.

10 Is It Still a Good Investment? – Part 1

Payback – Net Present Value – Profitability Index

This and the chapter that follows are really a single chapter divided into two, simply in order to have chapters of a reasonable length. The same practical example that we developed in Chapter 9 is used to illustrate the principles discussed in these two parts. At the end of Chapter 9 we reflected upon whether or not the proposed project whose cash flows we had estimated were a good investment. Invest £1 million, and over four years get your money back, plus £420k. The conclusion we drew was that it looked pretty good; not spectacular maybe, but certainly a better return than could be earned by putting the money in the bank for four years. As you might expect, however, financial people are unlikely to be satisfied with such a woolly-sounding judgement as "pretty good", and over many years they have developed various numeric methods for evaluating investment opportunities a little more objectively. It is these methods that we shall examine in these two chapters. We shall cover them in a convenient sequence rather than one that reflects their order of importance. Their relative importance will become apparent.

Payback

The first of these methods is both ridiculously simple and almost universally used. It is called *payback* or *break even*, and seeks to answer the following question: if we undertake this project, how soon will we get our money back? Suppose you have a friend who thinks that they are pretty smart at investing on the stock market, and they try to persuade you that if you will let them have £1,000 to invest, you will never regret it; in fact your fortune is as good as made. The shares are expected to quadruple in price in no time at all. Assuming that you trusted the friend (a big assumption), naturally the first question that you would ask is:

how soon will I get my money back? Share prices go down as well as up, and until you have got back at least the amount that you invested, you have not made your fortune at all; rather, you have lost money.

If your friend answered that the expected payback would not be until five years, you would, I suggest, almost certainly tell them, with greater or lesser politeness, to take their deal elsewhere. If, on the other hand, the expected payback was within three months, then you might be a little more interested. Why? For at least two reasons: first, because of risk; less is likely to go wrong in three months than in five years, although it is also often true that the biggest rewards come from taking the greatest risks. The second reason is that the sooner you get your money back the sooner you start to see the promised return.

We shall consider both of these factors in due course, but first let us work out the payback of our proposed project, and then discuss how the idea might be used in practice. The simple way to work out the payback period is to calculate the cumulative cash flows year by year, as shown in Table 10.1. £1,000k will be spent on the first day of the project – Year 0. Twelve months later, by the end of Year 1, if our estimates prove correct, there will have been benefits – cash inflows – of £206k. We obviously have not got our money back by the end of Year 1. We are still out of pocket by $1,000 - 206 = £794k$. How are we doing by the end of Year 2? During Year 2 there will have been further cash inflows of £554k. By the end of that year, we are still out of pocket, although of course by a smaller amount, $794 - 554 = £240k$. You will notice that the numbers have been cunningly designed to make it obvious that the payback or break-even

Table 10.1 Payback of cash flows in Table 9.14

	Ref	Year 0 £000	Year 1 £000	Year 2 £000	Year 3 £000	Year 4 £000	Total £000
Assumption: cashflows occur on last day of Year 0, and then evenly with Years 1 to 4							
Net cashflows from Table 9.14		−1,000	206	554	480	180	420
Cumulative net cashflows			−794	−240	240	420	

Break-even occurs during Year 3, the year in which the cumulative cashflow changes from negative to positive.

	Ref						
Net cashflow in Year 3	a				480		
Net cashflow per month during Year 3 (a/12)	b				40		
Positive cashflows in Year 3	c				240		
Months from break-even to end of Year 3 (c/b)	d				6.0		
Months in Years 1 to3	e				36.0		
Break-even occurs after (months) (e−d)					30.0		

point comes exactly half way through Year 3, £240k being of course exactly half of the net cash inflows receivable during Year 3. Table 10.1 shows the simple calculations necessary when the numbers are less easy.

Figure 10.1 shows our project in diagrammatic form. The bar chart does indeed represent the cash outflow and inflows of this particular project. However, it can also be thought of as a representation of any project, certainly any typical IT project. Spend money now in order to make money in the future. I happen to have chosen four years as the expected life of this particular project because IT projects will typically be valued over a four- or five-year period. Why do the expected benefits reach a peak and then diminish? To answer that question, consider again the debate about whether to keep your old car or to trade it in. What was the nature of the ongoing benefits? They represented decreases in fuel costs and in maintenance costs. Perhaps, however, there was a short-coming in that oversimplified example. We assumed that the differential between the "old" and "new" costs would increase over time in line with expected price increases. However, as the "new" car itself becomes older, its fuel-efficiency will diminish and its maintenance costs, relative to those of the old car, will almost certainly increase, so that the net benefit of new versus old will probably decrease over time.

With IT projects, a major factor delivering benefits will often be what is called competitive edge – stealing a march over your competitors by being first in the field with a new idea, or with a more efficient way of doing something, made possible by new technology. A few years ago, those companies first in the field to use image-processing technology – some insurance companies and utilities – gained a considerable advantage over

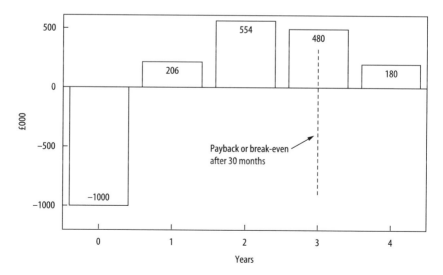

Figure 10.1   Payback of cash flows in Table 9.14

their competitors because of their newfound ability to handle customer enquiries more efficiently. For example, the person fielding an insurance query could call up that customer's insurance policy on the screen while the customer was on the telephone.

The business grapevine is itself usually quite efficient. Word gets around that Company X, who were known to be notoriously slow at handling customer enquiries, has now had a new lease of life and is a much better company to do business with. The result is more business for Company X – the estimated amount of which would have appeared as a benefit in the cost/benefit analysis for the "image technology" project – but only, of course, until Companies Y and Z get hold of the idea. They will then start to regain some of the business that they lost to Company X. So that particular benefit to Company X will tail off after a time. To regain its competitive edge it must then seek new ways of distinguishing itself from its competitors, based on the technology then available. At that point there will have to be another project evaluation, and so on.

At the time of writing, the Internet is one technology that is providing many companies with a competitive edge, as they develop innovative ways of using the communications opportunities that it offers. A few years from now there had better be something else, because by then everyone will be using the Internet. The point is that businesses have continually to find new ways of working, new ways to improve customer service, while containing or reducing costs. Those that stand still will fall behind. That is why there will always be a large number of possible projects, especially IT projects, for businesses to invest in, and never enough money available to take advantage of them all. To return from this digression, that in turn is why financial methods for choosing among all the possible alternatives are so important. The point of the digression was to explain why Figure 10.1 can indeed be taken as representing the financial profile of a typical IT project as well as, possibly, a typical personal one.

So, our particular project is estimated to payback, or break even, in 30 months. What do those two most useful words in the English language have to say about that? So what? Is 30 months good or bad, and by reference to what? Well, except for new businesses, companies thinking of investing in this particular project will almost certainly not be new to IT. Unless this is indeed truly "leading edge" stuff, they will have experience of past projects having at least some similar characteristics to this one in terms of size, innovativeness, risk and so on. How long did *they* take to pay back? What is this company's collected experience? If the answer is that such projects as this have typically paid back in 18 months, then, unless there are good reasons to the contrary, ours, which has a payback of 30 months, might be rejected with little or no further consideration. This is how the payback method is often used – as a blunt instrument for weeding out obviously unsuitable projects early on in the evaluation process.

You may feel that that sounds rather peremptory, but an analogy may be helpful. If a job is advertised, internally within a company or in the job market, there may well be a 100 or more applicants, at least if it is a job worth having. Does the company wish to conduct 100 or more interviews? No, it does not. Every manager has their particular ways of weeding out the 90% or so of job applicants who will never get as far as the interview stage, let alone the personality tests. Some will reject any application that is not printed, while some may require at least part of the application to be in the applicant's handwriting, which may itself be a yardstick for acceptance or rejection. The point is that, for most jobs at any rate, there are more applicants than vacancies. Similarly, the quantity of investment opportunities for companies usually exceeds the quantity of money available for taking advantage of them. Interviewing candidates takes time; so does evaluating projects. It is useful to have such a blunt instrument as payback for weeding out those that are more obviously unsuitable.

So, the advantages of the payback method appear to be its simplicity, the fact that in a common sense kind of way it gives some indication of project risk, and its use as a blunt instrument, the first hurdle over which candidate projects have to jump en route to acceptance or rejection. What are its disadvantages? The first is that, if used slavishly and without much thought, it could cause the rejection of projects that, if allowed, might indeed make the company's fortune. For example, suppose that the expected cash inflows of our project in Year 4 were not £180k, but £2 million. An exaggerated example, but enough to make the point that it would ridiculous, and therefore only too possible, by slavish concentration on the payback criterion, to ignore totally the cash flows expected to occur after the break even point.

The second disadvantage of the payback method, at least in its basic form, has already been hinted at. It is this: that money has a different value, depending on when it is received or paid. Surely not, I almost hear you say – a pound is a pound and a dollar is a dollar. How can they possibly change value? Unfortunately, in that very objection lies the reason why many people have some initial difficulty with the ideas that we shall shortly be discussing. A pound is indeed a pound, and a dollar is indeed a dollar, and each is different from the other. We know that they are different for the very good reason that different signs are used to represent them. We know immediately that £100 has a different value from $100 – the different signs portray this fact. But what sign is shown at the top of every column in Table 10.1? The pound sign in every case, and yet I repeat that the real values of the amounts in each of those six columns are as different as they would be if they were expressed in different currencies. However, because the same sign (£) is used for all of them, we are positively encouraged to believe that they have the same values. If only financial people had had the sense to invent different signs for "today pounds", "one-year future pounds", "two-year future pounds" and so on, just as they had the sense to invent different signs for different currencies, a great deal of confusion would have been avoided.

At this point, a simple example should at least make clear the nature of the problem. Suppose I say that I will give you £100. Would you rather have it today or in one year's time? If that is the choice, then almost certainly you would choose to have the money today. You would take it and run, not just because I might change my mind or not be around to deliver a year from today, but for two other reasons. What are the only two sensible things that you can do with money? The answer is that you can spend it, or you can invest it. I included the word "sensible" because the third option – keeping it in an old sock under the mattress is not generally regarded as a good idea.

In inflationary times, what happens to the purchasing power of money as time passes? It diminishes. In fact, a working description of inflation is the diminution over time of the purchasing power of money. So, if you wanted to spend my £100 gift, it would buy less of most things in the future than it would today. There are, of course, some exceptions – many IT goods among them. Some goods and services tend to become cheaper over time, because of competition, the nature of some of their components and increasing efficiency of production methods. However, that does not invalidate the description of inflation.

If, on the other hand, you decide to invest the money rather than to spend it, then you will earn interest, so that after one year it will be worth more. By waiting for a year to receive my gift you would have forgone one year's worth of interest. So on either count – inflation or interest – money received in the future is worth less than the same amount received today. Look again at Figure 10.1. It shows the future expected cash flows of our project, derived from Table 9.14 in the previous chapter. Now look at Figure 10.2. The shaded areas represent the fact that the future amounts, which happen to be the benefits, are worth less than they would be if receivable today. The further in the future, the less, proportionally, are they worth in today's terms. The question is – how much less? That is what we shall consider now.

First, we have already agreed that all the amounts shown are in units that are as unlike in real terms as they would be if expressed in different currencies. If they *were* expressed in different currencies, then what would we first have to do in order to be able to add up the amounts and get a meaningful answer? We would first have to decide in what currency we wanted the answer – pounds, dollars, yen or pesos – and convert the other currencies using appropriate exchange rates. We would then add up all the converted answers in order to arrive at a meaningful total.

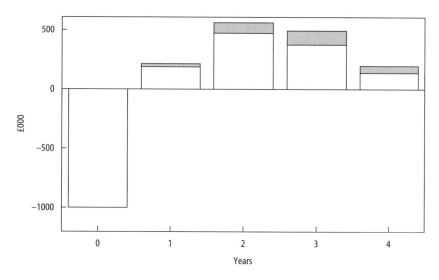

Figure 10.2   Diminution in real value of future cash flows

Net Present Value (NPV)

We have to do exactly the same with our different time-related "curren-cies" if we are to be able to add up the amounts and arrive at a meaningful answer. The only question is – in which "currency" do we want the answer? In theory, we could choose the "currency" of any one of our columns – one-year future pounds, two-, three- or four-year future pounds, or today pounds. In practice, "today pounds" or *present values* are always chosen, and various "exchange rates" or conversion factors are used to convert all the future values to that particular "currency". In other words, all future values are converted to their "today" equivalents, to their equivalent present values.

We agreed that if you chose to invest my gift, then you would earn interest. Let us choose a convenient interest rate of 10% per annum. At that rate, what will my gift of £100 have grown to after one year? The answer is, of course, £110. There was nothing very difficult about that, but to help us cover situations where the numbers are not so easy, for example £183 invested for 5 years at 7%, it will be worthwhile briefly reminding ourselves of the mental process we went through to get the answer of £110. What we did was to multiply the present value (£100) by an amount equal to one plus the interest rate, 1 + 0.1 or 1.1, to arrive at our answer of £110. To be pedantic we could say that we applied the multiplication only once because we wanted to know the future value at the end of one year. So we could express the multiplication factor as $(1.1)^1$. If we wanted to know the value of the investment after two years, assuming the same rate of interest, the multiplication factor would be

$(1.1)^2$, after three years $(1.1)^3$ and after n years $(1.1)^n$. We could now generalise the other terms as well, and say that the future value (F) after n years of a present value (P) invested at interest rate r is given by the following:

$F = P(1 + r)^n$, which is the *compound interest formula*.

Now let us ask the reverse question. Suppose that we want to have £110 one year from now. How much must we invest today, assuming an interest rate of 10%, in order to achieve that result? Of course, we know that the answer is 100, but by what process did we get there? The answer is by a process that is the inverse of what we have just done. Then, we derived a future value by multiplying a present value by an amount equal to one plus the interest rate, compounded n times. Now we derive a present value by *dividing* a future value by an amount equal to one plus the interest rate, compounded n times. £110 $\times$ 1/(1.1)^1 = £100. Generalising, we get the following:

$P = F \times 1/(1 + r)^n$ or $F(1 + r)^{-n}$, which is the *present value formula*.

Reverting to our specific example, 1/(1/1) is not a particularly easy fraction to work with, so let us convert it into a decimal. 1/(1/1) = 0.9091. To derive the present value of any cash flow occurring one year in the future, where the appropriate discount rate is 10%, we can now simply multiply the future amount by 0.9091. For example, the present value of £110 received (or paid) one year from today, discounted at 10%, is £110 $\times$ 0.9091 = £100. Not surprisingly, before the days of computers, spreadsheets and financial calculators, tables of a range of discount factors were published. Just such a table appears in Appendix 3, and for ease of reference an extract from it is shown in Table 10.2.

Table 10. 2   Present value of a lump sum of £1 receivable or payable n periods from today at rate r

	Periods										
%	1	2	3	4	5	6	7	8	9	10	11
5	0.9524	0.9070	0.8638	0.8227	0.7835	0.7462	0.7107	0.6768	0.6446	0.6139	0.5847
6	0.9434	0.8900	0.8396	0.7921	0.7473	0.7050	0.6651	0.6274	0.5919	0.5584	0.5268
7	09346	0.8734	0.8163	0.7629	0.7130	0.6663	0.6227	05820	0.5439	0.5083	0.4751
8	0.9259	0.8573	0.7938	0.7350	0.6806	0.6302	0.5835	0.5403	0.5002	0.4632	0.4289
9	0.9174	0.8417	0.7722	0.7084	0.6499	0.5963	0.5470	0.5019	0.4604	0.4224	0.3875
10	0.9091	0.8264	0.7513	0.6830	0.6209	0.5645	0.5132	0.4665	0.4241	0.3855	0.3505
11	0.9009	0.8116	0.7312	0.6587	0.5935	0.5346	0.4817	0.4339	0.3909	0.3522	0.3173
12	0.8929	0.7972	0.7118	0.6355	0.5674	0.5066	0.4523	0.4039	0.3606	0.3220	0.2875
13	0.8850	0.7831	0.6931	0.6133	0.5428	0.4803	0.4251	0.3762	0.3329	0.2946	0.2607
14	0.8772	0.7695	0.6750	0.5921	0.5194	0.4556	0.3996	0.3506	0.3075	0.2697	0.2366
15	0.8696	0.7561	0.6575	0.5718	0.4972	0.4323	0.3759	0.3269	0.2843	0.2472	0.2149

Above I used the words "appropriate discount rate". We shall delay, until later, discussion of what the appropriate rate is for any particular business. Meanwhile, why has the term "discount rate" crept in, rather than interest rate, which is the term that we have been using hitherto? The answer is that the word "interest" implies a present sum of money growing into a bigger future sum. With present value calculations we are concerned with the inverse process – deriving a smaller present value from a larger future one. For this process the word "interest" hardly seems appropriate. What word is commonly used to describe the process of reducing the size of a sum of money, a price, for example? The answer is "discount", and because in this case it is future cash flows that are being discounted, the term discounted cash flow is often used to describe the method that we are discussing.

Reverting to the table of discount factors in Appendix 3 and Table 10.2 what discount factor do you find when you look in the 1-year column at the 10% row? The answer, not surprisingly, is 0.9091. What is the discount factor for one year at 9%? The answer is 0.9174. And so on. Let us look at one or two hypothetical examples that illustrate the use of discounted cash flow. First, let us suppose that your employer is really pleased with your work, and wants you to stay with the company. As an incentive, the employer offers you a deal whereby, if you agree to stay with the company for a further three years, you will be paid a bonus of £10,000 at the end of that period. You are obviously pleased with this offer, but your mind quickly turns to your current large overdraft, that is approaching £10,000 and is costing you 11% per annum in interest, and how you might be able to turn the company's offer to even greater advantage.

Suppose you were able to persuade your employer that you would be willing to sign an agreement to stay with them for the required three years if they would agree to pay you immediately a sum that would put you in exactly the same financial position as would the £10,000 receivable in three years' time. What immediate sum would exactly satisfy that requirement? I am reasonably confident that the method of arriving at the answer is now obvious, but let us work through it anyway. Referring to the table of discount factors, what is the discount factor for three years at 11%? The number in the 3-year column at the 11% row is 0.7312. Multiplying the future sum of £10,000 by this discount factor gives the answer of £7,312.

Given your particular circumstances, receiving that sum now would put you in exactly the same financial position as would £10,000 in three years' time. To prove it, suppose that your overdraft is currently exactly £7,312. Assuming the interest rate charged by the bank remains at 11% and that interest is added to the overdraft, what will be the amount of the overdraft three years from now? Applying the compound interest formula, the calculation is as follows:

$$£7,312 \times (1.11)^3 = £10,000$$

So, you could exactly pay off your overdraft with £7,312 today or with £10,000 three years from today. Suppose that instead of having an overdraft you are "cash-rich" as the jargon has it, and that you are currently receiving 6% on money invested. What immediate sum would then put you in the same financial position as would the £10,000 in three years' time? The discount factor for three years at 6% is 0.8396, so the answer is £8,396. The proof, if needed, is similar to that above:

$$£8,396 \times (1.06)^3 = £10,000$$

If the deal is indeed as it was described, then it would obviously be to the company's advantage if you were to have the overdraft rather than being cash-rich. Clearly, the answer you get varies considerably according to the discount rate that you use. Let us consider one last hypothetical example before we use these ideas to evaluate our project. Suppose that a well-intentioned relation or friend has said that they plan to give you £100,000 twenty years from now, and that your mind turns to exactly the same train of thought as it did before. At a discount rate of, say, 8% what sum received today would put you in the same financial position as would receiving £100k in twenty years' time? The discount factor for twenty years at 8% is 0.2145, so the answer is £21,450. The proof is:

$$£21,450 \times (1.08)^{20} = £100,000$$

Now look again at Figure 10.2. When we left it, we had agreed, I think, that in real terms the future benefits are worth less than their cash value. We had also agreed on the desirability of being able to put numbers to the amount of the reduction. In discounted cash flow, we now have the mechanism with which to do so. I should like to hold in abeyance for just a little longer the discussion that we must have on what discount rate a company *should* use in discounting cash flows. Let us assume for the moment that the company currently uses a discount rate of 9%. What, to the nearest £000 are the present values of the project benefits receivable in Years 1, 2, 3 and 4 respectively? You may wish to do the calculations yourself before looking at the answer.

The cash flow in Year 1 is £206k; from the table, the discount factor for 1 year at 9% is 0.9174. Multiplying the cash flow by the discount factor gives £189k, which is the present value of the cash flow. The discount factors for 2, 3 and 4 years at 9% are respectively 0.8417, 0.7722 and 0.7084. The resulting present values for Years 2, 3 and 4 are respectively £466k, £371k and £128k. What about the cash outflow of £1,000 in Year 0? This, of course remains undiscounted, because Year 0 pounds are the currency into which we have decided to convert all the other "currencies", so the "today pounds" of Year 0 remain undiscounted. Purists would perhaps say that they are discounted, but using a discount factor of 1, derived from the special case of the formula:

$$P = F \times 1/(1 + r)^0$$

Table 10.3   Net present value of cash flows in Table 9.14 (discounted at 9%)

	Ref	Year 0 £000	Year 1 £000	Year 2 £000	Year 3 £000	Year 4 £000	Total £000
Assumption: all cashflows occur on the last day of each year							
Net cashflows	a	−1000	206	554	480	180	420
Discount factors (9%)	b	1.0000	0.9174	0.8417	0.7722	0.7084	
Present values (a × b)	c	−1000	189	466	371	128	
Net present value (NPV), the sum of all the present values in row (c)							154

The complete solution appears in Table 10.3, and it is shown diagrammatically in Figure 10.3. We have now achieved what we set out to achieve; we have converted the cash flows that were expressed in various future pounds into the common currency of "today pounds", and have derived a *net present value* (NPV). A net present value is simply the sum of a series of present values, some of which are positive and some negative.

We can now no longer escape the task of interpreting what the net present value tells us, and to do that we have first to answer the question: what discount rate should a company use in discounting cash flows? To answer the question we shall do what we have done many times so far, and start with a very simple analogy from personal finance.

We have already encountered your supposed grandparents in an earlier chapter. We shall now suppose that Granny 1 has decided to give you a further £10,000. Granny 1 is kindly disposed towards you, but she is also

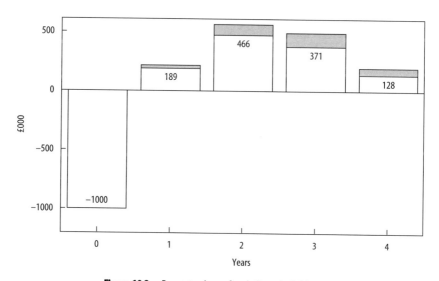

Figure 10.3   Present values of cash flows in Table 9.14

a shrewd businesswoman, and she has attached two conditions to the gift. One is that you may not spend it, but must invest it. The second condition is that you must pay her 11% simple interest per year for as long as she lives. In other words, she requires a return on her investment in you of 11% per year. She knows that this is more than you could get by just putting her money in the bank, so she is in fact encouraging you to start your own business – a commercial business this time. If Granny's gift is the only money you have, apart from your regular earnings which, unfortunately, all get spent quite quickly, we could then also say that your *cost of money* is 11%, the same as the return that Granny 1 expects to receive.

What is the minimum return that *you* must get each year from investing Granny's money in order to make it worthwhile accepting her gift? If your return is exactly 11%, then you would have gone to a lot of trouble to end up exactly where you started. If the best return you can get is less than 11%, then you would be out of pocket, and the only sensible alternatives would be either to give the money back or to try to renegotiate the terms. For the gift to be worthwhile accepting, the return you get from the investment must be at least a little higher than the cost to you of the money invested. A return of 11.1% would satisfy the demands of logic but, obviously, the higher the return the better.

Grannies are sometimes quite competitive with each other for the affections of their grandchildren, so let us now suppose that when Granny 2 gets to hear about Granny 1's gift, she decides that she will go one better. Granny 2 also gives you £10,000; this is clearly your lucky day. She imposes similar conditions to those imposed by Granny 1, except that Granny 2 only proposes to charge you 7% interest per year. So, you now have a total supply of money of £20,000, all of which has to be invested. Half of it costs you 11%, the other half 7%. What is now your *average* cost of money? The answer of course is 9%.

What is now the minimum return that you must get each year from investing your total supply of money in order that the whole deal be worthwhile? Before answering, for the purpose of the example, let us ignore the possibility that you could refuse the gift from Granny 1 but accept Granny 2's. You accept both offers. If now the return you get from investing the money is exactly 9%, then you would again have gone to a lot of trouble to end up exactly where you started. If the best return you can get is less than 9%, then you would be out of pocket. For the amounts to be worthwhile accepting, the return you get from investing them must be at least a little higher than the *average* cost of the money invested. A return of 9.1% would satisfy the demands of logic but, obviously, the higher the return the better.

Now let us translate the above into company terms. What are the two kinds of long-term money used by companies? The answer is equity – the money invested by ordinary shareholders, and debt – the money lent by banks. Which of these two kinds of providers of finance expect the higher return on their money, shareholders or banks? The answer is shareholders, but why? Which of the two is taking the higher risk with their money? Shareholders, because banks will usually only lend provided they have some security. This might be a mortgage on some of the company's specific assets, or a general "charge" over the assets as a whole that would give the bank priority over most other creditors and over shareholders were the company to fail, or for any other reason were to be wound up. Ordinary shareholders are right at the back of the queue for the share-out when a company is wound up.

Business is about risk and reward; the higher the risk, the higher the expected reward. Typically, over a broad spectrum of companies, and with possibly wide deviations from the average in particular cases, ordinary shareholders expect a return about 4 percentage points higher than that expected by secured lenders. So if banks are willing to lend to a particular company at 7% per year, then the ordinary shareholders in that company might expect a return of about 11%.

The "return" obtained by a lender is straightforward; it is the interest payable. Shareholders, however, get their return in one, or both, of two ways: by dividends and/or capital growth. By capital growth I mean an increase in the market price of a share over the price at which it was bought. The risks for shareholders lie in the facts that dividends are not compulsory – some companies rarely if ever pay a dividend – and that capital growth is not certain. Capital growth depends on supply and demand in the market for the shares. This depends on the market's expectation of the company's future earnings (profits), and this in turn depends partly upon what is sometimes called *systematic risk* – unpredictable factors in the economy, such as interest rates, taxation and consumer demand. If the market anticipates earnings in excess of what it would expect from companies in general of that kind in that industry, then demand for the shares will tend to increase and the price will go up; and vice versa. Notice that both dividends and capital growth depend on earnings. Dividends can only legally be paid out of earnings while, as just discussed, capital growth is dependent on whether future earnings exceed the norm expected for companies of that kind in that industry.

Suppose now that our company has equity of £100 million and debt of £100 million, and that lenders are currently charging the company 7% per annum for their loans. If our company is indeed typical, then, as suggested above, the return expected by shareholders would be about 11%. What is now the average return expected by all the providers of the company's total stock of money? The answer of course is 9%. If, as would usually be the case, the amounts of debt and equity are unequal, then we would need to take a weighted, rather than a simple, average. In the Granny example above, we saw that the return expected by the providers of money is often described as the cost of the money to its users. Because of the greater complexity of the way in which shareholders obtain their return, the connection between the two is less direct. Nevertheless, what I have referred to above as "the average return expected by the providers of the company's total stock of money" is in fact usually expressed, rather confusingly but more briefly, as the company's weighted average cost of money, or weighted average cost of capital or just *cost of capital.*

If our company's cost of capital is 9%, when what is the minimum return that it must obtain from investing that money? The argument is, of course, the same as that applicable to the Grannies. A return of 9.1% would satisfy the demands of logic but the higher the return the better. What are the things in which companies invest money? They are many, but they include projects of the kind that we are considering. It would seem, then, that the first criterion for deciding whether an investment such as our proposed project is worthwhile is whether the future returns or benefits will exceed the costs in real terms, that is after deducting the cost of the money invested to achieve them. That is exactly what discounted cash flow is doing when it is used to discount future net benefits. If the cash flows are discounted at the company's cost of capital, the discounting process is, in effect, reducing the benefits by the amount of that cost. So, what should be the basis of the discount rate used by a company in discounting future cash flows? By now, no doubt, the question hardly needs to be asked, but the answer is – the company's weighted average cost of capital.

A company's cost of capital will be different at different times, depending upon changes in prevailing interest rates and upon changes in the mix of equity and debt. If these things are indeed expected to change, then it could reasonably be argued that different discount rates should be applied to cash flows in different years. In theory that is right, but in practice it is rarely done. The only cost of capital that can be worked out with reasonable accuracy is that which applies today. Remember that every number in a cost/benefit analysis, sometimes called a "financial case", is already an estimate. It is difficult enough to estimate future cash flows; it would in most cases be much more difficult to estimate future costs of capital, so in most evaluations the current cost of capital is assumed to apply throughout the evaluation period.

Refer again to Table 9.14 at the end of the previous chapter. The message that the cash numbers give us is, as we discussed: invest £1 million, and over a four-year period we shall get our money back plus £420k. We have now discounted those cash flows. What the net present value (NPV) of £154k in Table 10.3 is telling us is: invest £1 million, and over a four-year period we shall get our money back plus, in real terms, after taking into account the cost of the money invested, £154k. It is also telling us that if we have, in effect, subtracted from the benefits the cost of the money used to earn them, then a positive NPV must mean that the interest rate or "rate of return" earned by the money invested in the project must be greater than the cost of that money.

We decided earlier that, in cash terms, the project looked reasonably good, but not spectacular. Does it now look so good? That depends. First, suppose that this is the only show in town, the only project that we can currently find in which to invest the company's money. With an NPV of £154k what advice is our unthinking, unfeeling mathematical model giving us? Invest or not? Invest, because by doing so we should be £154k better off in real terms than by not doing so.

Profitability Index

Now suppose that we are evaluating two mutually exclusive situations, of the kind typical of IT acquisitions. They may be mutually exclusive projects, or the kind of situation where two suppliers are responding to a request to provide quotations for a particular IT solution. Suppose that our numbers, with their NPV of £154k, represent one situation, and that the competing one, when all estimated cash flows were taken into account, gives an expected NPV of £180k. If all non-financial considerations as between one situation and the other were regarded as equal, then which of the two should be accepted? The answer, at first glance, is the one that has the highest positive NPV. However, suppose the initial investments required by the two alternatives were substantially different. Would it not be better to use a measure that related the NPV to the amount of the investment? Such a *profitability index* is sometimes used. The profitability index is usually taken as the sum of the present values of the future net cash flows, divided by the present value of the initial investment.

The initial investment (Year 0) required by our project is £1,000k and the NPV is £154k, so the sum of the present values of the future net cash flows (all the cash flows *except* Year 0) must be 1,000 + 154 = £1,154k. The profitability index of our project would be 1,154/1,000 = 1.154. If the initial investment needed by the alternative project were, for example, £1,400k, and the NPV were indeed £180k, then the sum of the present values of the future net cash flows must be 1,400 + 180 = £1,580k. Its profitability index would be 1,580/1,400 = 1.129. "Our" project has, marginally, the higher profitability index so, other things being the same, it should be accepted at the expense of the alternative. Profitability index is a way of using the powerful NPV concept to compare projects of different magnitudes.

Finally, for this chapter, suppose that the NPV of our project were not £154k but £1? What "advice" is the model giving us? Invest, says the model, because, by however small an amount, we should be better off in real terms than by not doing so. Just possibly, however, real people employed to make decisions might decide that investing £1 million in order to gain £1 in real terms is not a very good idea. Mathematical models are aids to decision making; they are not decision makers.

Now suppose that the NPV were not +£1, but −£1? What advice would our unthinking, unfeeling mathematical model then be giving us? Do not

Table 10.4 Net present value of cash flows in Table 9.14 (discounted at 25%)

	Ref	Year 0 £000	Year 1 £000	Year 2 £000	Year 3 £000	Year 4 £000	Total £000
Assumption: all cashflows occur on the last day of each year							
Net cashflows	a	−1000	206	554	480	180	420
Discount factors (25%)	b	1.0000	0.8000	0.6400	0.5120	0.4096	
Present values (a × b)	c	−1000	165	355	246	74	
Net present value (NPV), the sum of all the present values in row (c)							−160

invest, because if you do, then you would be £1 worse off in real terms than by not doing so. The bigger the negative NPV, the worse off we should be in real terms. You only have to look at the table of discount factors, and see how the factors decrease in value as the discount rate and the time period increase, to realise how sensitive project cash flows are to changes in discount rate. Just to make the point, what do you think would happen to the NPV of our project if we discounted the cash flows at 25%, rather than at our original 9%? Let us try it and see. Table 10.4 shows the answer – a negative NPV of £160k.

If 25% were really the company's cost of capital, the advice being given by the model is most certainly: don't do it, because if you do, then you will be worse off in real terms by £160k than you would be by not doing it. The model is also, however, saying the inverse of what it did when the NPV was positive. If we have, in effect, subtracted from the benefits, the cost of the money used to earn them, a negative NPV must mean that the interest rate or "rate of return" earned by the money invested in the project must be *less than* the rate representing the cost of money. It would be quite useful, would it not, if we could determine the *actual* rate of interest earned by the money invested in the project, because then we would know whether and by how much, it would earn a higher return than money invested in the bank. We would also have a familiar measure – a percentage rate of return – by which we could compare this project with others, present and past. How to do this will be the first item covered in Chapter 11.

Here is one last thought on this topic. Referring back to the car example in Table 9.2 in the previous chapter, and supposing your cost of money to be 10%, would trading in the old car for a newer one really be the best deal financially?

11 Is It Still a Good Investment? – Part 2

Internal Rate of Return – Risk – Return on Investment

In the previous chapter, of which this is a continuation, we have looked at two main methods of evaluating whether or not a proposed project is likely to be a good investment. Payback we may regard as giving some intuitive insights into a proposed project by comparison with projects that have gone before, and as a useful blunt instrument for weeding out apparently unsuitable projects early in the evaluation process. Incidentally, we now have a way of overcoming one of the criticisms of the payback method, namely that it took no account of the time value of money. Now that we know about discounted cash flow and present values, it becomes a simple matter to apply the payback method to the discounted cash flows in order to determine the *discounted payback* period or the discounted break-even point. As shown by Table 11.1, the discounted payback is 36 months. It occurs during the last month of Year 3. This result would then be subjected to the same "so what?" comparisons as already discussed in connection with the undiscounted payback.

By far the most important of all the evaluation methods, however, is that usually known as discounted cash flow. The aspect of discounted cash flow that we have considered so far is net present value (NPV), and its importance lies in the fact that it takes into account both the time value of money and the return expected by its providers. Profitability index is not really a method in its own right, but simply a way of interpreting the NPVs of projects of different magnitudes.

At the end of the previous chapter the following question was posed: would it not be useful if we could determine the actual rate of interest earned by the money invested in a project? To do this for a project is obviously more difficult than to do it in respect of money invested in a bank deposit account, because the cash flows are more complex. However it can certainly be done. If you are mathematically inclined, I am told

Table 11.1   Discounted payback of cash flows in Table 9.14

	Ref	Year 0 £000	Year 1 £000	Year 2 £000	Year 3 £000	Year 4 £000	Total £000
Assumption: cash flows occur on last day of Year 0, and then evenly within Years 1 to 4							
Net discounted cash flows (9%)		−1,000	189	466	371	128	154
Cumulative net cash flows			−811	−345	26	154	
Break-even occurs during Year 3, the year in which the cumulative cashflow changes, from negative to positive							
Net cash flow in Year 3	(a)				371		
Net cash flow per month during Year 3 (a/12)	(b)				30.9		
Positive cash flows in Year 3	(c)				26		
Months from break-even to end of Year 3 (c/b)	(d)				0.8		
Months in Years 1 to 3	(e)				36.0		
Break-even occurs after (months) (e–d)					――― 35.2		

that it can be done by solving polynomial equations, which I must confess I prefer to stay away from. Also, of course, spreadsheets and financial calculators have functions that do it automatically. However, as with much of what we discuss in this book, we learn little or nothing about a subject by simply letting the computer do the work. There is another way, albeit an approximation, that follows directly from the work that we have just done, and which gives us a little more insight into the principles involved.

Internal Rate of Return (IRR)

Table 11.2 compares the NPVs obtained in the previous chapter from using discount rates of respectively 9% and 25%. It reminds us that a 9% discount rate gave an NPV of + £154k, while a 25% discount rate gave an NPV of − £160k. The relationship between discount rate and NPV is not linear, but is nearly so, at least at relatively low discount rates. If we assumed for a moment that the relationship were linear, then it would become apparent that the discount rate that would give an NPV of exactly zero would be approximately 17%, the number midway between 9% and 25%.

The discount rate that gives an NPV of zero is the discount rate at which the discounted future net cash flows exactly equal the discounted investment. It is also the number that we are looking for – the rate of interest earned by the money invested in the project. It is called the *internal rate of return* (IRR). The actual IRR for the cash flows of our project, worked out by spreadsheet or financial calculator, is 15.8%. Figure

Table 11.2 Comparison of discount rates and resulting NPVs

	Discount Rate		NPV £000
A discount rate of	9%	gives an NPV of	+154
A discount rate of	25%	gives an NPV of	−160

Note: the above results refer to Tables 10.3 and 10.4

11.1 compares the actual NPVs given by all integer discount rates between 9% and 25% with our straight line approximation. The internal rate of return, whether exact or approximate is the discount rate at which the curve crosses the "0 NPV" line.

Looking at Table 11.2 and Figure 11.1 may have prompted you to notice that NPV and IRR are two sides of a single coin. It is the coin that is called discounted cash flow. With NPV, we choose a discount rate, the company's current cost of capital, or at least a rate based on it, and then discount the cash flows to derive a net present value. With IRR, we choose that the NPV should have a value of zero and then derive the discount rate that produces that value. Two sides of the same coin they may be, but are they equally valid? The short answer is that NPV always gives an answer that is an absolute number and that is unequivocal, whereas IRR can give confusing answers, for at least two reasons.

The first reason, mathematicians inform me, is that it can give multiple answers, depending on the number of times the sign of the cumulative cash flows changes – from negative to positive or vice versa. The second

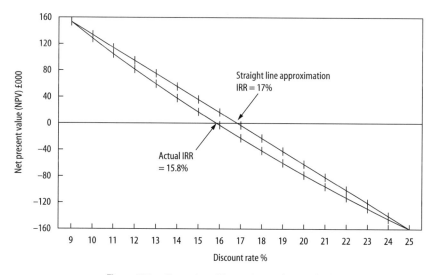

Figure 11.1   Illustration of internal rate of return (IRR)

reason for possible confusion lies in the interpretation. IRR is a percentage. Like any percentage, it may be a percentage of a very large number or of a very small number. Its significance needs to be verified in the light of the absolute numbers involved. For that reason, it would usually be prudent always to do both calculations – NPV and IRR. Now that you understand the principles, then let the computer do the work for you every time.

So, the internal rate of return of our project is 15.8%, if calculated precisely. As with our earlier discussion of payback, the next question should be: so what? The first answer is that in times of generally low interest rates, an internal rate of return of 15.8% is better than we would get by investing the money in a bank deposit account. That is just as well, because shareholders can do that for themselves. The reason they invest instead in companies is to get a higher return, and we have already agreed that if the business as a whole is to earn a high return, then so had the discretionary projects in which it invests. If the IRR of a discretionary project is less than could be obtained by virtually risk-free investment in a bank, then it is not a very sensible project.

As in our discussion of payback, the company will probably have experience of having undertaken projects in the past having at least some similar characteristics to this one in terms of size, degree of innovation, risk and so on. What, on average, was *their* internal rate of return? If the answer is that such projects as this have typically delivered an IRR of 25%, then this may be regarded as the next "hurdle" which projects like ours must clear if they are to be accepted. If this is so, then if ours is to stand a chance of getting accepted we had better try to increase its IRR, by finding more benefits or by reducing the costs. However, even that may not be enough.

Remember that not all of the things that a company spends money on are discretionary. Some of them are things that *have* to be done for legal reasons or that must be done for enabling reasons. That means that, together with sales of goods and services, those activities that *are* discretionary must collectively provide a sufficient return to carry those that are not, and still provide a return sufficient to ensure that the results of the business as a whole meet, and preferably exceed, its shareholders' expectations. Thus the *hurdle rate* that future projects are required to meet may be greater than the rate of return delivered by past projects.

Risk

So far we have not taken into account the risk inherent in some projects. *Project risk* is the risk of the extent to which the estimates of benefits and costs may prove to be wrong. Typically, but not necessarily, companies identify three levels of project risk. For example, straightforward technology replacement projects might be regarded as low risk, at least if the new technology has got beyond the stage of being "leading edge". A project that is a totally new venture, but of a kind that has been successfully implemented by other businesses in the industry, might be regarded as medium risk, while a project that is really pushing the frontiers in all directions would be regarded as high risk.

Suppose that our project is regarded as more risky, and therefore less certain in its outcome, than those in the past that contributed collectively to our assumed "normal" low-risk hurdle rate of 25%. Once again, business is about risk and reward; the higher the risk taken with a company's money, the greater the reward expected by its providers. So, what some companies do is to add a risk premium to their IRR hurdle rate. As an example, for projects regarded as medium-risk, the risk premium might be, say, 5%, so that the hurdle rate for such projects would, in our example be 25 + 5 = 30%. For high risk projects, the risk premium might be, say, 15%, so that such projects would have to deliver IRRs of at least 40%.

All of this is purely subjective, which leads me to repeat the common-sense caution that all of the numerical methods that we are considering are aids to decision-making; they are not decision-makers. The real decision-makers can and do override the "advice" given by financial models; they can and do make decisions that owe at least as much to gut-feel and entrepreneurial flair as to numbers.

If NPV and IRR are indeed two sides of the same coin, and if IRR can be used to take project risk into account, it would seem that it might be possible to do so using NPV also. Given that most projects involve expenditure now to achieve net benefits later – ongoing incremental cash inflows less outflows – and that it is therefore the net benefits that usually get discounted, how do you think that some companies adapt the NPV method to reflect the risk associated with a project, of the kind described above? We have already seen what happens to the NPV as the discount rates increases; it decreases, and may go negative. What, therefore, might be regarded as a near equivalent in the NPV method of raising the hurdle rate in the IRR method? The answer is that some companies apply a higher discount rate than normal to the evaluation of projects that are regarded as having a higher project risk than normal.

Using a similar example to the one we used when discussing IRR hurdle rates, the discount rate applied to a medium-risk project might be, say, five percentage points above the normal "cost of capital" discount rate; for high risk projects it might be, say, 15 percentage points. If so, if the project in our example were regarded as medium-risk, then it would be discounted at 9 + 5 = 14%; if it were regarded as high risk, then it would be discounted at 9 + 15 = 24%. A glance at Figure 11.1 will tell you that in either case the project would almost certainly be rejected. Discounted at 14% the NPV would be £38k; discounted at 24% it would be −£146k. Indeed we saw earlier the effect that increasing the discount rate has on the NPV of a project. This adaptation of the NPV method is quite often done, but it is open to some serious objections. First, although it may appear so, it is not true that the example we have just considered is the equivalent in NPV terms of how we took risk into account using IRR. With IRR, we are letting the result of the calculations be determined by the arithmetic of the cash flows, and then imposing certain subjective criteria against which that result should be judged. If we adjust the discount rate used in the NPV calculations, then we are tampering with the method itself, so that it will give a different result.

The second objection relates to the fact that it is the expected net benefits of the project – the net cash inflows – that are usually being discounted; the investment is usually upfront. By definition, net benefits are benefits less costs. It could be argued that it makes sense to apply a higher discount rate, and therefore lower discount factors, to benefits if it is felt that there is some risk of their not being achieved. Why? Because a higher discount rate will reduce the apparent value of the benefits. But if we wish to take into account the risk that is associated with costs, wherein lies that risk? It is not of an underrun, but of an overrun. So whatever method that we might adopt should have the effect of *increasing* the costs if it is desired to reflect the risk associated with them, not reducing them.

Project risk is real enough, however, and if the application of inflated discount rates to net cash flows is indeed inappropriate, for the reasons given, then in what other ways can it be taken into account? There are numerous methods, many of them described succinctly in Dixon (1994). Many of them are outside the scope of this book. Some such methods, however, are appropriate to consider because they are intuitive, they have the merit of simplicity and they may provide additional insights into the matters that we are discussing in this chapter.

Some companies take risk into account by applying what are sometimes called certainty equivalents or confidence factors to the cash flows before doing the NPV calculations. Sometimes this is done by recognising that cash flows are less predictable the further into the future they will occur. So, in our example, the total net cash flows in Year 1 might have a confidence factor of, say, 95% applied to them, the effect of which would be to reduce the total as presented by 5%. The confidence factors for Years 2, 3 and 4 might be respectively 90%, 85% and 80%. More sensibly, for the same reasons given above regarding inflated discount rates, the cash inflows might be reduced by applying such percentages, while the cash outflows might be correspondingly increased.

Recognising that some cash flows are less uncertain than others, it would be more sensible to examine each significant cash flow and apply an individual confidence factor to it. The cash flows thus having been risk-adjusted, the NPV calculations are then done using as a discount rate the normal weighted average cost of capital. The obvious danger of this kind of approach is that, if word gets around, then project sponsors will simply inflate their benefit numbers, knowing that they will be adjusted downwards, and deflate their costs, knowing that they will be adjusted upwards. Of course, all this is purely subjective, but I repeat – so are many of the numbers that go into the financial case in the first place. As someone said, forecasting is notoriously difficult, especially when it concerns the future. There are no legislated rules, and so it is not surprising that companies have their own particular ways of doing things.

For the kind of project whose outcome is highly sensitive to variations in one or more key factors, a method called "sensitivity analysis" is often applied. As an obvious example, an airline's plan to open a new route stands or falls by the number of passengers that will be attracted to use it. Spreadsheets make it a simple matter to run many iterations of the financial model, varying the number of passengers each time. Out of this analysis will come such insights as the minimum number of passengers required to break even, the number needed to meet any payback criterion, to exceed an IRR hurdle rate and so on. Out of such work, the company may then choose the outcomes that could be regarded as best case, worst case and average case, and these too will be used as inputs to the decision-making process.

Profit Impact

Let me remind you that all the investment evaluation methods that we have discussed so far have, in their different ways, been applied to the expected cash flows of a proposed project. We have not yet attempted to measure the effects that those cash flows will have on the profit and loss account, although we noted earlier the importance to some people of doing so. You may have noticed, in the project evaluation work that we have done so far, that having once determined what the relevant cash flows are, we have been able subsequently to work just with the totals. It has not been necessary to go back to the detail from which those totals were derived, and it has certainly not been necessary in using the evaluation methods considered so far, to differentiate between different kinds of cash flow and to treat them differently. Except, that is, when I suggested a little earlier that, *if* it is desired to apply inflated discount rates to reflect project risk, then a distinction should be made between benefits and costs.

The essential simplicity of cash flow analysis is in contrast with the rather greater complications involved when we attempt to measure the effect of a proposed investment on the profit and loss account. First, however, let us remind ourselves *why* it is often desired to show the effects of a proposed investment on the profit and loss account, even though for reasons already discussed this would usually not be regarded as the primary factor in the decision-making process. First is the understandable but artificial requirement, imposed by law, to chop businesses up into one-year chunks for reporting and taxation purposes.

For these purposes, profit is not only a very important measure, it is the best one yet devised. Second, quite apart from those external reporting requirements, divisional and departmental managers, including IT managers, are often measured and paid bonuses on the profit attributed to their business units, and they will wish to know, at least for significant projects, the likely effects on that profit, because their personal income may in turn be affected.

Look again at Table 9.14 in Chapter 9. This represents the incremental cash flows expected to result from a decision to undertake the project. To what extent can we use these same numbers in determining the effect of the project on the profit and loss account? The answer is that most of them can be used unchanged, provided we are willing to sacrifice a little accuracy, and in practice people are usually willing to make this sacrifice in the interests of simplicity. We know from earlier discussions that the profit and loss account reflects revenues *earned*, regardless of whether they have yet been received in cash, and expenses *incurred*, regardless of whether they have yet been paid in cash. Well, for our present purpose, these timing differences are usually ignored. What, I almost hear you say, do you mean that earlier on we went into all that detail about the difference between cash flow and profit, only to ignore it now? The answer is that we shall ignore what are usually small differences, but we shall take into account big ones.

Of all the cash flows shown in Table 9.14, there are two that will look substantially different when translated into profit and loss terms. Which are they, and why? They are the new fixed assets – the new equipment and the additional software licences, and the difference is that, unlike all the other cash flows, these represent assets that will be used up slowly – over the whole life of the project, in fact. What is the accounting mechanism for reflecting this fact? Depreciation. In both cases we were told that straight line depreciation would be used, £175k per annum for the equipment, £75k per annum for the software, a total of £250k per annum.

It looks as though a helpful first step would be to rearrange the list of project cash flows in Table 9.14 into the two categories, each of which will require different treatment in order to show its profit and loss effect – fixed capital items, and other items. *Fixed capital* is a term used to describe that part of a company's money, or capital, that is invested in fixed assets, in contrast with *working capital* is loosely used to describe that part of a company's money that is invested in net current assets. In practice, there could indeed also be a third category: changes to the level of current assets – especially stocks and debtors. For reasons that will become apparent later in the chapter, I have assumed no such changes in our example, although we shall later discuss how they should be handled when they occur.

Table 11.3 shows the results of this categorisation. Furthermore, because we no longer need the detail, only the category totals, let us now

Table 11.3 Categorised version of the cash flows in Table 9.14

	Year 0 £000	Year 1 £000	Year 2 £000	Year 3 £000	Year 4 £000	Total £000
Incremental cash flows arising from changes if new investment is undertaken:						
Changes to fixed capital cash flows						
Sale of old equipment	0					0
New equipment	−700					−700
Additional software	−300					−300
Subtotals:	−1,000					−1,000
Changes to other cash flows						
Cash inflows except the following		620	844	772	474	2,710
Old running costs saved		30	33	36	40	139
New running costs incurred		−10	−21	−22	−23	−76
Type 1 supplies		−48	−50	−53	−56	−207
Type 2 supplies		−20	−21	−11	0	−52
Type 2 opportunity cost		−3				−3
It specialists – Year 1		−240				−240
It specialists – Years 2 to 4			−105	−110	−116	−331
Non-specialists		−80	−168	−176	−185	−609
Stores personnel (1)		22	23	24	25	94
Stores personnel (2)		−15	19	20	21	45
Consultancy – paid for		0				0
Consultancy – invoiced		0				0
Consultancy – future		−50				−50
Space cross-charge		0				0
Subtotals:	0	206	554	480	180	1,420
Totals	−1,000	206	554	480	180	420

produce a summary that shows just those totals. *See* Table 11.4. Finally, using the arguments in the preceding paragraphs, we can produce a table that represents the expected profit and loss impact of our project over its four-year life. *See* Table 11.5. Taking the categories in turn, we have first taken the total of £1,000k spent on fixed assets, and instead shown £250k depreciation as an expense in each of Years 1 to 4. Second, by the expedient of ignoring timing differences, we have shown the remaining net cash inflows as though they were net revenues – earnings less expenses.

What information does Table 11.5 convey? First, the total operating profit is £420k. This is not surprising as, in this simple example, the only change we have made is to convert a cash outflow of £1,000k into four

Table 11.4 Summarised version of Table 11.3

	Year 0 £000	Year 1 £000	Year 2 £000	Year 3 £000	Year 4 £000	Total £000
Incremental cash flows arising from changes if new investment is undertaken:						
Fixed capital cash flows	−1,000					−1,000
Other cash flows	0	206	554	480	180	1,420
Totals	−1,000	206	554	480	180	420

Table 11.5 Summarised profit and loss account derived from Table 11.4

	Year 0 £000	Year 1 £000	Year 2 £000	Year 3 £000	Year 4 £000	Total £000
Incremental expenses and revenues arising from changes if new investment is undertaken:						
Depreciation		−250	−250	−250	−250	−1,000
Net revenues		206	554	480	180	1,420
Operating profit/loss		−44	304	230	−70	420

annual amounts of £250k depreciation. Second, Table 11.5 tells us the annual results that contribute to that net total of £420k. The operating profits or losses that the project is expected to deliver in Years 1 to 4 are, respectively, −£44k, £304k, £230k and −£70k. Notice that we have not yet taken into account the cost of the capital invested in the project. It is because this has so far been omitted that I referred above to the £420k as being the operating profit of the project. Operating profit, you will recall, is the name given in the profit and loss account to the profit before interest and other financial charges.

So the project is estimated to make an operating profit of £420k. As with the total net cash flow, we might think that that result looks pretty good, but what could we usefully compare it with as a way of seeing just how good, or bad, it is? We have earlier noted that one of the widely-used measures of the performance of a business as a whole, obtainable from its published accounts, is return on capital employed (ROCE), which is usually taken to be operating profit for the year as a percentage of capital employed during the year. So, if ROCE is an important measure of the performance of the business as a whole, is there a method of working out the ROCE of a project, which, as already discussed, we can think of as a subset of the business?

There is such a method, but we shall need to adapt ROCE to cope with the awkward fact that, unlike a business, whose results are always reported annually, projects usually extend over several years. The way in which the ROCE method is usually adapted is to compare the *average* annual profit with the *average* capital employed, and to express the result as a percentage; and because the method, although based on ROCE, is an adaptation of it, it is usually called by a different name – *return on investment* (ROI) or *accounting rate of return* (ARR).

Return on Investment (ROI)

So, what is the average annual operating profit expected to be delivered by our project? The total operating profit is £420k, and the project is being evaluated over four years, so the answer is £420k/4 = £105k. What will be the average capital employed in the project? Initially it will be £1,000k – the cost of the fixed assets. By the end of the project, the fixed assets will have been depreciated to zero and will be worth nothing; so will the capital – the money – spent on them. When the old car finally collapses in a worthless heap, it is not only the car that has been used up, but also the money that was spent on it. So if the capital employed at the beginning of the project will be £1,000k, and the capital employed at the end of it will be zero, then the average capital employed during the project will be half of £1,000k = £500k.

The final simple step is to express the average annual operating profit of the project as a percentage of the average capital employed. The result is shown in Table 11.6. What we might usefully call the operating return on investment is 21%. The question, as several times before, is: so what? One answer, as several times before, is that it depends on how this project, by this particular measure, compares with similar projects in the past. If the "hurdle" operating ROI for projects of this kind is currently 20%, then our project just scrapes over this particular hurdle. Some companies, in working out return on investment, compare average annual profit with *initial* capital employed rather than average capital employed. Using this method, the operating return on investment would be 105/1,000 = 10.5%. Provided whatever is done, is done consistently it hardly matters. Remember that, unlike the discounted cash flow evaluation methods, which are mathematically based, in considering the effect of an investment on profit there are no rules, there are only opinions.

Remember, however, that so far we have only looked at the expected *operating* profit of our project. We have not yet taken into account the

Table 11.6   Operating return on investment of the profits and losses in Table 11.5

	Ref		£000
Average annual operating profit (£420k/4)	(a)		105
Average capital employed (£1000k/2)	(b)		500
Operating return on investment (a/b)		21%	
(Before cost of capital, and ignoring tax)			

cost of the capital invested in it, and this we should now do. In evaluating the project cash flows, the cost of capital was taken into account in the discounting process, and you will no doubt recall how simple it was. Like every other, this particular aspect of profit analysis is more complicated than its cash flow counterpart. The questions are: how much capital – money – has been invested in the project during each year of its life? And what is the cost of that capital?

First, at the beginning of Year 1 of the project, £1,000k of capital was invested, the cost of the fixed assets. At the end of Year 1, one quarter of the fixed assets is deemed to have been used up, as is therefore one quarter of the capital invested in them. This is reflected in the £250k charge for depreciation, which reduces the value of the assets in the business and also, by reducing profit, the value of the capital. A similar thing happens in each of the following three years until, at the end of Year 4, the assets and the capital have both been depreciated by £1,000k. As for the cost of the capital, when doing our net present value calculations we have already assumed that to be 9%.

Therefore, taking the first year as an example, what is the cost of employing £1000k worth of capital during Year 1? The answer, in this context often called the *funding charge*, is 9% × £1,000k = £90k. Similar calculations apply for each of the remaining three years, giving results of, respectively, £67k, £45k and £22k. As shown in Table 11.7, subtracting the funding charge from the operating profit of each year gives the profit after funding charge. This is an approximation to the profit before tax for each year generated by the project. I use the word "approximation" because, in an actual profit and loss account, only interest – the cost of that part of the company's money that is borrowed – is deducted from operating profit to arrive at profit before tax. In evaluating projects we use an average cost of *all* the company's money.

So, what is the average annual profit after funding charge expected to be delivered by our project? From Table 11.7, the total profit after funding charge over the four years of the project is £196k, so the answer is £196k/4 = £49k. Expressing this as a percentage of the average capital

Table 11.7   Calculation of project profit after funding charge

	Ref	Year 0 £000	Year 1 £000	Year 2 £000	Year 3 £000	Year 4 £000	Total £000
Capital at beginning of year	(a)		1,000	750	500	250	
Project operating profit (from Table 11.5)			−44	304	230	−70	420
Funding charge (9% × a)			−90	−67	−45	−22	−224
Profit after funding charge			−134	237	185	−92	196

employed gives us the return on investment after funding charge, shown in Table 11.8 as 9.8%. Remember that, in practice using all the evaluation methods that we have explored, tax is usually also taken into account. Why? Because it is only after tax has been accounted for that we arrive at the figure of profit that finally belongs to the shareholders. Subject usually to a few adjustments, the profit before tax of the company as a whole is the profit on which tax is chargeable. If the project is to have the effect of increasing profit, then the tax chargeable will increase too. As already noted, however, the subject of tax is beyond the scope of this book.

The application of discounting to the numbers in a profit and loss account has no validity, precisely because many of them, depreciation being the most obvious, are noncash numbers. The very name "discounted cash flow" defines a method for evaluating cash flows. Nevertheless, using our simple example, an arithmetic connection can be shown to exist between the profit after funding charge of our project in Table 11.7 and the NPV of the project cash flows in Table 10.3. This connection can be demonstrated by applying the discount factors for 9% to the profits after funding charge in Years 1 to 4 respectively in Table 11.7. The results are as shown in Table 11.9. Adding up the "discounted" profits of Years 1 to 4 gives a total of £154k, which is the same number as the NPV of the project cash flows.

In real situations this arithmetic equivalence of discounted cash flows and "discounted" profits is usually less easy to demonstrate. Especially is this so when one or more of the cash flows attributable to a project results from changes to the quantities of current assets such as stocks or debtors used in the business. For example, suppose that one expected benefit of a project is the more efficient control and collection of trade debts, and that as a result, for the same level of sales, the average amount of debts outstanding would be reduced from, say, £500k to £450k. This would represent a one-time cash inflow of £50k, a conversion of part of the asset called trade debtors into cash, that would be shown as a cash inflow in the cash flow cost/benefit analysis. We know, however, that the mere conversion of one asset to another has no effect on operating profit, at least no direct effect. That only happens when an asset becomes an expense by being used up.

Table 11.8   Return on investment (after funding charge)

	Ref		£000
Total profit after funding charge (from Table 11.7)	(a)		196
Average annual profit after funding charge (a/4)	(b)		49
Average capital employed (£1,000k/2)	(c)		500
Return on investment after funding charge (b/c)		9.8%	
(Ignoring tax)			

Table 11.9 Arithmetic connection between net profit after funding charge and NPV

	Year 0 £000	Year 1 £000	Year 2 £000	Year 3 £000	Year 4 £000	Total £000
Profit after funding charge (from Table 11.7)		−134	237	185	−92	196
Discount factors (9%)		0.9174	0.8417	0.7722	0.7084	
"Discounted" profits*		−123	199	143	−65	154

Note: The application of discounting to non-cash numbers, such as profits and losses, has no validity. This is nothing more than a demonstration that, with the data in this particular simple example, an arithmetic connection can be shown to exist between profit after funding charge and NPV.

Let us suppose that the one-time cash inflow of £50k, resulting from a reduction in debtors, had been an item in our project cost/benefit analysis. For the sake of simplicity we shall assume that the cash inflow occurred instantaneously on Day 1 of the project, that is "Year 0". Table 11.10 shows the NPV calculations, that we originally did in Table 10.3, revised for the new situation in which only net capital of £950k is invested in the project, the original £1,000k cash to be spent on fixed assets, less the £50k of cash to be liberated by the reduction in debtors. Not surprisingly, the NPV of the project has now increased by £50k, from £154k (in Table 10.3) to £204k. This is because the discount factor for "Year 0" cash flows is 1, so the £50k is undiscounted. The profitability index will also have increased from 1,154/1,000 = 1.154 to 1,154/950 = 1.215, and the internal rate of return, from 15.8% to 18.4%.

We have already established that there will be no effect on operating profit, at least no direct effect. There will, however, be an effect on operating return on investment. Why? Because the initial net capital employed in the project is now no longer £1,000k but has been reduced to £950k, and the average capital employed to (£1,000k/2) − £50k = £450k. Table 11.11 shows the revised operating ROI calculation, and its result, 23%. If we reflect on the alternative way of doing ROI calculations – the one that uses initial, rather than average, capital employed, then you will understand the desirability of assuming, as we have done, that all "capital cash flows", those concerned with current assets as well as those concerned with fixed assets, be deemed to occur in Year 0. If this were not the case, then in our example, the benefit resulting from the reduction in debtors would not find its way into an "initial capital" ROI calculation.

Because the net capital employed in the project has been reduced from £1,000k to £950k, there will be a reduction in the funding charge and a corresponding increase in the consequent profit after funding charge. Table 11.12 shows the revised calculations. Because less capital is employed, the funding charge is reduced and so the profit after funding charge has increased, from £196k to £212k. Predictably, Table 11.13 shows

Table 11.10   NPV calculations revised to reflect reduction of £50k in debtors

	Ref	Year 0 £000	Year 1 £000	Year 2 £000	Year 3 £000	Year 4 £000	Total £000
Assumption: all cash flows occur on the last day of each year							
Net cash flows from Table 9.14		−1,000	206	554	480	180	420
Reduction in debtors		50					50
	(a)	−950	206	554	480	180	470
Discount factors (9%)	(b)	1.0000	0.9174	0.8417	0.7722	0.7084	
Present values (a × b)	(c)	−950	189	466	371	128	
Net present value (NPV), the sum of all the present values in row (c)							204

Table 11.11   Operating ROI calculations revised to reflect reduction of £50k in debtors

	Ref		£000
Average annual operating profit (£420k/4)	(a)		105
Average capital employed ((£1000k/2) − £50k)	(b)		450
Operating return on investment (a/b)		23%	
(Before funding charge, and ignoring tax)			

that the return on investment after the funding charge has also increased, from 9.8% to 11.8%. Finally, were you to redo the calculation of "discounting" the project profit after funding charge, that we did in Table 11.9, you would find the answer to be £182k. This is, predictably, different from the revised NPV of the cash flows of £204k shown in Table 11.10. The reason, as we discussed at the outset, is that attributable changes to such current assets as debtors affect cash flow but have no effect, at least no direct effect, on operating profit.

In the above, we have used a reduction in trade debtors as an example. We noted that, if the level of credit sales remains the same, then a reduction in debtors – the result of customers paying their bills more quickly on average – represents a one-time conversion of the asset debtors into the asset cash. Suppose, instead, we were to consider what is a quite frequent aim of some IT applications – a reduction in stock levels. Although stocks of goods or raw materials may be bought on credit, ultimately they have to be paid for in cash. Therefore a permanent reduction in stock levels, for the same level of production or sales, has exactly the same financial effect as does a reduction in debtors. When the reduction in stock level occurs, there is a one-time avoidance of the cash outflow that would have occurred to replenish the stock to its original level. However, it has already been shown that the avoidance of a cash outflow has the same financial effect as an increase in cash inflow of equivalent amount. Therefore, all the

Table 11.12   Project funding charge revised to reflect reduction of £50k in debtors

	Ref	Year 0 £000	Year 1 £000	Year 2 £000	Year 3 £000	Year 4 £000	Total £000
Capital at beginning of year	(a)		950	700	450	200	
Project operating profit (from Table 11.5)			−44	304	230	−70	420
Funding charge (9% × a)			−86	−63	−41	−18	−208
Profit after funding charge			−130	241	189	−88	212

Table 11.13   Return on investment (after funding charge) revised to reflect reduction of £50k in debtors

	Ref		£000
Total profit after funding charge (from Table 11.12)			212
Average annual profit after funding charge (£212k/4)	(a)		53
Average capital employed ((£1000k/2) − £50k)	(b)		450
Return on investment after funding charge (a/b)		11.8%	

(Ignoring tax)

above arguments concerning a reduction in debtors would apply if used to illustrate a reduction in stocks.

There is usually, however, an additional benefit to be had from reducing stocks. Holding stocks costs money, over and above the cost of the stock itself. These holding costs include space costs, people costs, insurance and – depending on the nature of the stock – obsolescence, deterioration and theft. Generally, these holding costs are proportionate to the quantity of stocks held. Therefore, a consequence of reducing stocks will often be a proportionate reduction in holding costs, a corresponding increase in operating profit and a resulting increase in operating ROI.

At this point, let us summarise the results obtained from the various methods of evaluating our proposed project and, for comparison, how those results would have changed had our project included an expected reduction of £50k in trade debtors. *See* table 11.14, which also reminds us of the basis for each of the evaluation methods – cash flow or profit. If you think of a project as a building, then these various results could be thought of as windows, each giving a different view into the building. Remember that, with the exception of NPV, which is an absolute number, these results only make sense when compared with something else – usually a company's past experience of projects of this kind.

It is also vital to know which of the results is actually giving "advice" most likely to contribute towards achieving the objective of the business,

Table 11.14   Summary of evaluation results

	Basis	Original project	After reduction of £50k in debtors
Net cash inflows		£420k	£470k
Operating profit		£420k	£420k
Net present value (NPV)	Cashflow	£154k	£204k
Profitability index	Cashflow	1.154	1.215
Internal rate of return (IRR)	Cashflow	15.8 %	18.4 %
Payback	Cashflow	30 months	29 months
Discounted payback	Cashflow	36 months	34 months
Operating return on investment (ROI) (*operating profit/average capital employed*)	Profit	21 %	23 %
ROI after funding charge (*profit after funding charge/average capital employed*)	Profit	9.8 %	11.8 %

which is the maximization of shareholders' wealth – ultimately cash wealth. Let me reiterate that, unless all the authorities have missed an important trick, then it is the discounted cash flow methods – net present value (NPV) and internal rate of return (IRR), but especially NPV – of which this is true. Return on investment (ROI) has, or should have, a different objective – to show what the effect on profit or loss – company or departmental – would be if a proposed investment were to be undertaken.

At this point we have come full circle. We started the book with an assertion that the point of a business is to maximize the wealth of its proprietors, and that ultimately that means cash wealth. We have concluded this part of it with a detailed examination of the various methods which are used to assist the process of deciding whether or not a proposed investment is the best way of achieving that aim at a particular time. I have tried to relate the various topics to each other, first because they *are* related, but second, because understanding one topic provides insights into others. Indeed, that is the main reason why I have, in this chapter, devoted more space to the subject of return on investment than is really merited by its importance relative to other topics.

This concludes the main part of the book. I believe, based on considerable experience, that if you have fully understood all the arguments and explanations that have been presented here, then you will have achieved an understanding of many of the essential principles of business, and of finance – the language of business. In the next, and final, chapter I offer you a brief taste of some other important financial aspects of business – budgeting, costing and pricing.

12 Tasters

Budgeting – Costing and Pricing

The purpose of this chapter is to provide a brief taste of some other financial aspects of business – budgeting, costing and pricing, each of which could be, and indeed is, the subject of whole books.

Budgeting

In the opening chapters of this book we spent time studying how all business transactions can be recorded in the primary accounting document, namely the balance sheet. We also looked at the role of the profit and loss account as an explanation of how the profit or loss made since the start of the business, or since the previous balance sheet, was arrived at; and the similar role played by the cash flow statement, but with respect to cash. We went on to see how various comparisons – of numbers within the accounts, and with past years, industry averages and so on – can yield a lot of information about how a business is performing.

However, that information concerns the past. We as individuals may find it useful, even if possibly depressing, to find out from our personal "accounts" that our expenditure exceeded our income last year, and what caused the excess. However, would it not have been even more useful if we had had some idea in advance that that was likely to be the case? If so, then we might have had a chance to do something about it. The same is true of businesses. Sometimes individuals do try to work out their personal finances in advance, however approximately. The process of doing so is called budgeting, and the same word is used to describe the very similar activity carried out by almost all businesses.

For a small business, the budgeting process may be as simple as it would be for most individuals, consisting of estimates of income and expense, and the resulting profit or loss, and of cash availability month by month, highlighting periods during which overdraft facilities might be needed.

The business would also need to budget for any planned capital expenditure, such as new premises or equipment, just as an individual would if buying a house or a car. This is for two reasons: The first is to determine whether the necessary financial resources are already available, or can be borrowed, and the second is that capital expenditure always has an effect on subsequent year-by-year income or expense. If existing resources such as cash deposits or investments are to be used, then there will in future be less income from interest or dividends; if a loan is to be taken out, then there will be higher expense in the form of interest, and increased cash outflow on both the interest and the repayments. Either way, if the asset to be acquired is one that will depreciate in value, then this too will be an expense that will further reduce profit.

As a business gets bigger, there comes a point at which the owner or owners or, in the case of a company, the board of directors, can no longer take all the decisions themselves. They have no choice but to divide the business up into manageable parts, and to appoint a director or manager to be in charge of each part. The three most common ways of carving a business up are by function, by product or by region, or possibly all three. Division by function distinguishes between the major functions of a business. What these are will depend on the kind of business it is, but they might typically include research and development, manufacturing, sales, distribution and finance. They might also include IT, although in some businesses the person in charge of IT reports to another functional head, typically but not necessarily, finance. Division by product distinguishes between the major products of a business. For example, a large IT manufacturer might have separate divisions for its main hardware and software products and its services. Division by geography may be by continent, country or region within a country. As you can image, a worldwide multi-product company that carries out most of its functions in most or all of the countries in which it operates, will have a quite complex divisional or departmental structure. At the other end of the scale, the successful owner of a shop, who buys another shop and appoints a manager to run it, would have a quite simple structure – the two shops.

Mention of a manager highlights the main point here, which is that however complex or simple the way of dividing up the business, if you are going to give someone responsibility for managing a part of it then you had better also provide them with the resources with which to do so, including financial resources. To do this we can expand slightly the original idea of a budget as simply an estimate of future income, expense and cash flow, to become a way of allocating financial resources to the managers of various parts of the business and delegating authority for managing those resources. Eventually the sum of the income, expense and cash flow budgets of all the divisions and departments will give the totals of those budgets for the business as a whole, although as a bargaining position, revenue budgets may be initially overstated, while expense budgets may be understated.

Exactly what financial resources are delegated depends upon the nature of the division or department. For this purpose, let us dispense with the rather cumbersome "division or department" and coin the term "centre" to mean either. Many centres do not earn revenue for the business but simply incur costs, and so are called "cost centres". An example would be an accounting department, which is necessary for the running of the business, but which would be most unlikely to earn revenue. The obvious requirement for such a centre therefore is that its costs should be minimised, and its budget would reflect that fact.

If there were such a thing as a centre that earned revenue without incurring any cost, then it would no doubt be called a "revenue centre". The obvious example of a centre whose purpose is to produce revenue is a sales division or department, Since, however, such a centre does indeed incur costs – salespeople's salaries, commissions and travel, for example – then it is clearly important to budget not just for the revenue required to be earned by that particular centre but for its costs also. Since those costs become expenses when "used up" (see earlier chapters) and since profit is the difference between revenue and expenses it is perhaps not surprising that such a centre would usually be called a "profit centre".

Some functions in a business, for example the IT function, may be cost centres or profit centres. If, as well as serving the company, IT services are provided to other businesses for a charge, then the IT function or part of it might be regarded as a profit centre; if not, then it would be regarded as a cost centre. Sometimes, even where no external services are provided, notional amounts are "charged out" to user departments within the business. Charge out may be at cost, or at a marked up amount yielding a notional profit to the IT department. The purpose of such an approach is to encourage functional management to operate their function as though it were indeed an independent business. Especially is this so if the amounts charged to user department are reasonably accurate, which is more easily said than done, and if user departments are free to use external IT services if they can be obtained more cost-effectively. Such calculations may eventually be the basis for deciding whether to outsource part or all of the IT function.

There would be little point in doing the considerable amount of work involved in budgeting if account were not kept of how individual centre managers actually perform when measured against their budgets. Budget-holding managers are indeed judged on, among other things, their performance against budget, and it is but a small further step to reward or penalise them on the basis of such performance. Many managers are in fact paid bonuses based on their performance against budget. In this way managers responsible for divisions or departments are held accountable for the performance of those centres. Not surprisingly, therefore, the term "responsibility accounting" is sometimes used to describe this whole process.

As in the example above of the sales division, it is usually obvious which centres in a business should be held responsible for generating revenues. However, if managers are to be held responsible for costs, then it is important that any particular manager is only measured on those costs over which they can have control. Many costs are obviously directly attributable to a particular centre. For example, the rent and insurance of a factory building are obviously "direct costs" of the manufacturing division as a whole, which may be the responsibility of the manufacturing director. It is therefore reasonable to include those costs in the total by which that person is measured. By contrast, the manufacturing director is likely to have no control over whether extra money required by the company is raised by borrowing or by issuing further shares. This kind of decision is the responsibility of the financial director or chief financial officer, who would, therefore be held accountable for interest payable.

One reason why operating profit is an important number in the profit and loss account is that it represents the revenues earned less all the operating, or non-financial, expenses of the business. These expenses are the ones that are usually capable of being charged to the responsibility of the operating, as distinct from financial, managers within the business, even if the process of assigning responsibility is not necessarily easy. Interest, tax and dividends belong in deep finance territory. There is one respect, however in which an operating manager, such as an IT manager, may be given discretion to encroach into deep finance territory, and that is in the matter of leasing. Managers may be given authority to incur capital expenditure up to a given amount. While in some companies the decision as to how equipment (for example) is to be financed is always left to the finance function to decide, in others managers are given discretion whether to purchase or lease.

It should by now be apparent that much of the information needed to determine the actual revenues and costs of individual divisions or departments is the same as that needed to determine the financial results of the business as a whole, but analysed in different ways. For example, the sales achieved by Supermarkets A and B in J Sainsbury plc will no doubt be used to measure the performance against budget of their respective managers. However, together with the sales achieved by all the other shops operated by the business, they will be part of the total sales of the business that will be shown in the group profit and loss account. The various costs and expenses of manufacturing at a particular factory of a worldwide manufacturing company will be used to measure the performance against budget of the manager of that particular factory. They will also be incorporated in the company's group accounts. However, they may also be part of the performance measurement of the company's European Region, its UK operation, and of a particular product line that is manu-

factured in several different parts of the world. The essence of the requirement is to be able to analyse the same data in many different ways, a
task greatly facilitated by IT systems.

In the above brief description, it should have become apparent that
budgeting is a combination of several things: the delegation of responsibility, forecasting, and the measurement of performance again forecast.
It is also a means of influencing the behaviour of managers and provides
a basis for rewarding them according to their performance. However, just
as a business is itself a dynamic entity which needs to adapt to meet
changing circumstances, so should budgeting systems also be adaptable.
By their nature, budgets are formulated before the period to which they
relate. Budgeting procedures should be sufficiently flexible to allow
managers to take advantage of opportunities or react to situations that
could not have been foreseen.

Costing and Pricing

In the previous section we discussed the fact that at the heart of budgeting is the process of estimating in advance the revenues likely to be
achieved and the costs likely to be incurred by a business and by its various
subdivisions during some future period. However, to a considerable extent
we glossed over just how difficult it can sometimes be to determine what
those costs might be. "What did it cost?" A simple enough question, you
might think, when applied to a recent purchase. "£15,000", you might
answer in the case of a new car, or "£1" for a loaf of bread, or "£40" in
the case of a software package. That is indeed what those items might cost
us, the cost to us being the price charged by the supplier. However, the
question: "What did it cost the supplier to *produce* the car, or the loaf of
bread or the software package?" – is not nearly so easy to answer.

There are several reasons why it is important to understand cost. First,
and most obviously, if we do not know how much a product or service
costs to produce or provide, then how can we know how much to charge
for it in order to make a reasonable profit? Second, in a competitive world
there is always pressure to reduce prices. The only way to improve or
maintain profit may be to reduce costs. If we do not know which costs
are attributable to which product or service, then we cannot know which
costs we should try to reduce, or which products should be discontinued
because they can never be profitable. Third, some businesses have a choice
of making or buying certain parts or components, while most businesses
can choose whether to provide certain functions in-house, for example
IT, or to buy them externally, to outsource. Not knowing the cost of in-
house provision would make it impossible to exercise that choice sensibly.

To get a taste for some aspects of this subject we shall look briefly at
some simple examples, starting with the simplest kind of business imag-
inable. Mary sells tins of beans from a market stall. Suppose that the stall

is rent free; that her supplies are delivered from the supplier each day; that she sells all the tins that are delivered and that she has no other costs. Each tin costs her £1 and she sells it for £1.50, that is at a profit of 50p. Her markup – profit as a percentage of purchase price – is therefore 50%. Probably not bad for tins of beans, but the numbers are only for illustration. Her profit margin – profit as a percentage of sales – is therefore 33.3%. The more tins she sells the more profit she makes. If she sells 1,000 tins, then her cost of sales would be £1,000, her revenue would be £1,500 and her profit £500. If she sells 10,000 tins, then her cost of sales would be £10k, her revenue would be £15k and her profit £5k. Let us suppose that she actually sells 100,000 tins in a year. Her cost of sales would be £100k, her revenue would be £150k and her profit £50k.

Let us also suppose that from to time Mary draws out some of her profit in cash to live on. The tax authorities have not yet caught up with her. For the purpose of the examples that follow we shall avoid the debate about whether proprietor's "salary" is a charge against profit or a distribution of profit, and we shall treat it as the latter, that is as a distribution of profit, the same view that the tax authorities take. So the profit of Mary's business is indeed £50k.

Why were these calculations so easy? The reason is that all the costs of the business vary directly with the quantity of goods sold; in other words, all the costs are variable costs, in this case, simply the costs of the daily supply of tins. The more Mary buys and sells, the more profit she makes, ad infinitum. A *variable cost* is defined as a cost that varies proportionally with a chosen unit. In this case, the unit is the number of tins purchased. In a manufacturing business, the chosen unit might be the

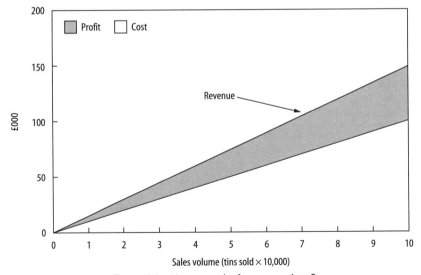

Figure 12.1   Linear growth of revenue and profit

number of items manufactured; in a software house it might be the number of lines of code written. The relationship between Mary's revenue, costs and profit can be represented by the chart in Figure 12.1.

All businesses try to reduce their costs. Suppose that Mary were able to find a new supplier who would only charge her 80p per tin instead of £1. If she were able to maintain her selling price of £1.50, then her profit per tin sold would increase from 50p to 70p. What would be the effect of all this on Mary's profit at her current volume of sales of 100,000? Her only expense – cost of sales – will be reduced by 100,000 × 20p = £20k for her current volume of sales. What is this reduction worth to Mary's business? Since profit is the difference between revenue and expenses, and what Mary has done is to reduce her cost of sales, the benefit to her is to increase her profit by the same amount, that is by £20,000, but only at her current volume of sales. Halve the sales, and halve the benefit; double the sales, double the benefit, and so on.

Now let us assume that the local council has caught up with Mary and that she is being charged £20k per year rent for her pitch. You might think that this is rather excessive, and indeed it is, but the purpose is to illustrate a point, not to reflect the true economics of running a market stall. As long as Mary chooses to park her stall she must pay the £20k even if she never sells a single tin of beans. In other words, her business has joined the vast majority of businesses which, in order to earn revenue, incur *fixed costs* as well as variable. See Figure 12.2.

Before, every tin of beans that Mary sold yielded a profit of 50 pence, which she regarded, with only the occasional glance over her shoulder at the tax authorities, as her own. Now, however, the surplus from the first

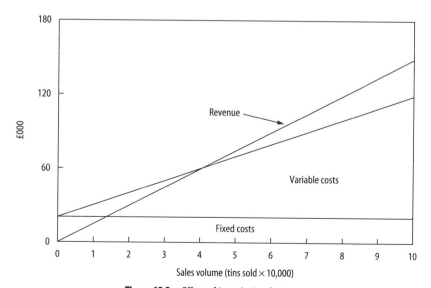

Figure 12.2 Effect of introducing fixed costs

few tens of thousands of tins sold does not belong to her at all, but has
to go towards paying her rent. The sums are easy – each tin sold, starting
with the very first, contributes 50p towards paying the rent, the fixed cost.
However, by itself the "contribution" from selling the first tin is obviously
nowhere near enough.

How many tins are required to make the total contribution required
in this case? Well, if the rent comes to £20k and if each tin contributes
50p, then the required number is £20k divided by 50p = 40,000. This is
the number of tins that must be sold in order that the business can just
pay its fixed costs. At this level of sales Mary's business makes neither a
profit nor a loss. Sales are just sufficient to cover the total costs. The business is said to "break even". *See* Figure 12.3. Sell one tin fewer, and the
business makes a loss of 50p. This in turn means that Mary must pay
the last 50p of the rent out of her own pocket. Sell one tin more and her
business has made a profit of 50p; all subsequent tins sold add to
her profit. Notice that the fixed costs represent a direct reduction in profit,
and the reduction is the same regardless of the level of sales. The profit
had been £50k; the introduction of fixed costs of £20k has directly
reduced the profit – to £30k. Had the original profit been £35k, then it
would be reduced to £15k, and so on.

Suppose now that Mary complains about the amount of the rent and
succeeds in having it reduced from £20k to £10k. What is the benefit of
this reduction to her business? The answer is probably obvious. Precisely
because fixed costs are, by definition, fixed and independent of the level
of sales, the benefit of a reduction in fixed costs is an increase in profit
of the same amount, regardless of the level of sales. If the fixed costs
have decreased by £10k, then the profit must have increased by £10k.

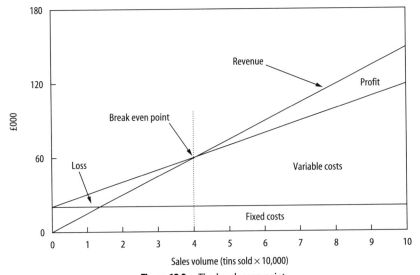

Figure 12.3   The break even point

Furthermore, if the fixed costs are now less than they were, a correspondingly smaller contribution is required to cover them. So, the break-even point must now occur at a lower sales volume.

As before, the break-even point can be worked out arithmetically or by means of a simple diagram. How many tins must be sold in order to make the total contribution to fixed costs now required? The fixed costs – the rent – now come to £10k. Each tin sold contributes 50p; therefore the number of tins that must be sold is £10k/50p = 20,000. This is now the number of tins that must be sold in order for Mary to break even, as shown in Figure 12.4. The term "fixed cost" is frequently used, but can be misleading. If Mary were to become really successful she might acquire another stall, at which point her fixed costs would go up, because she would have to pay rent on that too, as well as having to pay wages to someone to serve on it. Ultimately, all fixed costs become variable. We could say as a general rule that the benefit of a reduction in fixed costs is an increase in profit equal to that reduction. The amount of the benefit per year will be independent of the level of sales but only up to a certain point. Beyond that point the fixed costs may increase.

Given the simple definition of profit to which we have reverted in this chapter, namely that it is revenue less expenses, then it follows that there are two ways of increasing profit – reducing expenses or increasing revenue. Mary has already had considerable success in reducing both her variable and fixed costs. If she wants further to increase her profit, then the only remaining option is to increase revenue, and there are two ways in which this might be done: she could sell more tins at the same price or she could increase the selling price.

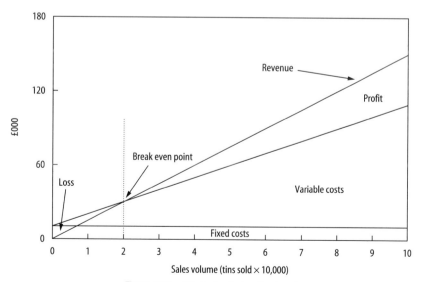

Figure 12.4   Effect of reducing fixed costs

Before deciding upon either approach, it would make sense for Mary to conduct a little market research, which means finding out what customers want and what they are prepared to pay for it. The fact that she already sells all of her stock every day suggests that if only she could accommodate some more stock she might well be able to sell it at the current price. Does she have space for storing more stock during the day, free of charge; perhaps on the ground under her stall? If so, then she would be in the ideal position of being able to increase her sales at no extra cost other than the obvious cost of additional purchases. In particular, she would not have the awkward job of trying to forecast in advance whether she could make enough extra sales in order to recoup extra fixed costs. This would be for the good reason that no extra fixed costs would be incurred.

If, on the other hand, Mary could not find any free storage space, then her options would appear to be as follows: she may be able to sub-rent some currently unused space under a neighbouring stall, or she could start a second stall. Both of these options would, however, incur additional fixed costs. In the first case she would almost certainly have to agree a contract for sub-rent payable to the other stallholder. In the second case, as already discussed, she would have to pay both rent for her second stall and the wages of an employee to run it. In either case, she would need to do a little break-even analysis in order to work out how many additional tins she would need to sell in order to recoup her additional fixed costs.

Suppose on the other hand, that her market research suggests to Mary that at least most of her customers would indeed be prepared to pay more for her beans. She would now need to do a pricing exercise. Pricing simply means setting the price at which you will sell a product or service, and it is about three things – cost, customers and competition. If your prices do not yield revenue that exceeds your total costs, then you make no profit. If your prices are higher than customers are prepared to pay, then you have no business. Competition is what gives customers the choice. Suppose Mary believes that all her customers would be prepared to accept a 5% price increase, but that if the increase were 10%, then customers representing an estimated 10% of her business would go elsewhere. What should she do? For what follows we revert to the original situation where the rent was £20k, as shown in Table 12.1. We can use this simple spreadsheet to test the effect of Mary's various assumptions.

First, suppose that Mary were able to increase her prices by 5% and keep all her customers. Table 12.2 shows the result, an increase in profit of £7,500 to £37,500. Now let us suppose that she were to increase her prices by 10% but in so doing were to lose 10% of her customers. *See* Table 12.3. In this case her profit, at £38,500, would be slightly more than that yielded by the price increase of only 5%. However, she might well

Table 12.1 The original situation

		Ref	£	% of revenue
Sales volume	100,000 tins			
Revenue	100,000 × £1.50	(a)	150,000	100.0
Variable costs	100,000 × £1.00	(b)	100,000	66.7
Contribution	(a–b)	(c)	50,000	33.3
Fixed costs		(d)	20,000	13.3
Profit	(c–d)		30,000	20.0

Table 12.2 Increase price by 5%, keep all customers

		Ref	£	% of revenue
Sales volume	100,000 tins			
Revenue	(100,000 × £1.50) × 1.05	(a)	157,500	100.0
Variable costs	100,000 × £1.00	(b)	100,000	63.5
Contribution	(a–b)	(c)	57,500	36.5
Fixed costs		(d)	20,000	12.7
Profit	(c–d)		37,500	23.8

Table 12.3 Increase price by 10%, lose 10% of customers

		Ref	£	% of revenue
Sales volume	90,000 tins			
Revenue	(90,000 × £1.50) × 1.1	(a)	148,500	100.0
Variable costs	90,000 × £1.00	(b)	90,000	60.6
Contribution	(a–b)	(c)	58,500	39.4
Fixed costs		(d)	20,000	13.5
Profit	(c–d)		38,500	25.9

conclude that it would not make long-term business sense to risk losing 10% of her customers for the very small short-term gain of an extra £1,000 in profit.

At this point, suppose that Mary is indeed favouring the option of raising prices by 5%. Before deciding, however, it would make sense to revisit the option of selling more tins at the same price. The question now is: How many extra tins would she have to sell in order to make at least the additional profit of £7,500 that she believes the 5% prices increase would produce? Once again, you would use the spreadsheet to do the work for you. However, if you prefer to do the arithmetic, here are the calculations. At the original price, the contribution made by each tin sold is 50p, or 33.33% of selling price. In order to obtain an extra £7,500 of contribution, and therefore of profit, she would have to sell £7,500/50p = 15,000 extra tins. If she has to pay a sub-rent of, say, £2,000 per year for her neighbour's spare space, then Mary would have to sell a further £2,000/50p = 4,000 tins to cover her increased fixed costs. 19,000 extra tins in all. So, her final decision might be: Should she increase prices by 5% with no increase in fixed costs, and risk losing some customers (even though her gut feeling tells her she wouldn't lose any) or should she try to increase sales volume, but with the risk that she might possibly not even cover the additional fixed costs incurred?

At this point we shall leave Mary to her decision-making, with which we can probably help her no further. Notice that all the calculations that she has done so far, and the financial statements that she has produced, have all been entirely for her own purposes, to help her manage her business and make decisions about it. They are all purely for internal consumption, and because of that you would not, I think, be surprised to know that there are no laws or any other rules that govern what they contain, or indeed dictate that they have to be produced at all. If we wanted to give a collective name to all these statements, accounts and charts that are purely for management purposes, and the process of producing and using them, then perhaps management accounting might come to mind. Whether it did or not, that is what those activities are usually called.

For a look at another aspect of the large subject of costing we shall turn to the manufacturing industry. Think of a business that assembles PCs from bought-in components. Suppose each PC uses £300 of components and takes one person three hours to assemble. If the cost of the person is £20 per hour, then the labour cost per PC is £60, and the cost to the business of assembling it is the materials plus the labour, a total of £360. However, is this the full cost of assembling the PC? It might be, but only if the assembly work were being done in a rent-free field, if the components found their way there automatically without being ordered or checked on delivery, if those components could be used immediately without being stored somewhere until they were needed, and if the business could somehow survive without any administration or accounting staff.

In reality, of course, the assembly work is done in a building, for which rent, insurance, power and cleaning costs have to be paid; the components have to be ordered, and checked on delivery, moved into a store and eventually issued to the production line – all by people who would quite like to be paid. There are, additionally, other costs, more remote from the production process, but costs nevertheless, – the costs of selling the product, such as advertising and sales staff; and the costs of administering the business – accounts and secretarial staff, and office costs and equipment.

All these costs are also part of the total costs of all the PCs assembled. What is the essential difference between these costs and the costs of labour and materials? The answer is that labour and material costs are obviously related directly to the assembly of the PCs, whereas the others are not. We can *see* the person assembling that particular PC, measure how long the work takes, and therefore *easily* work out the labour cost of producing it. We can see the materials being put into that particular PC and therefore, knowing what the materials cost, can *easily* work out the materials cost of producing it. The emphasis is deliberately on the word "easily". These costs, labour and materials can easily be directly related to the product being assembled. For this reason, they are called direct costs.

All the other costs that we considered are called, not surprisingly, indirect costs or sometimes overhead costs. Indirect costs or overheads are simply those costs that cannot *easily* be related directly to the product. Suppose that, just because it was too difficult to relate these indirect costs to an individual PC, they were simply ignored. Would we base our prices on just the direct costs? Of course not. Remember that in order to make a profit a business has to earn revenue that exceeds its *total* costs. Total means what it says – all costs, both direct and indirect.

"Easy", we might be tempted to say. "At the end of the year we shall know exactly what all the costs are, indirect as well as direct, and we'll simply apportion the indirects equally among the products that have been made. If we've made 10,000 products and supposing that the total of the indirect costs is £2 million, then the proportion of indirect costs attributable to each produce will be £2 million/10,000 = £200. As long as wage rates and material costs remain the same, then the direct costs of each product will be £360. Each product's share of the indirect costs would be £200, so its total cost would be £360 + £200 = £560. Suppose we are aiming for a profit margin (which is, you may remember, profit as a percentage of revenue) of 20%? To achieve it, our selling price would have to be £560/0.8 = £700.

Unfortunately, there are some fairly obvious flaws in the above argument. Chief among them is that if we wait until the end of the year to know the actual indirect costs before fixing our selling price we shall no longer have a business. It helps to have a price in order to make a sale. What is the solution to this little problem? The answer is provided by the activity described in the first section of this chapter, it is: estimate in advance, as accurately as possible, what the indirect costs will be, and how many products will be made, and use the estimated or budgeted numbers. So, the budgeted indirect cost of each product would be the result of dividing the total budgeted indirect costs by the estimated number of products to be produced. For pricing purposes, such calculations might be adequate. Indeed, since pricing has to be done in advance, such calculations would usually have to be adequate.

But accounting is a continuous process. Business managers want to know as they go along what the costs and revenues of the business are, and therefore what its profit is to date. So, for each product that is made, the accounting system should ideally record its total cost there and then or, rather, its total budgeted cost. Since the direct costs are, by definition, those that can easily be attributed directly to an individual product, one way of doing this would be simply to work out what percentage the indirects bear to the direct costs, and apply a corresponding percentage uplift each time that direct costs are recorded. In the example above, the budgeted direct costs of each product were £360 and the budgeted indirects were £200. 200 as a percentage of 360 is 55.56%. So a simple way for the accounting system to do what management requires would be always to add 55.56% of the direct costs as an uplift.

So far so good, provided of course that we actually produce the estimated number of products. However, the question then becomes – should we base the uplift on the total of the direct costs, or would it be better to base it on only one of them? What is wrong with using total direct costs? In some businesses, there is nothing wrong at all. However, in others, the price of materials is quite volatile. For example, oil prices are subject to considerable fluctuation based on both supply and, sometimes, political pressures; the prices of crops, whether cocoa beans or carrots, vary according to whether the harvest has been good or bad. So, businesses manufacturing chocolate or baby food may find the price of their most important raw materials changing considerably during a year. Should the amount added for overheads fluctuate in sympathy with rises and falls in the price of materials? Of course not.

Are labour rates as volatile as the prices of some materials? Usually not. Certainly they do not often come down, and increases, although modest, especially in times of low inflation, are reasonably predictable. For this reason, and because in past times direct labour accounted for the major part of product costs, direct labour is what has historically been the main basis for allocating indirect costs. In our example, direct labour costs are £60 per product. Using the same "percentage uplift" method that we used above, the budgeted direct labour costs of each product were £60 and the budgeted indirects were £200. 200 as a percentage of 60 is 333.33%. So the way the accounting system might allocate indirects on the basis of direct labour would be always to add 333.33% of the direct labour costs as an uplift. However, direct labour costs now represent a much lower proportion of total costs than they once did.

Many manufacturing businesses are becoming more and more automated, with machines doing much of the work previously done by people. Just as you can *see* a person assembling a PC, so you can see a machine doing the same thing if the assembly process has been automated. Therefore, as the cost of employing the person to do the work is known and reasonably predictable, so is the cost of employing the machine. The purchase price of the machine is known, and its likely number of productive hours will also be known, from which a cost per hour used can be derived. Add its power costs and maintenance costs, which are also reasonably predictable, and you have an estimated total cost per machine-hour. If the machine is solely used for working on one product, then the cost of machine-hours is a direct cost attributable to that product, just as the cost of labour-hours was. If the machine is used for two hours per product and costs £15 per hour of use, then the direct machine cost attributable to each product is £15 × 2 = £30. If the machine is used in the manufacture of several different products, then the cost of machine-hours devoted to each product are direct costs attributable to each of the different products.

If a particular machine is used for short but varying periods on a very large number of different products, then it may be neither easy nor economically feasible to determine with sufficient precision the time spent upon each individual item. In this case, the costs of the machine no longer satisfy our criteria for being treated as direct costs, so they would be treated as indirect, and added to all the other indirect costs, to be allocated to particular products in whatever way has been determined.

Every different kind of business has its own particular kind of costing problems. This section can have done no more than give an idea of just a few of the problems that costing tries to answer. If by now you have gained the impression that costing is a subject that is both quite complex and more art than science, then you would be right, and we have only considered quite simple examples. One thing that can be said, however, to close our brief excursion into this topic, is that the power of IT systems economically to record and analyse large amounts of individually quite small data items is helping to take just a little of the art out of costing and replace it with science.

For example, in the case of the machine, cited above, which is used for varying periods on a very large number of different products, it *may* now be economically feasible to allocate the costs of its use directly to the products on which it is used whereas it would not have been in earlier times. To the extent that costs previously treated as indirect, and therefore subject to some estimated basis of allocation, might now be economically treated as direct, so costing becomes more accurate. The more accurate the data used for business decision-making, the better the decisions are likely to be.

Tailpiece

At the beginning of this book I expressed some frustration at the extent to which generations of finance and accountancy students have suffered from the fact that an essentially simple subject has been made unnecessarily complicated by those two wretched terms – debit and credit. If you have got this far in the book, then I hope and believe that you will have understood the essential simplicity of financial concepts, and of accountancy, which is nothing more than the means whereby the application of those concepts is recorded. If so, you will have done so without any mention of those terms. However, perhaps I owe it to you to explain how terms on which I have poured such vitriol came about.

It happens that in the United Kingdom, and in some other countries, balance sheets are today usually set out as described in the early chapters of this book. Assets are shown at the top, liabilities at the bottom, and this is sometimes referred to as the "vertical format". However, in former times, when accounting was done by hand rather than by computer, and in some countries still today, balance sheets were set out differently, being divided into two columns. Assets were shown on the left-hand side and liabilities on the right – the "horizontal format". The same was true of profit and loss accounts. Instead of the vertical format often used today, the horizontal format was used for them too. Expenses were shown on the left-hand side and revenues on the right.

This was all a natural consequence of the way in which, in those days, individual transactions were recorded in a book, often a beautifully bound book, that was called a "journal". For example, the two sides of the transaction representing the sale of goods to J Bloggs for £10 would have been recorded in the journal of the selling business, inessential details being omitted, as shown in Table 13.1. People to whom goods or services were sold, and who therefore owed a debt to the business – the obligation to pay for them – were called "debitors", different by only one letter from the word used today. Those *to* whom a business owed a debt – in this example, the obligation to deliver goods – were called creditors,

Table 13.1   Illustration of an entry in a journal

Date	Details of transaction	Debitor £	Creditor £
November 25	*J Bloggs, for goods sold*	*10.00*	
	Sales		*10.00*

as they still are. By convention, the debitors were always shown in the left-hand column, the creditors on the right. Over time, "debitor" and "creditor" became abbreviated to "debit" and "credit", and eventually to "dr" and "cr". Notice from the example that, even in those more leisurely days, the intermediate recording as a "creditor" of the obligation of the seller to actually deliver the goods would have been omitted, the transaction being instead immediately "credited" to sales.

Because the two-column format was obviously a convenient way of recording two-sided transactions, it came to serve as the medium for recording *all* transactions, not just those involving actual debtors and creditors. So, all assets came to be recorded as "debits", and all liabilities as "credits". It was then only a small step also to use the "debit" column to record expenses – the using up of assets, you will recall – and the "credit" column to record revenues, the money earned when the obligation to actually deliver goods or services had been fulfilled.

Thus it was that generations of finance and accountancy students came to be told that "assets and expenses are debits, while liabilities and revenues are credits". This might possibly have contributed to understanding if it had been explained to those same students that expenses were used-up assets and that revenues represented money earned when a liability – the obligation to deliver – had been fulfilled. Usually, there was no such explanation.

Appendix 1 – the 1999 Accounts of J Sainsbury plc

In this Appendix are reproduced, with permission, the Group and holding company balance sheets of J Sainsbury plc as at 3 April 1999, and the Group profit and loss account and cash flow statement for the 56 weeks ended 3 April 1999. Usually, published accounts represent a period of one year. The 56-week period arises from the fact that J Sainsbury changed their accounting date.

As stated in its Annual Report 1999, J Sainsbury was founded in 1869, and is one of the world's leading retailers. Its main business is Sainsbury's supermarkets, which has over 400 stores throughout the United Kingdom, offers over 23,000 products and employs in excess of 129,600 people. The Group's other businesses are: Sainsbury's Savacentre, which sells clothing and electrical items as well as food; Sainsbury's Homebase, which sells do-it-yourself (DIY), home enhancement and gardening products; Shaw's Supermarkets Inc., which has 127 stores in the New England states of the USA, and Sainsbury's Bank, which opened in 1997, and was the first bank to be opened by a British supermarket company.

Frequent references are made in the main text of the book to these extracts from the J Sainsbury accounts. The Group balance sheet (Figure A1.1) is referred to mainly in Chapter 4. The Group profit and loss account (Figure A1.2) and the Group cash flow statement (Figure A1.3) are both referred to mainly in Chapter 5.

There are further references to J Sainsbury plc at the beginning of Chapter 7. The purpose of Chapter 7 is to compare and contrast the financial characteristics of various different kinds of business. The four kinds of business referred to in that chapter are: supermarkets (represented by J Sainsbury plc); manufacturing (Glynwed plc); a water company (Severn Trent plc), and an IT solutions company (Logica plc). Since it is primarily in the balance sheet that the main differences between such diverse businesses can be discerned, only the balance sheets of Glynwed, Severn Trent and Logica have been reproduced, also with permission. They appear as, respectively, Figures 7.1, 7.2 and 7.3 in Chapter 7.

Balance sheets

3 April 1999 and 7 March 1998

		Group		Company	
	Note	1999 £m	1998* £m	1999 £m	1998 £m
Fixed assets					
Tangible assets	11	**6,409**	6,133	**226**	228
Investments	12	**41**	151	**5,726**	5,023
		6,450	6,284	**5,952**	5,251
Current assets					
Stocks	15	**843**	743	**-**	-
Debtors	16	**249**	229	**72**	67
Investments	17	**17**	14	**-**	-
Sainsbury's Bank	18	**1,766**	1,584	**-**	-
Cash at bank and in hand		**725**	270	**1**	-
		3,600	2,840	**73**	67
Creditors: due within one year					
Sainsbury's Bank	18	**(1,669)**	(1,502)	**-**	-
Other	19	**(2,880)**	(2,499)	**(835)**	(518)
		(4,549)	(4,001)	**(835)**	(518)
Net current liabilities		**(949)**	(1,161)	**(762)**	(451)
Total assets less current liabilities		**5,501**	5,123	**5,190**	4,800
Creditors: due after one year	19	**(804)**	(949)	**(767)**	(926)
Provisions for liabilities and charges	23	**(8)**	(9)	**-**	-
Total net assets		**4,689**	4,165	**4,423**	3,874
Capital and reserves					
Called up share capital	24	**480**	476	**480**	476
Share premium account	24	**1,359**	1,295	**1,359**	1,295
Revaluation reserve	25	**38**	38	**-**	-
Profit and loss account	26	**2,767**	2,318	**2,584**	2,103
Equity shareholders' funds		**4,644**	4,127	**4,423**	3,874
Minority equity interest		**45**	38	**-**	-
Total capital employed		**4,689**	4,165	**4,423**	3,874

* Restated for new accounting standard (see note 23).

Notes to the accounts are on pages 40 to 57.

The Accounts on pages 34 to 57 were approved by the Board of Directors on 1 June 1999, and are signed on its behalf by

Sir George Bull Chairman

Dino Adriano Group Chief Executive

Figure A1.1   Balance sheets of J Sainsbury plc as at 3 April 1999

Group profit and loss account

for the 56 weeks to 3 April 1999

	Note	1999 56 weeks £m	1998* 52 weeks £m
Group sales including VAT and sales taxes		**17,587**	15,496
VAT and sales taxes		**1,154**	996
Group sales excluding VAT and sales taxes	1	**16,433**	14,500
Cost of sales	1	**15,095**	13,289
Exceptional cost of sales – Texas Homecare integration costs	23	**21**	28
Gross profit		**1,317**	1,183
Administrative expenses	1	**406**	357
Year 2000 costs	1	**30**	20
Group operating profit before profit sharing	1	**881**	806
Profit sharing	2	**45**	44
Group operating profit		**836**	762
Associated Undertakings – share of profit		**12**	16
Profit on sale of properties		**11**	3
Profit/(loss) on disposal of an associate/subsidiary	3	**84**	(12)
Profit on ordinary activities before interest		**943**	769
Net interest payable	4	**55**	78
Profit on ordinary activities before tax	5	**888**	691
Tax on profit on ordinary activities	8	**292**	226
Profit on ordinary activities after tax		**596**	465
Minority equity interest		**2**	4
Profit for the financial year		**598**	469
Equity dividends	9	**294**	264
Retained profit	26	**304**	205
Earnings per share	10	**31.4p**	25.1p
Exceptional cost of sales		**0.7p**	1.0p
(Profit)/loss on sale of properties and disposal of an associate/subsidiary		**(2.9p)**	0.5p
Earnings per share before exceptional cost of sales, profit/loss on sale of properties and disposal of an associate/subsidiary	10	**29.2p**	26.6p
Diluted earnings per share	10	**31.1p**	25.1p
Diluted earnings per share before exceptional cost of sales, profit/loss on sale of properties and disposal of an associate/subsidiary	10	**29.0p**	26.6p

*   Restated for new accounting standards (see notes 10 and 23).

Figure A1.2   Group profit and loss account of J Sainsbury plc for the 56 weeks to 3 April 1999

Group cash flow statement

for the 56 weeks to 3 April 1999

	Note	1999 56 weeks £m	1998 52 weeks £m
Net cash inflow from operating activities	27	**1,322**	1,149
Dividends received from Associated Undertakings		**3**	6
Returns on investments and servicing of finance			
Interest received		**46**	22
Interest paid		**(113)**	(83)
Interest element of finance lease rental payments		**(16)**	(14)
Net cash outflow from returns on investments and servicing of finance		**(83)**	(75)
Tax paid		**(287)**	(177)
Capital expenditure and financial investment			
Payments for tangible fixed assets		**(803)**	(672)
Receipts from sale of tangible fixed assets		**107**	96
Purchase of investments		**(2)**	(7)
Net cash outflow from capital expenditure and financial investment		**(698)**	(583)
Acquisitions and disposals			
Investment in Sainsbury's Bank by minority shareholder		**9**	38
Investment in Egyptian Distribution Group SAE		**(11)**	-
Proceeds from disposal of Giant Food Inc.		**345**	-
Proceeds from disposal of other fixed asset investments		**3**	13
Net cash inflow from acquisitions and disposals		**346**	51
Equity dividends paid		**(249)**	(221)
Management of liquid resources		**3**	-
Financing			
Issue of ordinary share capital		**38**	41
Debt due within a year			
Increase/(decrease) in short-term borrowings		**188**	(629)
Debts due beyond a year			
(Decrease)/increase in long-term borrowing		**(9)**	343
Capital element of finance lease rental payments		**(6)**	(7)
Net cash inflow/(outflow) from financing		**211**	(252)
Increase/(decrease) in cash in the period		**568**	(102)
Reconciliation of net cash flow to movement in net debt			
Increase/(decrease) in cash in the period		**568**	(102)
Cash (inflow)/outflow from (increase)/decrease in debt and lease financing		**(173)**	293
New finance leases		**(17)**	(13)
Currency translation difference		**(5)**	11
8.5% Capital Bonds conversion		**-**	156
Movement in net debt in the period	22	**373**	345
Net debt at the beginning of the period	22	**(1,077)**	(1,436)
Prior year reclassification	22	**-**	14
Net debt at the end of the period	22	**(704)**	(1,077)

Figure A1.3   Group cash flow statement of J Sainsbury plc for the 56 weeks to 3 April 1999

Appendix 2 – Glossary

Accounting rate of return (ARR) *or* return on investment (ROI)
Average annual profit generated by a project as a percentage of the capital employed on it.

Accrued expense *or* accrual
A service received for which payment has not yet been made.

Accrued income *or* accrued revenue
Work done for which payment has not yet been received.

Acid test ratio
Same as *quick ratio*

Administrative expenses
In a published profit and loss account, the sum of all the non-financial expenses of the business except cost of sales.

Annual accounts
Financial statements of a business produced annually to comply with statutory obligations.

Asset
Something of value that is owned or to which an individual or business has a right, that may be tangible or intangible, long-term (*fixed* or *capital asset*) or short-term (*current asset*).

Asset turnover
See *capital productivity*.

Associated undertakings
Other companies, of whose shares a company holds a significant minority, usually at least 20%.

Auditor
A person appointed to report to the shareholders of a company on the accuracy of its annual accounts.

Balance sheet
A summary of the assets and liabilities of a business at a point in time.

Bankruptcy
The state of being unable to pay one's debts; a legal procedure for giving public notice of that fact.

Book value
The value at which an asset appears on the balance sheet; for fixed assets, usually cost less accumulated depreciation.

Capital
1. Money contributed by the proprietors of a business to enable it to function.
2. As (1) but including profits made using that money.

Capital assets
Same as *fixed assets*.

Capital employed
Usually all the long-term money – proprietors' capital and long-term loans – being used in a business.

Capital productivity *or* asset turnover
Sales divided by capital employed; a measure of the sales being generated by the (long-term) capital employed in the business.

Cash flow
A movement of cash into or out of a business; also the net total of such movements during a period.

Cash flow statement
A summary of cash inflows and cash outflows during a period of time, usually a year.

Company
A corporate enterprise that has a legal identity separate from that of its members.

Consolidated *or* group accounts
Combined accounts of a group of companies.

Cost/benefit analysis
A method of deciding whether or not a particular project or investment should be undertaken, by comparing its relevant likely costs and benefits over its estimated lifetime.

Cost of capital
The return expected by the providers of capital; in a company, the weighted average of the costs of equity and debt.

Cost of sales
Usually the production costs incurred in getting goods or services to the point at which they are capable of being sold to the customer.

Creditor
A person or business to whom a debt is due.

Current assets *or* circulating assets
Short term assets that are turned over (used and replenished) frequently, usually within one year, in the course of business; mainly stock, debtors and cash.

Current ratio
Current assets divided by current liabilities.

Debtor
A debt due to a business or individual.

Debtor days
Trade debtors divided by (credit sales/365); the number of days, on average, that credit customers are taking to pay their bills.

Debt/equity *or* gearing ratio
Usually the total of interest-bearing debt (long-term borrowing plus overdrafts) divided by equity (total capital and reserves), expressed as a percentage.

Deferred income *or* deferred revenue
Cash received in advance of goods or services delivered.

Depreciation
An amount representing approximately the decline in value due to the wearing out or obsolescence of a fixed asset, charged to the profit and loss account as an expense.

Diluted earnings per share
What the earnings per share would have been if the exercise of certain options or the occurrence of certain events had resulted in more shares being in circulation.

Direct costs
Costs, for example materials and labour, that can be traced to a particular unit of cost, for example a product, a batch of products or a process in an economically feasible way.

Director
A person appointed to carry out the day-to-day management of a company.

Discounted cash flow (DCF)
Two related methods for comparing the values of cash flows occurring at different times, by taking into account the time value of money: net present value (NPV) and internal rate of return (IRR).

Discounted payback
The application of the payback method to discounted cash flows.

Dividend
That part of the profit of a company paid to its shareholders.

Dividend yield
The dividend per share divided by the current share price, expressed as a percentage.

Drawings
Amounts drawn out of an unincorporated business by the proprietor or proprietors.

Earnings per share
Profit after tax and minority interest of a company over a stated period, usually one year, divided by the number of ordinary shares issued by the company.

Equity dividends
Dividends on ordinary or equity shares.

Equity *or* equity shares
The ordinary shares of a company.

Exceptional item
Something falling within the ordinary activities of a business but which is a "one-off" occurrence or sufficiently unusual to warrant being shown separately.

Expense
The extent to which an asset has been used up during a period of time, usually shown as a charge against profit in the profit and loss account.

Extraordinary items
Items possessing a high degree of abnormality which arise from events outside the ordinary activities of a business and which are not expected to recur, for example natural disasters.

Factoring *and* invoice discounting
Buying the trade debts of a company in return for a discounted lump sum.

Finance
Money resources.

Finance lease (capital lease in the US)
A lease that transfers all or substantially all the risks and rewards of ownership of an asset to the lessee.

Financing
The process of obtaining the money resources for something that it is wished to acquire or have the use of.

Fixed assets, *also* capital assets
Assets that are expected to be used for a considerable time, usually more than one year, in a business.

Fixed capital
That part of a company's capital that is invested in fixed assets.

Full payout finance lease
A finance lease under which the lessee, during the primary period, pays the lessor the full cost of the leased asset plus interest; a lease whose residual value is zero.

Funding charge
The cost of capital in the context of return on investment (ROI) calculations.

Gearing
The relationship between the amount of borrowed money and the amount of proprietors' money in a business; the equivalent US term is leverage.

Gearing ratio
See *debt/equity ratio*.

Gilt-edged securities or gilts
United Kingdom government stocks or bonds on which a fixed rate of interest is usually paid.

Goodwill
The amount by which the price paid for a business exceeds the market value of the assets less liabilities acquired.

Gross profit
The difference between sales and cost of sales.

Group accounts
Same as *consolidated accounts*.

Group of companies
A holding or parent company together with its subsidiaries.

Hire purchase
A lease with a purchase option.

Holding company *or* parent company
A company that holds the shares of other companies, which it then controls, and which are then known as subsidiaries.

Hurdle rate
The minimum rate of return that a proposed project is required to deliver; usually refers to internal rate of return (IRR) or return on investment (ROI).

Interest cover
Operating profit divided by interest payable; the extent to which profit is available to cover interest payable.

Internal rate of return (IRR)
The rate of return earned by the money invested in a project; the percentage discount rate r that must be applied in the present value formula to a series of cash flows if the net present value of the series is to equate to zero.

Investment
The purchase of assets or the depositing of money with a primary view to their financial return, either as income or capital gain.

Joint venture
An undertaking by which its participants expect to achieve some common purpose or benefit, controlled jointly by two or more venturers.

Lease
A contract under which the owner of an asset (the lessor) permits someone else (the lessee) to use it during a defined period in return for agreed payments.

Liability
Something that is owed; an obligation.

Limited company, *also* **limited liability company**
A company whose members are legally responsible only to a specified amount for its debts.

Liquidity
A term describing the ease with which an asset can be turned into cash.

Loan capital
Usually the long-term money provided to a company by lenders.

Manufacturing overheads *or* **indirect production costs**
Manufacturing costs, for example factory insurance, heating and cleaning costs that cannot be traced to a particular unit of cost in an economically feasible way.

Materiality
The state of having sufficient significance to require separate disclosure in a company's accounts.

Minority interest
In a group of companies, the proportion of group capital and group profits or losses attributable to shareholders outside the group.

Multiple
Same as *price/earnings (PE) ratio.*

Negative equity
An asset that has a market value less than the sum of money borrowed to purchase it.

Net current liabilities *or* net current assets
The difference between current assets and current liabilities.

Net present value (NPV)
The sum of a series of positive and negative present values.

Net worth
What is left when the external liabilities have been deducted from the value of the assets of an individual or a business.

Nominal *or* par value
The face value of a share.

Off balance sheet
Of an operating lease, descriptive of the fact that neither the leased asset nor the obligation to make payments appear on the balance sheet of the lessee.

Operating lease
A lease other than a finance lease (in the US a lease other than a capital lease); usually a lease that includes a guaranteed residual value.

Operating margin *or* return on sales
Operating profit over sales, expressed as a percentage.

Operating profit or loss
The difference between gross profit and administrative expenses; the profit or loss from business operations before interest and tax.

Opportunity cost
The benefit lost by not employing an economic resource in the most profitable alternative activity.

Ordinary *or* equity share
Part ownership in a company that confers a legal right to a proportionate part of the company's profits.

Outsourcing
The arranging of work previously done within an organisation to be done by an outside contractor.

Partnership
An association of two or more people carrying on a business.

Payback *or* **break even**
The length of time that it will take for the net cash inflows of a project to equal the initial cash outlay.

Payable
A US term meaning the same as trade creditor.

Plc
See *public limited company.*

Preference share
A share in a company that entitles the holder to a fixed rate of interest rather than a variable dividend.

Prepayment, *also* **payment in advance**
Payment for goods or services before they have been received.

Present value formula
$P = F(1 + r)^{-n}$ represents the present value (P) of a cash flow (F), receivable or payable n periods in the future, discounted at a required rate of return r.

Present value
The value derived by applying the present value formula to a future cash flow.

Price/earnings (PE) ratio *or* **multiple**
The market price of a share divided by the earnings per share of the company.

Pricing
The process of determining the price at which a product or service is to be sold.

Private limited company
Any company that is not a public limited company.

Profit *or* **loss**
The difference between the earnings and expenses of a business.

Profit and loss account
In a balance sheet, the reserve representing the amount of accumulated profits and losses of a business to date after dividends or drawings; also an account showing how the profit or loss during a year was arrived at.

Profit after tax *or* net profit
The profit that, subject in group accounts to any necessary adjustment for minority interest, belongs to the shareholders.

Profitability index
Usually the sum of the present values of the future net cash flows of a project, divided by the present value of the initial investment.

Project risk
The risk of the extent to which estimates of the benefits and costs of a project may be wrong.

Provision
An amount set aside for a known liability, the amount of which cannot be precisely determined.

Public limited company (plc)
A company that is authorised to offer shares to the public either directly or by trading on a stock exchange.

Quick *or* acid test ratio
Usually the sum of all current assets except stock, divided by current liabilities.

Receivable
A US term meaning the same as trade debtor.

Reserve
Anything that is part of proprietor's or shareholders' capital but needs to be shown separately from the original capital.

Residual value
An amount, based on the expected value of an asset at the end of a lease, deducted by the lessor from the asset's value in determining the payments due.

Retained profit
The accumulated profit that belongs to the shareholders that has not yet been paid to them as dividends.

Return
The yield or profit from an investment.

Return on capital employed (ROCE)
Profit (usually operating profit) over capital employed (usually all the long-term money used in a business), expressed as a percentage.

Return on equity (ROE)
The profit that belongs to the shareholders (profit after tax) compared with the equity or capital that belongs to them (the total capital and reserves) expressed as a percentage.

Return on investment (ROI)
Same as *accounting rate of return.*

Return on sales (ROS)
Same as *operating margin.*

Revaluation reserve
The increase in capital representing an upward revaluation in the balance sheet of one or more of a company's assets.

Revenue
Earnings, especially from the sale of goods or services.

Risk capital
A term used to describe money invested in ordinary or equity shares because with the right to a share of profits comes the risk of a share of losses.

Share
Part ownership of a limited company conferring on its owner the right to a proportionate part of the company's profits.

Share capital *or* shareholders' capital
The capital contributed by the shareholders of a company.

Share premium
The amount by which the price at which a share is issued by a company exceeds the nominal or par value of the share.

Share premium account
A reserve representing the accumulated sum of share premiums.

Share certificate
A document that provides evidence of ownership of shares in a company.

Shareholder
Owner of shares in a limited company.

Sole trader
An individual who is the sole owner or proprietor of a business.

Stock exchange
A place in which stocks and shares are bought and sold, prices being determined by supply and demand.

Stock turnover *or* stock turn
Sales divided by stocks; a measure of the sales being generated relative to the stocks held.

Subsidiary company *or* subsidiary
A company controlled by another which holds all or a majority of its shares.

Sunk cost
Money already spent that cannot be recouped, and that therefore should not affect financial decision making.

Systematic risk
The risk represented by unpredictable factors in the economy such as interest rates, taxation and consumer demand.

Time value of money
A term descriptive of the fact that money received or paid in the future is worth less than money received or paid today.

Trade creditors
Suppliers of goods and services to whom money is owed in the ordinary course of trade.

Trade debtors
Customers who owe money for goods and services supplied in the ordinary course of trade.

Transaction
A piece of business done, especially commercial business.

Turnover
Same as revenue; also used to describe the rate at which assets, or particular classes of assets, are used and replenished, or "turned over".

Working capital
That part of a company's capital that is invested in net current assets.

Work in progress
Partly manufactured goods.

Appendix 3 – Table of Present Values

Table A3.1 gives the present value (P) of a lump sum of £1 receivable or payable n periods in the future discounted at rate r.

$$P = £1/(1 + r)^n = £1(1 + r)^{-n}$$

Example:
The present value of a lump sum of £1 receivable or payable three years in the future discounted at 8% is given by

$$£1 \times (1 + 0.08)^{-3} = £0.7938$$

Table A3.1 Present value of a lump sum of £1 receivable or payable n periods from today discounted at rate r

%	Periods 1	2	3	4	5	6	7	8	9	10	11	12	13	14	15	16	17	18	19	20
5	0.9524	0.9070	0.8638	0.8227	0.7835	0.7462	0.7107	0.6768	0.6446	0.6139	0.5847	0.5568	0.5303	0.5051	0.4810	0.4581	0.4363	0.1455	0.3957	0.3769
6	0.9434	0.8900	0.8396	0.7921	0.7473	0.7050	0.6651	0.6274	0.5919	0.5584	0.5268	0.4970	0.4688	0.4423	0.4173	0.3936	0.3714	0.3503	0.3305	0.3118
7	0.9346	0.8734	0.8163	0.7629	0.7130	0.6663	0.6227	0.5820	0.5439	0.5083	0.4751	0.4440	0.4150	0.3878	0.3624	0.3387	0.3166	0.2959	0.2765	0.2584
8	09259	0.8573	0.7938	0.7350	0.6806	0.6302	05835	0.5403	0.5002	0.4632	0.4289	0.3971	0.3677	0.3405	0.3152	0.2919	0.2703	0.2502	0.2317	0.2145
9	0.9174	0.8417	0.7722	0.7084	0.6499	0.5963	0.5470	0.5019	0.4604	0.4224	0.3875	0.3555	0.3262	0.2992	0.2745	0.2519	0.2311	0.2120	0.1945	0.1784
10	0.9091	0.8264	0.7513	0.6830	0.6209	0.5645	0.5132	0.4665	0.4241	0.3855	0.3505	0.3186	02897	0.2633	0.2394	0.2176	0.1978	0.1799	0.1635	0.1486
11	0.9009	0.8116	0.7312	0.6587	0.5935	0.5346	0.4817	0.4339	0.3909	0.3522	0.3173	0.2858	0.2575	0.2320	0.2090	0.1883	0.1696	0.1528	0.1377	0.1240
12	0.8929	0.7972	0.7118	0.6355	0.5674	0.5066	0.4523	0.4039	0.3606	0.3220	0.2875	0.2567	0.2292	0.2046	0.1827	0.1631	0.1456	0.1300	0.1161	0.1037
13	0.8850	0.7831	0.6931	0.6133	0.5428	0.4803	0.4251	0.3762	0.3329	0.2946	0.2607	0.2307	0.2042	0.1807	0.1599	0.1415	0.1252	0.1108	0.0981	0.0868
14	0.8772	0.7695	0.6750	05921	0.5194	0.4556	0.3996	0.3506	0.3075	0.2697	0.2366	0.2076	0.1821	0.1597	0.1401	0.1229	0.1078	0.0946	0.0829	0.0728
15	0.8696	0.7561	0.6575	0.5718	0.4972	0.4323	0.3759	0.3269	0.2843	0.2472	0.2149	0.1869	0.1625	0.1413	0.1229	0.1069	0.0929	0.0808	0.0703	0.0611
16	0.8621	0.7432	0.6407	0.5523	0.4761	0.4104	0.3538	0.3050	0.2630	0.2267	0.1954	0.1685	0.1452	0.1252	0.1079	0.0930	0.0802	0.0691	0.0596	0.0514
17	0.8547	0.7305	0.6244	0.5337	0.4561	0.3898	0.3332	0.2848	0.2434	0.2080	0.1778	0.1520	0.1299	0.1110	0.0949	0.0811	0.0693	0.0592	0.0506	0.0433
18	0.8475	0.7182	0.6086	0.5158	0.4371	0.3704	0.3139	0.2660	0.2255	0.1911	0.1619	0.1372	0.1163	0.0985	0.0835	0.0708	0.0600	0.0508	0.0431	0.0365
19	0.8403	0.7062	0.5934	0.4987	0.4190	0.3521	0.2959	0.2487	0.2090	0.1756	0.1476	0.1240	0.1042	0.0876	0.0736	0.0618	0.0520	0.0437	0.0367	0.0308
20	0.8333	0.6944	0.5787	0.4823	0.4019	0.3349	0.2791	0.2326	0.1938	0.1615	0.1346	0.1122	0.0935	0.0779	0.0649	0.0541	0.0451	0.0376	0.0313	0.0261
21	0.8264	0.6830	0.5645	0.4665	0.3855	0.3186	0.2633	0.2176	0.1799	0.1486	0.1228	0.1015	0.0839	0.0693	0.0573	0.0474	0.0391	0.0323	0.0267	0.0221
22	0.8197	0.6719	0.5507	0.4514	0.3700	0.3033	0.2486	0.2038	0.1670	0.1369	0.1122	0.0920	0.0754	0.0618	0.0507	0.0415	0.0340	0.0279	0.0229	0.0187
23	0.8130	0.6610	0.5374	0.4369	0.3552	0.2888	0.2348	0.1909	0.1552	0.1262	0.1026	0.0834	0.0678	0.0551	0.0448	0.0364	0.0296	0.0241	0.0196	0.0159
24	0.8065	0.6504	0.5245	0.4230	0.3411	0.2751	0.2218	0.1789	0.1443	0.1164	0.0938	0.0757	0.0610	0.0492	0.0397	0.0320	0.0258	0.0208	0.0168	0.0135
25	0.8000	0.6400	0.5120	0.4096	0.3277	0.2621	0.2097	0.1678	0.1342	0.1074	0.0859	0.0687	0.0550	0.0440	0.0352	0.0281	0.0225	0.0180	0.0144	0.0115

References

Dixon R (1994). *Investment Appraisal – A Guide for Managers*. Kogan Page, in association with The Chartered Institute of Management Accountants, London.

Horngren CT, Foster G and Datar SM (1997). *Cost Accounting – A Managerial Emphasis (International Edition)*. Prentice Hall-International, New Jersey, USA.

Lumby S and Jones C (1999). *Investment Appraisal and Financial Decisions*. International Thompson Business Press, London.

Index